Kahiki Supper Club

A Polynesian Paradise in Columbus

David Meyers, Elise Meyers Walker, Jeff Chenault & Doug Motz

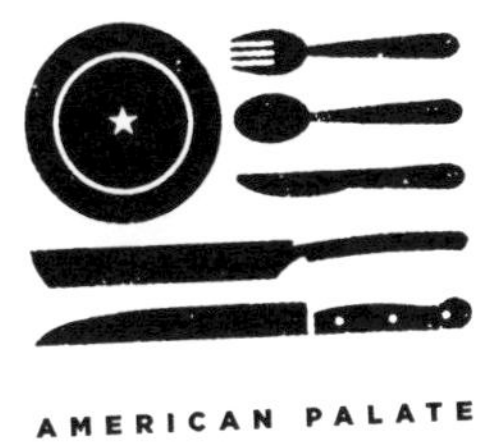

Published by American Palate
A Division of The History Press
Charleston, SC 29403
www.historypress.net

Front cover: An artist's rendition of the Kahiki showing the "fire-fish" along the roof ridge. *Courtesy Sapp/Henry.*

First published 2014

Manufactured in the United States

ISBN 978.1.62619.594.3

Library of Congress Cataloging-in-Publication Data

Meyers, David, 1948-
Kahiki Supper Club : a Polynesian paradise in Columbus / David Meyers, Elise Meyers Walker, Jeff Chenault and Doug Motz.
pages cm
Includes bibliographical references and index.
ISBN 978-1-62619-594-3 (paperback)
1. Kahiki Supper Club (Columbus, Ohio)--History. 2. Columbus (Ohio)--History. 3. Columbus (Ohio)--Social life and customs. 4. Art, Polynesian--Influence--History. 5. Cooking, Polynesian. I. Walker, Elise Meyers. II. Chenault, Jeff. III. Motz, Doug. IV. Title.
TX945.5.K34M49 2014
641.5996--dc23
2014035001

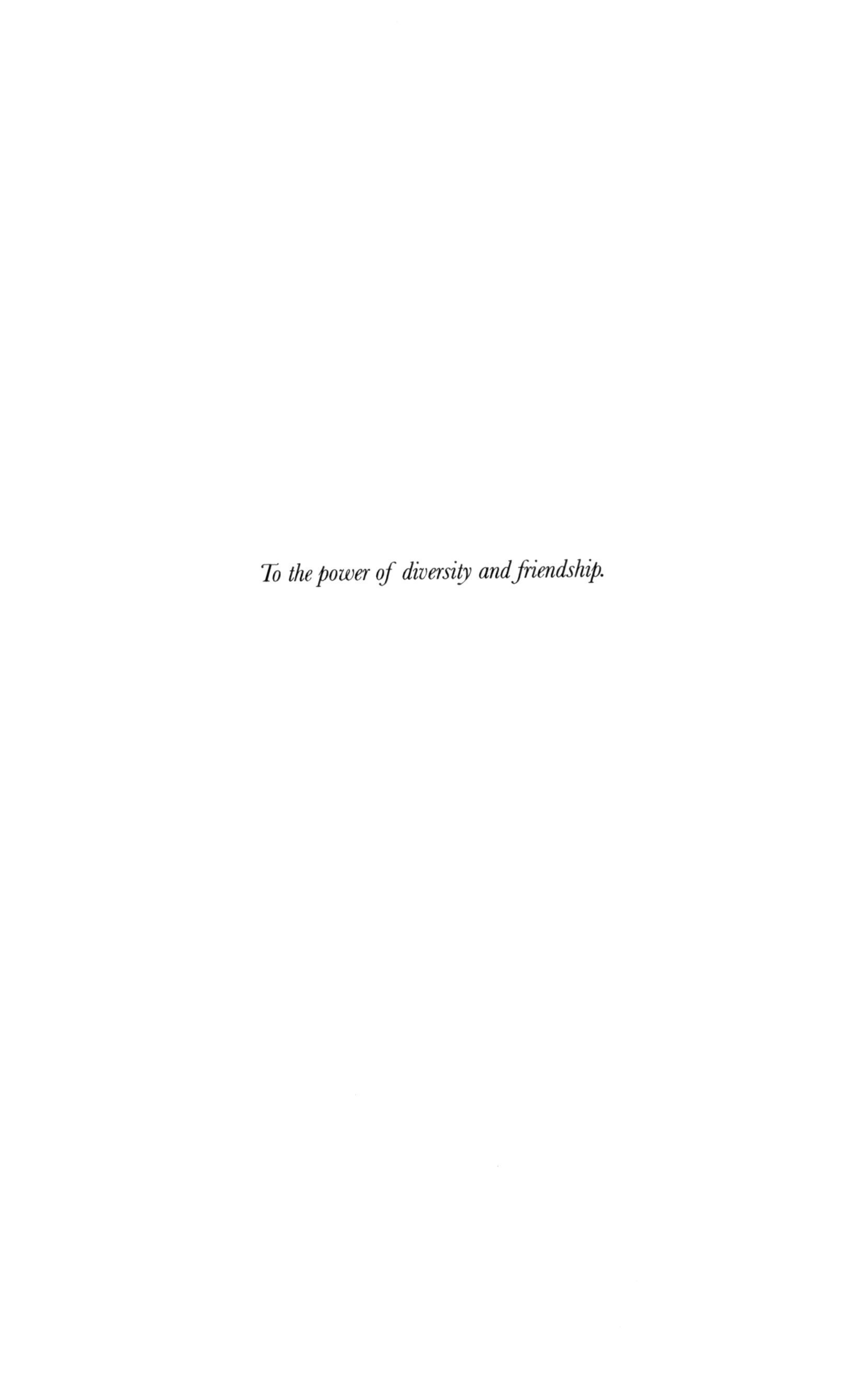

To the power of diversity and friendship.

CONTENTS

FOREWORD

As the daughter of Bill Sapp, co-founder with Lee Henry of the celebrated Kahiki Supper Club, I found a playground at the Kahiki, which provided me with an escape from the cold, gray skies of Columbus, Ohio. It was also my own little piece of paradise—all twenty thousand square feet of it!

The restaurant was a truly magical place, where you were transported to a tropical oasis from the moment you pulled into its parking lot. First you passed the towering moai, fire spewing from their topknots. They guarded and lighted the way across the bridge spanning the moat. Then, opening a pair of giant doors, you entered a passageway with roaring waterfalls on either side. Arriving in a circular cavern, you had to choose which path to follow to continue on your journey.

To the right were the Tiki Hut Coatroom, the Beachcomber Gift Shop and the Outrigger Bar. To the left were the bamboo-wrapped telephone booths that you could spiral into like a shell for privacy—an excellent place to hide—or the restrooms with their conch shell sinks and cowrie shell faucet knobs that made water flow from the mouth of a protectant tiki.

Circling the center wishing well with its sacramental pig fountain, you would reach the grand entrance. As you looked down the palm tree–lined main dining room, you would see the fierce-looking fireplace moai with glowing eyes and a flaming mouth. On the left side of the dining room were booths lining a wall of the aquariums with a plethora of tropical fish from faraway seas. In the center were tiki statues and intimate dining huts with exotic rattan peacock chairs fit for royalty. And on the right were the booths that overlooked the rain forest with live tropical birds flying among exotic plants and trees. Periodically, lightning would flash and thunder would boom as a shower fell on your window, providing a glimpse into an exotic land.

As magical as the décor was, the restaurant staff, representing twenty-one different nationalities, were more so. During frequent visits to Cuba, my parents and Sandro Conti, the bar manager, had come to know doctors, lawyers and business people who lost everything when Castro came to power. Some of them came to work at the Kahiki. This was a time of turmoil for many countries around the world. It was this coming together of so many people from such diverse backgrounds, all working cooperatively, that made the Kahiki such an extraordinary creation.

A Cuban doctor delivered me. The chef would babysit both my brother and me. They were joined by many Japanese and Korean women, often wives of servicemen fighting for our country. The Kahiki was in many respects a global village. Of course, I became particularly attached to several members of the staff. I loved to spend time with Tilly, our horticulturalist, who also took care of all the birds in the rain forest. He worked as the groundskeeper at the Columbus Country Club as well. Sometimes, when my dogs, Chi-Chi and Cha-Cha, brought a baby bunny home, we would nurse it back to health and then take it to Tilly's to live in his fantastic backyard. He was an amazing man.

At the age of thirteen, I started working at the restaurant at the urging of my father's secretary, Wanda Stevens. I joined the ranks of the employees who had become my friends, family and mentors. Over the years, I held nearly every job I was old enough to do. I got to know many wonderful people at the Kahiki and learned the value of hard work. I remember busboy Jimmy, who worked there through the middle 1970s. By the time my daughter was two, he had become manager, having climbed his way up the ladder from waiter to captain to *maître d'* before reaching the top. My dad and his partner, Lee, take pride in the many success stories that have their roots in the Kahiki.

For much of my life, I thought my childhood was normal. After I got married, my husband, Craig, told me that he was fascinated by how blind I was to my father's legacy. When my dad and Lee sold the Kahiki, they kept nothing. Everything was part of the business. Some of the most sought-after pieces of pottery and china that were later sold on eBay had, in fact, been "appropriated" by customers who wanted a souvenir.

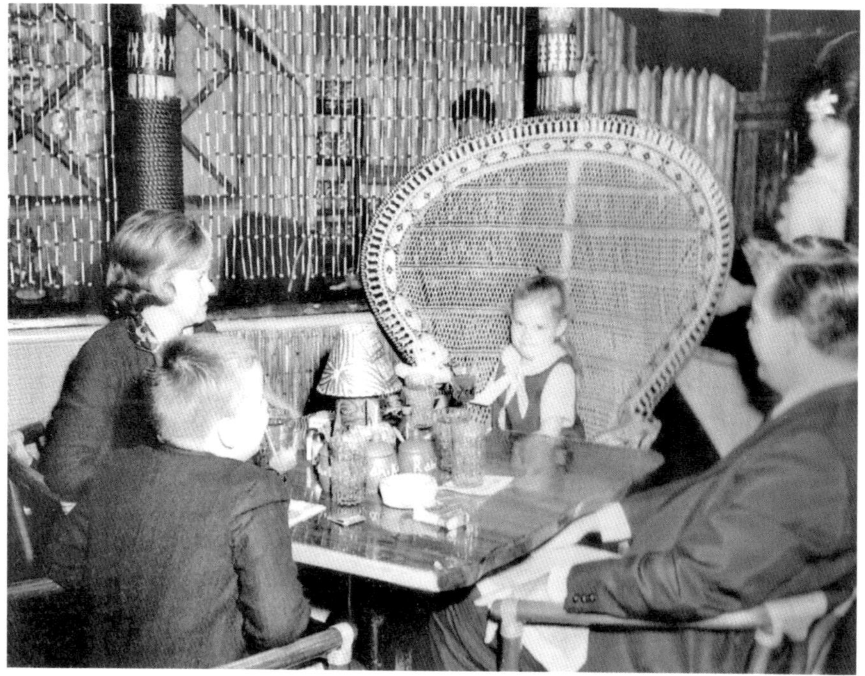

As the daughter of the co-owner, Linda Sapp Long (center) has many happy memories of the Kahiki. *Courtesy Sapp/Henry.*

When I was contacted by David and Jeff about doing a book on the Kahiki, I was excited by the prospect of finally having a definitive history of the place I loved so much. Over the years, I have learned that the feelings I hold for the Kahiki are shared by many others who worked or dined there. If anything, the legion of Kahiki fans seems to have increased since it fell to the wrecking ball nearly fifteen years ago. It is for them that this book was written. I feel very lucky to have played a small part in its story.

Linda Sapp Long

PREFACE

The palm-clad isles of the South Sea bear a closer resemblance to the description of the Garden of Eden than any other of the many parts of the world that I have ever seen; and of these, Tahiti is a real paradise on earth. There is no country nor other isle where Nature has been so liberal in the distribution of her gifts. No other island can compare in natural beauty with Tahiti, the gem of the South Pacific Ocean. It is the island where life is free of care. It is the island where the natives are fed, clothed and housed by nature. It is the island where man is born, eats his daily bread without being forced to labor, sleeps and dreams away his life free from worry, and enjoys the foretaste of the eternal paradise before he dies.
—Nicholas Senn, 1906

Once upon a time, not too long ago, a little corner of paradise—heaven, Eden, Shangri-La or whatever term you prefer—occupied a three-acre plot of ground on the east side of Columbus. It was called the Kahiki Supper Club, and no one had ever seen the likes of it before or since. Although it is gone, the Kahiki is without a doubt the most fondly remembered restaurant in the city's history and, arguably, in all the tiki universe. That is why the *Kahiki Supper Club: A Polynesian Paradise in Columbus* came to be written.

My daughter, Elise, and I have previously collaborated on five books of local history. When we were casting about for a follow-up to *Look to Lazarus: The Big Store*, first Doug Motz of the Columbus Historical Society and then Jeff Chenault of the Fraternal Order of Moai urged us to do one on the Kahiki. While we both were fans of the fabled Polynesian Palace, we were reluctant to embark on such a venture without taking Jeff and Doug along with us as coauthors. It's safe to say it would have been a lesser book without their contributions.

As we soon discovered, there is more to the story of William "Bill" Sapp and Leland "Lee" Henry than just the Kahiki. Even without it, they still would have been responsible for creating a handful of the best dining establishments to ever grace the local scene. A book of this sort would not be complete without some mention of these restaurants as well.

However, as both Lee and Bill would be the first to point out, what made the Kahiki such a success was not the incredible building—a veritable Polynesian shrine—but the wonderful people who worked there. Their diversity was its greatest asset. While there are far too many to mention by name, we hope that they will feel they are well represented by the various vignettes and anecdotes we have included in these pages.

David Meyers

ACKNOWLEDGEMENTS

One of the great joys of writing a history book such as this is having the opportunity to meet some of the people who actually made the history. The story of the Kahiki Supper Club is the story of two men: Bill Sapp and Lee Henry. Lifelong friends and longtime business partners, there would have been no Kahiki without their vision and industry. We owe both an enormous debt of gratitude for allowing us to revisit those days with them and their families. We would also like to thank Bill's wife, Dianna; his daughter, Linda, and her husband, Craig Long; and Lee's wife, Marilyn. All of them were instrumental in coaxing stories out of Lee and Bill. Others who assisted us in one way or another include Lynn and Cris Wehr, Candi Spencer, Bill Harrison, Bruce Nutt, Eric Hoffman, Greg Dumais, Doral Chenoweth, Deborah Diez, Susie Gehrisch, Autumn Shah, Jo Hannah Ward, Julia Turner, Karen Wilcox, Linda Becker, Robert D. Thomas, Donna Newman, Syble Humphreys, the Cloyes family, the Delcamp family, Todd Popp, Jeff Lafever, Deb Chenault, John "tikiskip" Holt, Sam Walker, Evelyn Keener, Beverly Meyers and the Columbus Historical Society.

1
THE RISE OF TIKI CULTURE

Tiki culture is a 20th-century theme used in Polynesian-style restaurants and clubs originally in the United States and then, to a lesser degree, around the world. Although inspired in part by Tiki carvings and mythology, the connection is loose and stylistic, being an American kitsch form and not a Polynesian fine art form.
—Wikipedia, "Tiki culture"

The year was 1934.

The funny papers became a little funnier with the debut of Li'l Abner, the Three Stooges started n'yuk-n'yuk-n'yukking their way across the silver screen, gangster John Dillinger was gunned down outside a Chicago movie house and a madman-in-the-making became Führer of Germany. Meanwhile, a former adventurer, bootlegger and world traveler, Ernest Gantt, age twenty-seven, had recently opened a bar called Don's Beachcomber Café on North McCadden Place in Hollywood. (The exact date is unknown, but it is believed to have been shortly after Prohibition ended on December 5, 1933). In 1937, he moved it across the street and renamed it Don The Beachcomber.

Gantt adopted a tropical theme and a menu that relied heavily on Cantonese dishes. "If you can't get to paradise, I'll bring it to you," he told his customers, who soon began to include such celebrities as Charlie Chaplin and Howard Hughes. However, it was for his "Rhum Rhapsodies" (rum cocktails) that he quickly rose to fame. The Zombie, Tahitian Rum Punch, Vicious Virgin, Missionary's Downfall and Navy Grog, among many others, inspired countless imitators. Since patrons of his establishment assumed Gantt was Don the Beachcomber, he officially changed his name to Donn Beachcomber—or, simply, Donn Beach.

Farther up the coast, thirty-one-year-old Victor Bergeron opened a small bar and restaurant in San Francisco on November 17, 1934, with a $500 loan from his parents. It was located at San Pablo Avenue and Sixty-fifth Street, directly across from the family grocery. He called it Hinky Dink's, possibly after a notorious Chicago bar of that name. In order to drum up business, he would let customers stick an ice pick in his wooden leg. After a visit to Don The Beachcomber, Bergeron completely reorganized his own watering hole in 1938. According to Michael Stern, "He tore down the old deer horns and moose heads and covered the walls with green, grassy fabric and bamboo." He also changed the name to Trader Vic's, an obvious nod to the 1931 movie *Trader Horn*, which was notable for its on-location filming in Africa.

By 1940, Bergeron had begun rolling out franchises, the first in Seattle. Others soon followed.[1] At one point, there were more than two dozen Trader Vic's worldwide. It is said to have been the first successful chain of themed restaurants in the United States.[2]

Meanwhile, Gantt/Beach was serving in the U.S. Army, assigned to operate officer R&R (rest and recreation) centers. Apparently, this was more dangerous than it sounds, for he was awarded a Purple Heart and a Bronze Star for his gallantry. While he was in the military, his wife, Sunny Sund, transformed his popular business into a sixteen-restaurant chain. However, when they subsequently divorced, he was prohibited from any further expansion in the United States. So Gantt relocated to Hawaii, which was then a U.S. territory, and opened several businesses, including the famed International Marketplace in Waikiki.[3]

The competition between Trader Vic's and Don The Beachcomber's was generally friendly, but Bergeron and Beach did have a falling out over the historically "important" issue of which one deserved credit for developing the Mai Tai (from *maitai*, the Tahitian word for "good"). While there are numerous recipes for the Mai Tai, including three different ones at Trader Vic's, Beach was the one who came up with most of the original drink recipes (his *New York Times* obituary mentions eighty-four), and others copied or improved them.[4]

Just as Don The Beachcomber and Trader Vic's were getting started, the Hawaii Visitors' Bureau began sponsoring a live weekly radio broadcast from Honolulu. For forty years (1935–75), *Hawaii*

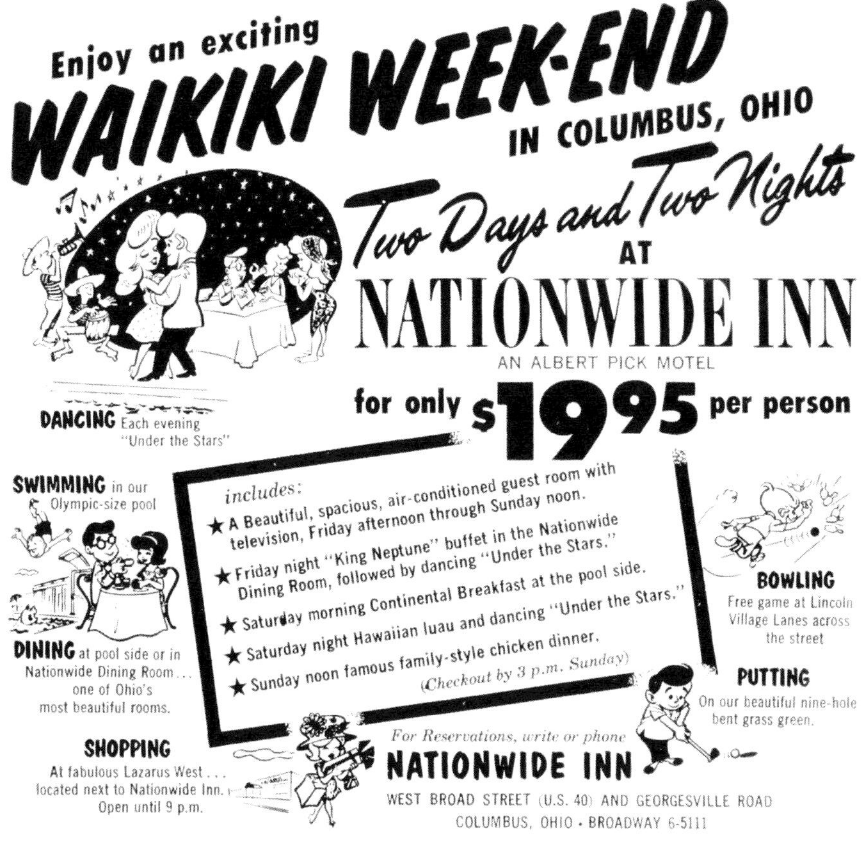

The public's interest in all things Polynesian led the Nationwide Inn to host a "Waikiki Weekend." *Authors' collection.*

Calls extolled the virtues of the islands. With the sound of the surf at Waikiki in the background, Webley Edwards would announce, "This is a call from Hawaii," followed by a segue into Hawaiian music "and the trumpeting of conch shells." Broadcast live from Moana Hotel's Banyan Court, *Hawaii Calls* featured many guest stars, including Al Jolson and Arthur Godfrey. It also made stars of Hawaiian performers such as Alfred Apaka and John Kameaaloha Almeida. At its peak, the program was carried by 750 stations. However, after 2,083 broadcasts, it came to an end.[5]

The popularity of *Hawaii Calls* undoubtedly led to the making of a number of films with Hawaii as the setting. Harry Owens, music director for the radio broadcasts, won an Oscar for his original song "Sweet Leilani," sung by Bing Crosby in *Waikiki Wedding*. Two years later, Eleanor Powell burned up the silver screen in her drum dance/hula/tap number for *Honolulu*.

Once Hollywood discovered Hawaii, it was just a matter of time before tiki culture had permeated the arts. Tiki culture is characterized by exotic drinks, island or even jungle décor, flaming torches, rattan furniture, bamboo screens, flower leis, brightly colored patterned fabric and carved wooden and stone moai and tiki statues. In the long run, Trader Vic's has proven to be the more enduring of the original chains, but both it and Don The Beachcomber had an undeniable influence on those that followed in their footsteps, such as the famed Mai-Kai in Fort Lauderdale, Florida.[6]

Opened on December 28, 1956, the Mai-Kai was the first of the so-called Grand Polynesian Palaces of Tiki. Built by brothers Bob and Jack Thornton at a cost of over $300,000, they raided Chicago's Don The Beachcomber, hiring away number-two chef Kenny Lee, number-two bartender Mariano Licudine (and his book of drink recipes), head *maître d'* Andy Tanato and other assorted staff.[7] Standing alone in a field along Federal Highway, the Mai-Kai earned over $1 million in its first year despite being open only during the winter tourist season. Its success did not go unnoticed.

The Mai-Kai became the inspiration for many other Polynesian-themed restaurants, although few equaled it. It contained multiple dining rooms, a bar, tropical gardens, waterfalls, a stage for the floor show and a gift shop, all enclosed in an A-frame building. Originally, the roof in the main dining room was open to the stars, but this proved to be impractical due to the need to move diners under cover whenever it rained. Nevertheless, its location in a tourist mecca and a subtropical climate are no doubt major reasons why the Mai-Kai is also the last surviving establishment of its type.

Then and now, the waitresses at Mai-Kai's Molokai Bar were attired in bikini tops and wraparound sarongs. This costume was a Mai-Kai innovation, probably inspired by the example of the "sarong Queen," movie star Dorothy Lamour, who had first donned her trademark outfit in *The Jungle Princess* (1936). For many years, a calendar was published featuring the attractive young women of the Mai-Kai. The restaurant also introduced the ritual of the Mystery Drink, a smoking concoction delivered by a Mystery Girl.

The 1936 MGM blockbuster movie *Mutiny on the Bounty*, starring Clark Gable, helped awaken the broader public's interest in the islands. It was partially filmed in French Polynesia and gave moviegoers a glimpse of paradise in the form of Tahiti. Three years later, the Golden Gate International Exposition in California provided a showcase for Polynesian culture with the theme "Pageant of the Pacific." It was symbolized by an eighty-foot statue of Pacifica, goddess of the Pacific Ocean.

However, more significant was the December 7, 1941 Japanese air assault on the U.S. naval base at Pearl Harbor, Hawaii, which ushered the nation into a world war. A U.S. territory at the time, Hawaii became the locus of all military operations in the Pacific Theater. And for the first time, Americans began looking at the Hawaiian Islands as a part of the larger United States. The country, not just some remote piece of turf in the middle of the ocean, had been attacked. Returning American soldiers brought home stories, souvenirs and, occasionally, wives from the South Pacific.[8]

A couple years after the war ended, explorer Thor Heyerdahl floated across the Pacific Ocean from South America to the Polynesian islands, demonstrating that such an expedition could have been possible in pre-Columbian times. Heyerdahl believed that the Easter Islands had been settled by migrants from Peru. His 1948 account of his voyage, *The Kon-Tiki Expedition: By Raft Across the South Seas*, became a bestseller and the subject of an Academy Award–winning documentary film. The same year, James Michener won the Pulitzer Prize for his collection of short stories *Tales of the South Pacific*, which was turned into the Rodgers and Hammerstein musical *South Pacific* the following year. A darling of the critics, the show would go on to win the Pulitzer Prize for drama in 1950, at least in part due to its attack on racial bigotry.

As the decade was winding down, President Dwight D. Eisenhower signed a 1959 act by Congress admitting Hawaii into the Union as the country's fiftieth state. Soon U.S. tourists began flocking to Hawaii, and America's love affair with all things tiki flourished. With the islands' supply of real souvenirs soon exhausted, people made do with ersatz ones. Architects began incorporating Polynesian design elements into buildings, from single-family homes to shopping districts. And designers capitalized on Polynesian aesthetics in everything from clothing to furniture.

Of course, the role of three Elvis Presley films—*Blue Hawaii* (1961), *Girls! Girls! Girls!* (1962) and *Paradise, Hawaiian Style* (1965)—cannot be overestimated in marketing the islands' allure.[9] Americans seemingly could not get enough of Polynesian culture, much of it manufactured to order.

Meanwhile, back in Columbus, Ohio, two guys who had been friends since college took note of this trend and began to make some plans to construct their own little piece of Polynesia out on the far east side of town, near the sleepy suburb of Whitehall.

2
THE VIEW FROM THE TOP

All great deeds and all great thoughts have a ridiculous beginning. Great works are often born on a street corner or in a restaurant's revolving door.
—Albert Camus

The decade following World War II was the "Golden Age" of downtown dining in Columbus. While most of the city's best restaurants were concentrated within a few blocks of the Ohio Statehouse, a few notable establishments had begun popping up in the outlying bedroom communities as well. The 1953–54 city directory lists some nine hundred eateries, serving a growing population in excess of 400,000. Among the best were the Chintz Room, the Clarmont, the Clock, the Crystal Room, the Desert Inn, Far East Restaurant, Hoover's Restaurant, Ionian Room, Kuenning Brothers "19" Restaurant, Marzetti's, the Maramor and the Jai Lai—none of which has survived. Although many were quite nice and occasionally bordered on chic, most served up typical midwestern cuisine in a relaxed setting.

The Maramor and the Jai Lai were two of the most notable. The Maramor was started in 1920 by twenty-nine-year-old Mary Love in a house at 112 East Broad. The name was a contraction of Mary and *amour*, the French word for "love." A home economist who had managed the tearoom at the F&R Lazarus Department Store, Love married, moved to California for a time and then returned to Columbus with her husband, Malcolm McGuckin, to resume operating the restaurant, now located at 137 East Broad Street.

The Maramor garnered accolades not only for its food (critic Duncan Hines gave it a four-star rating) but also for its candy and gift shop and, in time, its entertainment. The McGuckins sold the restaurant to Maurice Sher in 1945, and a dozen years later, he hired Danny Deeds to manage it. During the 1960s, as many of Maramor's downtown competitors started gravitating to the suburbs, Deeds gave the restaurant a bit of a makeover in the form of a nightclub that brought in nationally known entertainment, such as Phyllis Diller, John Davidson, the Smothers Brothers and even the "Velvet Fog," Mel Torme. However, it did not survive the decade.

The Jai Lai, by comparison, started life as a saloon in the Short North at the corner of Poplar and North High Streets, its opening coinciding with the end of Prohibition. No more than a hole-in-the-wall, it was founded by south-sider Jasper Wottring with $1,500 he borrowed. He took the name from the Jai Lai Club in New Orleans and stuck a sign outside advertising "Genuine Turtle Soup." Its focus was more on selling whiskey than its delicious salt rolls. As *Columbus Citizen Journal* columnist Ben Hayes once wrote, "Opposite the bar, with its stools, the café had a few tables and chairs. A strip of new linoleum ran down the floor like a highway of refinement."

It wasn't long before the Jai Lai expanded from 581 North High into the Old Vienna Café at 589. However, by 1955, it had outgrown both spaces and relocated to Olentangy River Road between Fifth and King Avenues. Built to resemble a Spanish castle with turrets on the north and south corners, the nine-thousand-square-foot building featured Old World décor with dark wood, tapestries and high-backed booths, as well as parking on the roof.

Wottring had dreamed of having a flotilla of Jai Lai boats sail up the Olentangy River, carrying patrons to Ohio Stadium on Buckeye football game day. While this never came to pass, the restaurant's final owner, Dave Girves, founder of the Girves Brown Derby chain of restaurants, arranged for a helicopter to do it during the 1974 season. Of course, the Jai Lai's biggest fan was Ohio State football coach Woody Hayes. For years, his image was used to promote the restaurant with the slogan "In all the world, there's only one!"

This was the dining landscape when William "Bill" Sapp and Leland "Lee" Henry joined forces to create what quickly became a Bexley landmark: the Top Steakhouse (or the Top, for short). Friends since their undergraduate days at Ohio State University, Bill and Lee continued to pal around after Lee had graduated. While Bill was taking pre-law classes, Lee was working as an assistant buyer at the Union Department Store. "I realized I didn't want to do that the rest of my life," Lee said.

"We would hang out at different places downtown and talk the bar and restaurant business," Bill recalled. "I had been in the restaurant business for

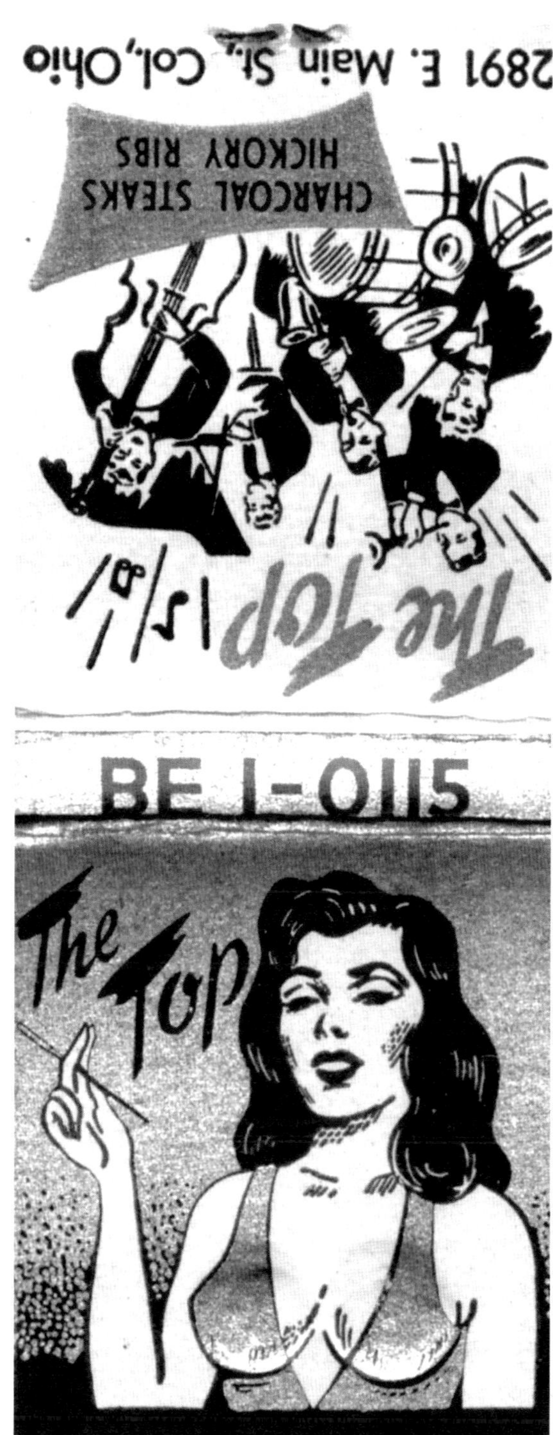

An early matchbook cover from the Top Steakhouse. *Courtesy Sapp/Henry.*

a small time in Florida. I told Lee I think it's a great business, and so we got together and looked at different restaurants."

"Columbus had no supper clubs, just restaurants and night clubs," Lee noted. "A supper club is a home away from home, where you can move from dinner to the piano bar and leave at 2:00 a.m." Rather than starting from scratch, they sought out the cheapest place they could find that already had a D-5 liquor license. Otherwise, they would have to get on a waiting list to obtain one.

The friends would often hang out at Tops, a bar on the far east side of Columbus, because, to quote Bill, "That's where the girls were." It had a spinning sign that resembled a child's toy top. Impressed with how busy the place always seemed to be, they set their sights on buying it.

Located at the corner of East Main Street and Chesterfield Avenue, Tops was a neighborhood (or "hillbilly," to quote Lee) bar owned by Buddy DeLong and Roy Stingley. Bill and Lee borrowed the $60,000 purchase price, installed a kitchen, built a piano bar and opened for business in April 1955. Bill claimed they had to "run off a bunch of hooligans," but many of those same "hooligans" grew up to be regular customers. Their business also helped the partners to pay off their loan in one year.

Then and now, the Top's time-traveling décor wallowed in the 1950s with dark wood paneling, a fireplace, a copper-top bar and Naugahyde booths. Exuding a "Rat Pack" (or, in modern parlance, "Mad Men") ambience, the restaurant immediately established itself as the place to go for surf, turf and martinis in the Midwest and, if Bexley native Bob Greene is to be believed, the entire country.

It did not take long for the Top to become a hangout for businessmen, politicians and powerbrokers of all kinds. To facilitate deal making, phone jacks were installed at each of its sixty tables (it seats another thirty-two at the bar). Its dedicated fan base has kept it going strong for nearly sixty years and several changes of ownership, the first occurring in 1980, when Bill bought out Lee's interest.[10]

Although they owned the building outright, Bill and Lee leased the land from Tony Agiesti. Each year, when it came time to negotiate a new lease agreement, they would pay a visit to their landlord. During their negotiations, they would be invited to drink some of Tony's homemade wine and did not feel they were in a position to turn him down. According to Lee, Bill would go in until he got drunk and then come out and say, "It's your turn."

With three years of "charbroiled success" (as Doral Chenoweth put it) under their belts, Bill and Lee decided to explore the possibility of creating another destination restaurant. This time, however, they would own the land as well. They began traveling throughout the United States and even the South Pacific in search of inspiration. No matter where they went, they were struck by the fact that all the Polynesian restaurants they visited were thriving while many others weren't. So they went looking for a piece of real estate—one that already had a liquor license, of course—to build their dream restaurant. On the east side of Columbus near Whitehall and not far from the Top, they found a barbecue rib joint that fit the bill.

With the addition of various grasses to enhance the décor, they turned the restaurant into the Grass Shack, a tiki bar, and installed Sandro Conti as bar manager. It opened for business in June 1958 and quickly became a popular place for World War II veterans to meet and reminisce about their war experiences. According to Lee, Sandro would sleep until noon and then get up and begin mixing drinks and inventing new ones. When he wasn't busy trying out new recipes for Polynesian dishes, Jerry, the Chinese chef, would walk around on his hands. He owned a car that had no heater, so he installed a coal stove inside it and cut a hole through the roof for a chimney. Jerry later opened his own restaurant on Oakland Park Avenue. Another employee was Alex Tsitouris, a Greek immigrant, who went on to become co-owner of Zorba's and Alex's Restaurant and Lounge.

The Grass Shack resembled a typical grass shack found on many ocean beaches. From the start, it was intended as the pilot for a much grander enterprise. Using a house on the property as their office,[11] Bill and Lee began planning a million-dollar Polynesian supper club. In creating the Grass Shack, they had employed many of the same materials (e.g., grasses, bamboo, thatch) they would later use in construction of the Kahiki by treating them with a fire retardant, Flame-Art, manufactured in California.

Then on June 14, 1959, the day before the groundbreaking for the new venture was to take place, the Grass Shack burned down. It was Bill's birthday. He had left the party at the Grass Shack while it was still in progress. Soon after he arrived home, he got a call from Sandro, who said, "Boss, we got a fire here."

Bill responded, "Well, put it out. I'll see you tomorrow."

A short time later, Sandro called back. "Hey, Boss, this thing's getting pretty big."

Bill asked, "Sandro, are we going to open tomorrow?"

The response was "Well, maybe."

An hour went by, and the bar manager called one more time. "Boss, we no open tomorrow."

Nevertheless, Bill and Lee pressed on. What they had in mind was a themed restaurant unlike any ever created anywhere. However, it was not the first themed dining and/or drinking establishment in Central Ohio. For a time, "America's Most Unique Night Club" (as it was billed) could be found at Spring and High Streets. The Catacombs was located in the Chittenden Hotel and accessed by a small building that resembled a subway kiosk. Customers would descend a flight of stairs to enter an "elevator" car to continue their downward descent another three hundred feet. In actuality, the elevator traveled nowhere, and after its passengers had been shaken about a bit, the door in the rear of the car would open into the nightclub. Greeted by employees wearing skeleton costumes, the patrons made their way through the Chapel of a Thousand Skulls.

An article in *Life* magazine stated that the Catacombs was opened by Illinois hotel magnate Albert Pick in the fall of 1940. It was an instant hit, although at least one reader of the magazine found it quite distasteful.[12] The nightclub used a folded, coffin-shaped postcard as an advertising mailer: "Thrills and Spills for Jacks and Jills. Enjoy an unforgettable evening...Be insulted and like it."

After passing down a hallway lined with caskets and plaster skeletons dressed in monks' habits, customers entered the Nut House Bar. The bar eschewed the macabre décor, replacing it with the madcap antics of a magician, Dr. Marcus, who would cut the sleeve off an unsuspecting customer's shirt and waitresses who would throw peanuts in their faces, all in the name of good fun. Former vaudevillian Mary Brant enjoyed a long engagement at the nightclub with her "dead-pan waitress" routine.

Using the Catacombs as the yardstick, other themed-venues in the region didn't quite measure up. For example, Nick Albanese, whose résumé included stints as a circus executive, fight promoter and celebrity publicist, operated several east side night spots during the 1930s–'50s. Around 1935, he, along with his partner, Tom Worlen, transformed the Broad-Manor nightclub at Norton Field into the Arabian Gardens. This upscale club featured entertainment ranging from Duke Ellington and his Orchestra to Zorine and her Nudist Colony in a vaguely Middle Eastern setting. However, the real attraction was the gambling casino, which "had the blessing of Sheriff Jacob Sandusky."

According to Nick's daughter, Donna Newman, the roulette wheels, slot machines and gaming tables either flipped over or retracted into secret compartments when there was a raid, just like in the 1973 movie *The Sting*. Across East Broad Street from the Gardens, Nick built another "swanky"

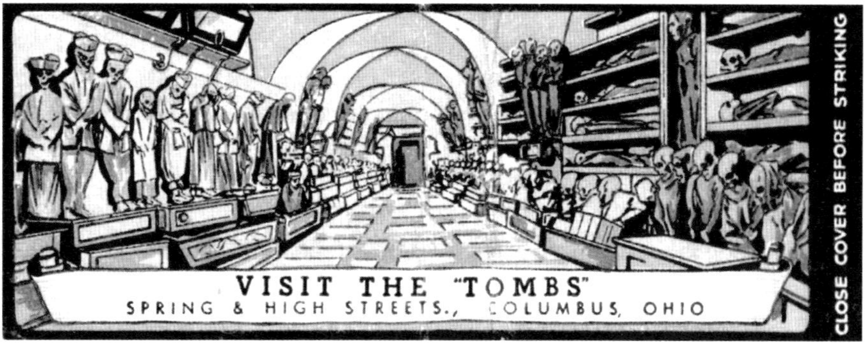

The Catacombs, a themed restaurant once featured in *Life* magazine, was also known as the Tombs, as this matchbook cover shows. *Authors' collection.*

club: the Showboat (4500 East Broad Street). Although it looked like a cruise ship on the outside, "in the main bar, a colorful circus train with carved animals circled continuously around the room's ceiling." In Bexley, you could also patronize the Glass Bowl. This eatery was built like an upside-down champagne glass and sat only twelve folks inside, requiring most patrons to order via drive-in service.

Among the many dining spots housed in the downtown Lazarus Department Store was the Colonial Room. Modeled after the Raleigh Tavern in Williamsburg, it opened in 1926 and had a nearly seventy-year run before closing in 1995. While the surroundings were evocative, little effort was put into re-creating an eighteenth-century dining experience. It wouldn't be until a couple decades after the Kahiki debuted that such themed restaurants as Baby Doe's Matchless Mine, the 94th Aero Squadron, the WaterWorks (where you could have dinner in a claw-foot bathtub and order from a menu shaped like a manhole cover!) and JoAnn's Chili Bordello began dotting the Columbus landscape. Other eateries, such as Max & Erma's, tried novelty approaches by installing closed-circuit telephones at each table so you could make dinner plans and a date all at the same time. Most of these restaurants, however, quickly died as a result of placing more emphasis on the concept than the food. Over the years, Planet Hollywood, Dick Clark's American Bandstand Grill, Made in America, the Buckeye Hall of Fame Café and similar efforts to use pop cultural artifacts as a lure for diners cycled through the city.

Columbus acquired its own Playboy Club on December 7, 1982, when the latest bunny hutch opened in the old Desert Inn, directly across the street from the Kahiki. Thirty-four women were hired and provided with six weeks of training to augment the décor. Bill Sapp was one of the first people to buy a Playboy Key (at twenty-five dollars each). Syndicated columnist Bob Greene's ninety-six-year-old grandmother was another. But despite widespread support across generations, it closed four years later.

None of these establishments, however, approached the Kahiki in terms of total commitment to a theme, which is why it remains the gold standard.

3
SAIL TO TAHITI

The ultimate goal of the architect…is to create a paradise. Every house, every product of architecture…should be a fruit of our endeavour to build an earthly paradise for people.
—Alvar Aalto

The loss of the Grass Shack did not deter Bill and Lee from moving forward with their original plan, which, according to Bill, was simply to "build a nice Polynesian restaurant." They were not thinking in terms of constructing the most magnificent Polynesian supper club in the country and, perhaps, the world, although few would argue that the result was anything less.

The local restaurant scene had not changed appreciably since the Top opened in 1954. There were now roughly 840 dining establishments listed in the city directory. Most of the major ones were still thriving. However, there was still very little variety—meat and potatoes or Italian were the options. The few "oriental" or Asian restaurants to be found were Aloha Restaurant, Far East Restaurant, Ho Toy Restaurant, Jong Mea, Mandarin Restaurant, Ming's Chop Suey, Lem's, New China Restaurant, Olentangy Village Tavern, Oriental Restaurant, Tropics East Restaurant and Tropics North Restaurant. Columbus was clearly ripe for something new.

To assist them in realizing their vision, the partners hired architect Bernard C. "Bernie" Altenbach. As Bill Sapp recalled:

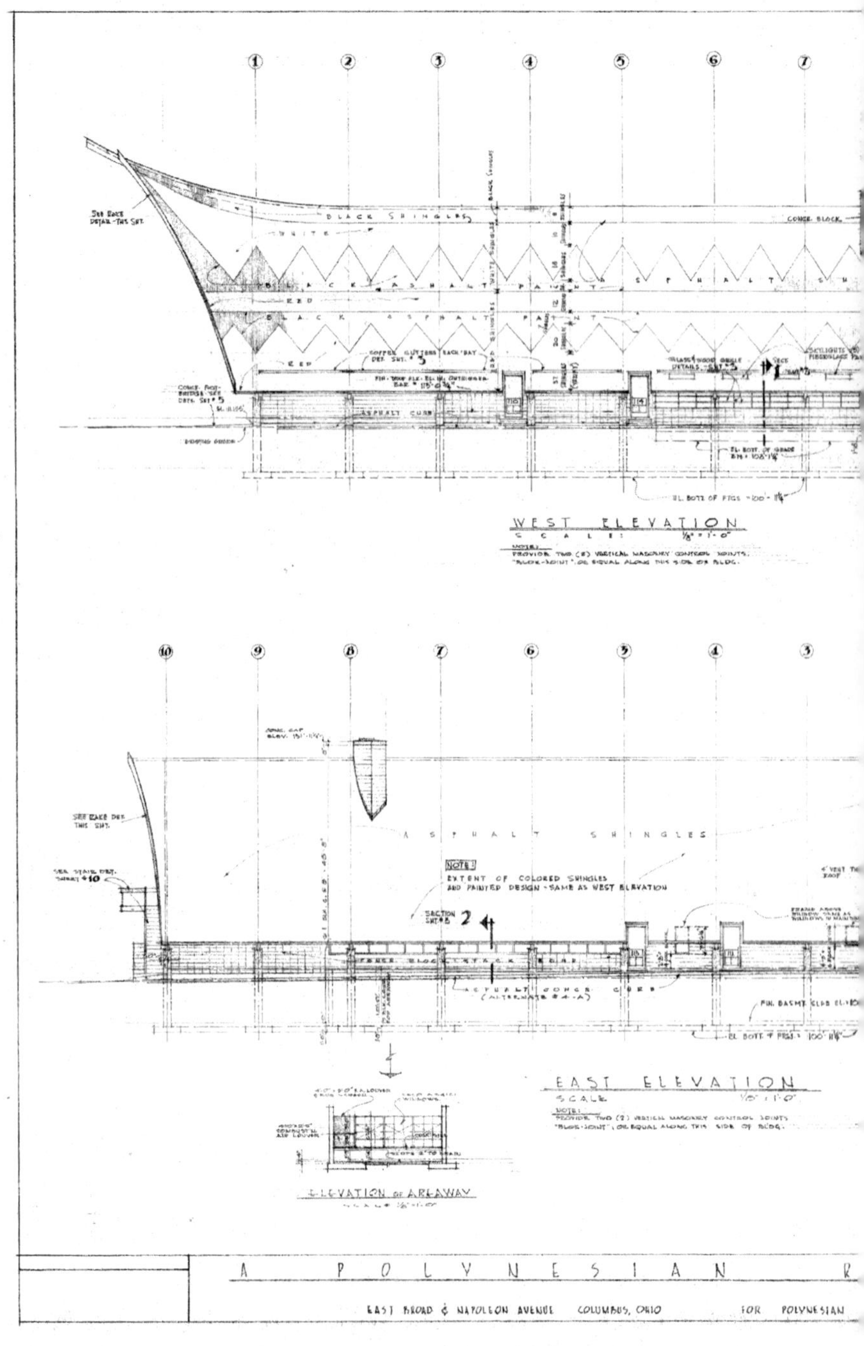

The design of the Kahiki went beyond the standard A-frame construction. *Fraternal Order of Moai Archive.*

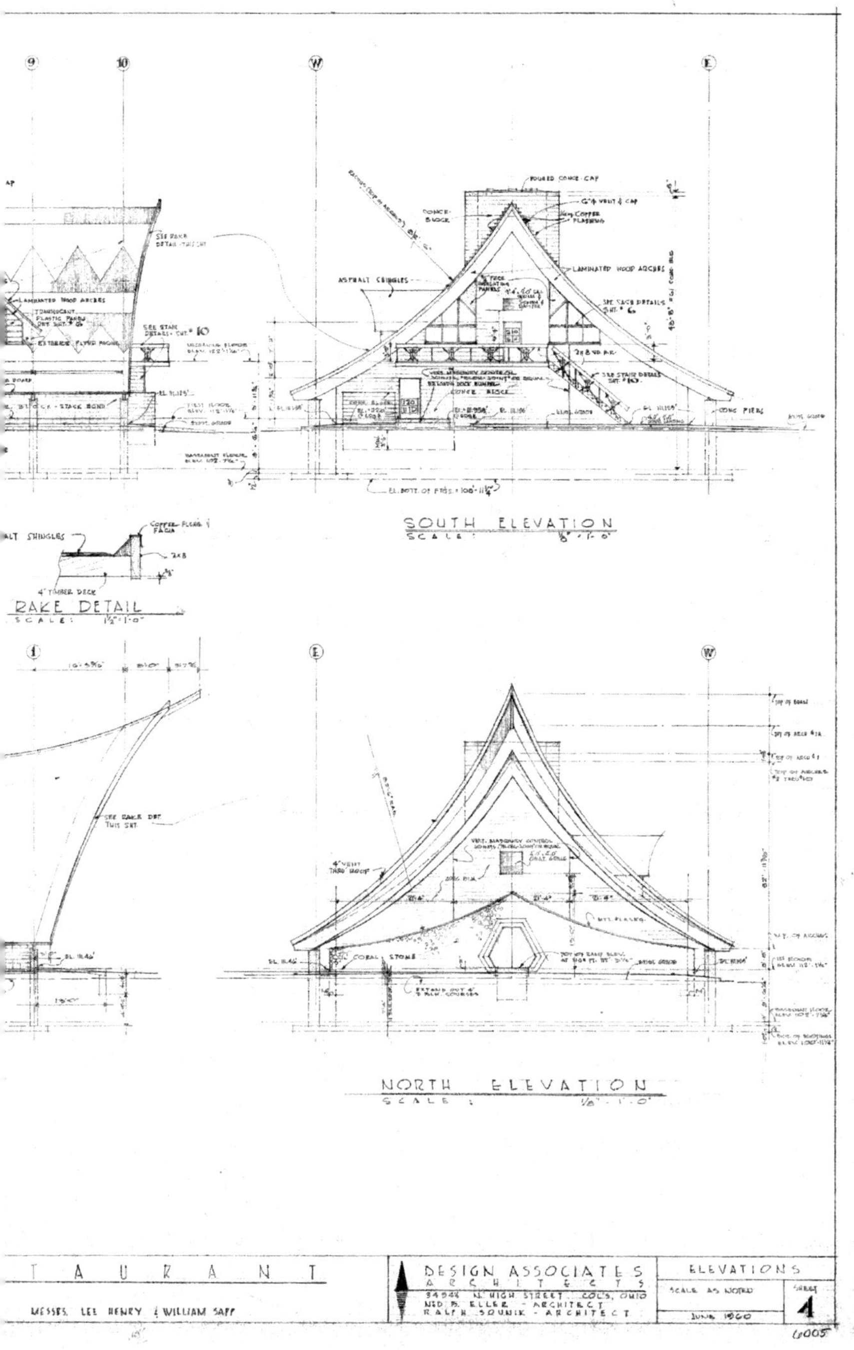
SOUTH ELEVATION
SCALE: 1/8" = 1'-0"
LAMINATED WOOD ARCHES
ASPHALT SHINGLES
CONC. PIERS
RAKE DETAIL
SCALE: 1½" = 1'-0"
4" TIMBER DECK
NORTH ELEVATION
SCALE: 1/8" = 1'-0"
CORAL STONE
T A U R A N T
MESSRS. LEE HENRY & WILLIAM SAPP
DESIGN ASSOCIATES
ARCHITECTS
3454½ N. HIGH STREET COL'S, OHIO
NED B. ELLER - ARCHITECT
RALPH SOUNIK - ARCHITECT
ELEVATIONS
SCALE AS NOTED
JUNE 1960
SHEET 4
6005

> *Bernie came up with the idea of the Polynesian meetinghouse, and he got it started and well on its way. Coburn Morgan came in as the decorator. Bernie Altenbach designed the different rooms inside the Kahiki but never really got the credit that he deserved. Bernie had just finished remodeling the Top at that time. We hired Bernie to do it, but when he got too busy, he had Coburn take over. Coburn Morgan was very outgoing and got all the credit.*

A resident of Columbus, Bernie was fifty-six years old when he undertook the project, which he modeled on a "New Guinea meetinghouse." Chris Altenbach recalled that his father's "intention was to showcase 'the four forces of nature—earth, wind, water and fire—in a South Pacific island setting.'" Bernie had been friends with Bill and Lee since their college days. However, after he passed away on July 24, 1995, at the age of ninety-one, the memory of his contribution to the restaurant began to fade.

Ned B. Eller and Ralph Sounik took over for Bernie. Fraternity brothers at Ohio State, the two men had formed S.E.M. (Sounik, Eller and Harry W. Martin) Partners in 1959, specializing in educational and religious architectural projects. They were responsible for creating the final construction blueprints. Ned eventually relocated to West Virginia, and Ralph passed away on March 17, 2012.

While traveling through Lexington, Kentucky, Bill and Lee saw a Polynesian mural. "We learned it was painted by Coburn Morgan, who was in Columbus doing a job for Nationwide Insurance," Lee said. "He was selling a ceiling material called Tectum." Coburn was a brilliant but difficult guy, Bill would later say. A talented artist, he often relied on others to execute his ideas. For example, he sculpted a miniature of the moai that guarded the main door of the Kahiki and shot gas flames from the tops of their heads, but Philip Kientz constructed the actual full-size statues. As a result, it is sometimes difficult to identify who was responsible for what.

"He devised a method to make the water in the fountain glow," architect Barry Follmer recalled, "and he put together the sound and light effects for the thunderstorms that occur periodically in the glass aviary. He fashioned the knots in the ropes that hold the bamboo huts together. He even designed the tin lamps that sit on each table." With Lee, Coburn traveled to the West Coast to handpick many of the numerous artifacts that were not his original creations.

"We were traveling all over the world and all doing research on Polynesia," Bill recalled. "I went through the Polynesian dictionary and found the word *Kahiki*, which means 'sail to Tahiti.' It sounded like it would work." Coburn

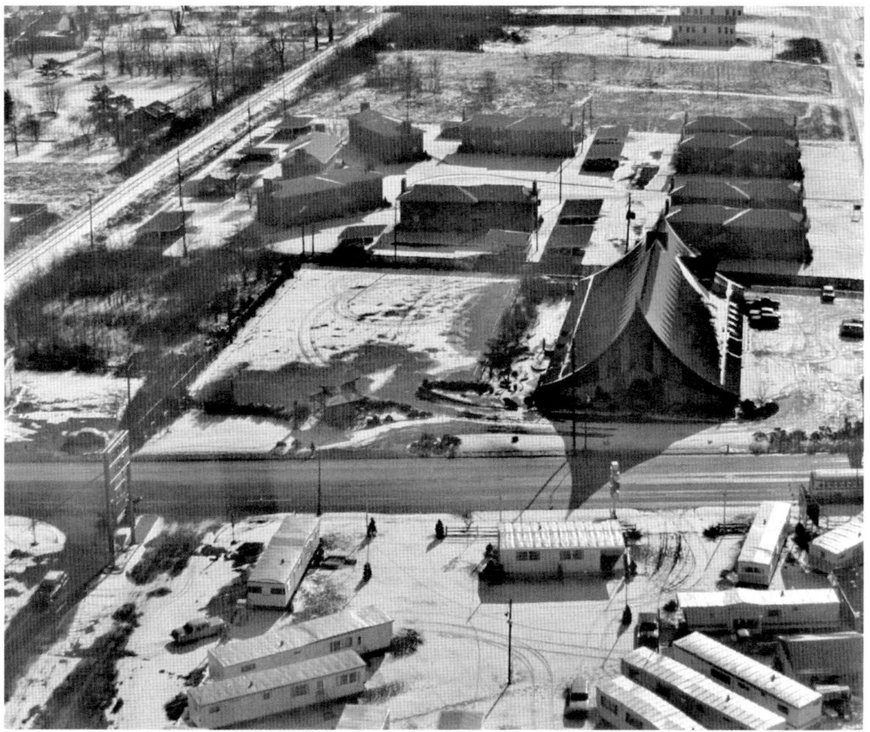

An aerial photo of the Kahiki Supper Club during construction. *Authors' collection.*

sketched hundreds of ideas for the Kahiki's décor and hired teenage art students to fabricate handmade lamps and wall designs.

Ground was broken in July 1960 on the former site of the Grass Shack. Those in attendance included Bill Sapp, Lee Henry, Robert Henry, Coburn Morgan, Ned Eller, Ralph Sounic, model Marsha Gleaves and L.M. Berry, Henry's stepfather, who operated an advertising agency in Dayton and had a financial interest in the project.

Because the Grass Shack had burned, fire chief McFadden wasn't going to allow Bill and Lee to use any grasses or thatch in the construction of the Kahiki. However, examining the ruins of their tiki bar, they pointed out to the chief that everything had been consumed except those materials that had been treated with Flame-Art. They were only charred. After that, McFadden said, "It's alright with me."

Not surprisingly, Central Ohio carpenters did not have much experience working with bamboo and palm fronds, so they had to learn on the job,

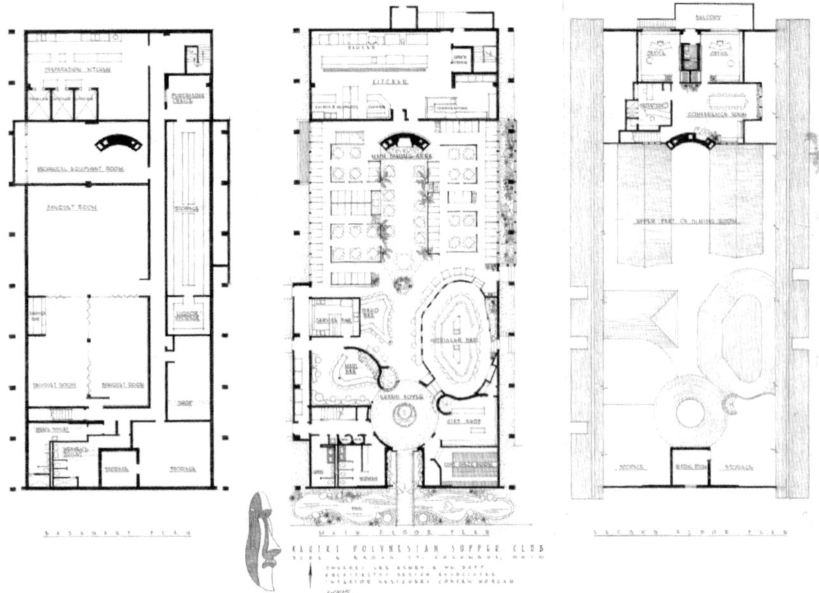

These blueprints show the layout of the restaurant's main floor and basement. *Fraternal Order of Moai Archive collection.*

Linda Becker remembered. Her father was one of them and made the "flaming" plywood fish that ran along the ridge of the roof. Years before, he had worked on the Desert Inn across the street (which would later benefit from the Kahiki's overflow business).

General contractor Jack Liberatore's involvement ended when construction was done. Herman L. Leitwein, who had worked on the Grass Shack, Top of the Isle, Desert Inn and Larry Flynt's Hustler Clubs, continued to work for them. "He was our guy," Lee said. He remained as the restaurant's building and maintenance superintendent while Jesse Howard handled all the electrical installation. Majestic Paint created a custom color—Kahiki Brown—that was used throughout the restaurant.

Leitwein recalled that when the bamboo dried out, it would split with a loud crack that sounded like a gun being fired. On two occasions, live snakes purportedly emerged from the bamboo. He also said that the live palm trees and other tropical plants had to be replaced on a yearly basis.

"I remember when we had just brought up some palm trees from Florida, and I took my mother to the Kahiki for the first time," Bill said. "A little green snake fell out of one of the palm trees onto the table, which of course made a lasting impression on my mother." During its heyday, the restaurant required a truckload of banana tree leaves each month to meet its needs.

When the doors opened in February 1961, "Polynesian was the theme; pineapple was the flavor; Far East eclectic was the cuisine; Kahiki was the name," to quote Doral Chenoweth, the Grumpy Gourmet. It was an immediate hit. And as a result, some thought was given to opening another one.

"We were so tired from all this and the way it went over and everything. We were making money like we never dreamed of. We really didn't think of any others," Bill said. "At one time, though, after we had been open a year we got a call from some people in Hawaii that wanted us to open up over there, but we didn't. We thought about that pretty seriously, but in the meantime, we were working on plans to open a Kahiki in Cincinnati. We applied for a liquor license and did everything down there, but we were never able to make any kind of deal for a lot down there. So it just fell through."

The scramble to build tiki bars and restaurants included several other notable Buckeye State establishments. In 1953, sometime actor Stephen Crane, best known for his two marriages to film star Lana Turner, bought Lucy's, a popular Hollywood hangout on Rodeo Drive. Reopened as the Luau, it quickly became a magnet for celebrities, who were attracted by its exotic décor, beautiful table and dinnerware and flamboyant cocktails. Five years later, Crane began parlaying his "tiki oasis" into a small chain of restaurants. Taking a cue from Trader Vic's, he formed a partnership with Sheraton hotels to open Polynesian-themed restaurants in more than a half dozen Sheratons. He called them Kon-Tiki after purchasing the rights to the name from Thor Heyerdahl, author of the bestselling book. For the third outlet in his chain, Indiana-born Crane chose the Sheraton-Cleveland Hotel. Located on Public Square, it opened in 1961 and seated 230. It closed in 1976. In 1965, Crane opened his seventh Kon-Tiki in Cincinnati's Sheraton-Gibson Hotel, occupying what had formerly been the Florentine Room. Situated on the edge of Fountain Square, the hotel closed in 1974 and was demolished three years later.

Toledo's contribution to "tiki culture" was AkuAku, located in the Town House Motel. Between its opening in 1960 and its closure ten years later, this "Polynesian Room" hosted many major acts, including Frank Sinatra, Tony Bennett, Count Basie, Buddy Rich, Duke Ellington, Henny Youngman and Phyllis Diller. The club was owned by Irving "Slick" Shapiro, a gambler and bookmaker with a number of arrests under his belt by the time the AkuAku opened. "There's no question: He ran the last of the great clubs in this

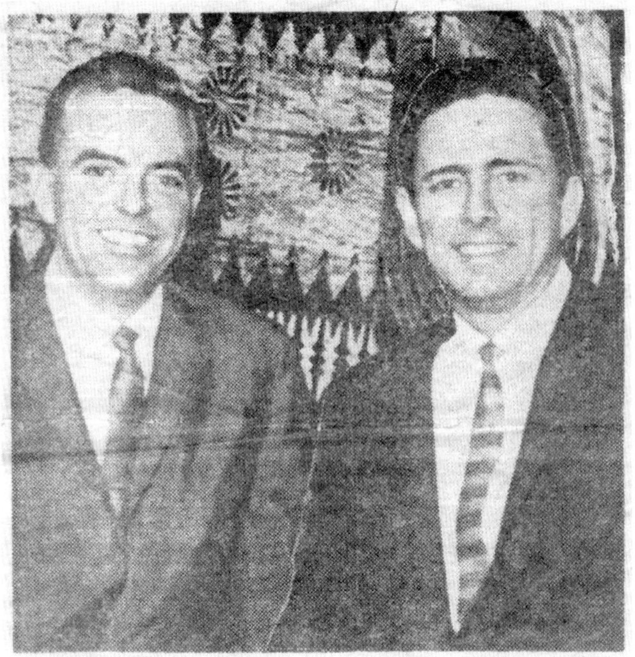

OWNERS of the fabulous Kahiki, 2583 E. Broad St., are Bill Sapp annd Lee Henry. Designed and founded in 1961 according to their own specifications and architecture, it has the reputation of being the largest Polynesian restaurant in America. It has achieved popularity both for its cuisine of island dishes as well as American foods and for the hospitality of its personnel.

Bill Sapp (on left) and Lee Henry promoted the Kahiki throughout Central Ohio and beyond. *Courtesy Sapp/Henry.*

town," Seymour Rothman, retired *Toledo Blade* columnist, recalled. "There's never been any place like that since. Not even close." As might be expected, the club was popular with both city leaders and well-known mob figures. It also had the same logo tiki as the Luau 400 in New York City. It is unclear if the logo was lifted or if the two locations had a relationship. Shapiro also owned several other Toledo eateries: Guiseppe's Italian, the Embers, the Gas Light Club (later the Lamplite Club) and the Granada Gardens.

Dayton was also home to a Kon-Tiki of its own, but rather than a tiki bar, it was a Polynesian-themed movie palace. A longtime landmark at 4100 Salem Avenue, the Kon-Tiki was built in 1968 by the local Levin family, specifically Samuel Levin, who owned three other movie houses and thirteen drive-in theaters. Also decorated by Coburn Morgan during the peak of the tiki-craze, the Kon-Tiki was patterned after Grauman's Chinese Theater in Hollywood. It featured illuminated tiki faces on the façade, volcanic rock and abalone shells on the walls and enormous seashells for sinks in the restrooms. There was also an enormous marquee and tiki torches studding the parking lot. Unbelievably, the theater did not have a concession stand when it first opened because Sam felt it would cheapen the experience. However, since concessions are often more important than film revenues to a theater, one was soon installed. In 1987, the Kon-Tiki became part of the Lowes movie house chain. Twelve years later, it closed and was demolished in 2005 to make way for a medical center.

A meat cutter by trade, George Rudin opened a Dayton grocery in 1946 at 1721 North Main Street. Within two years, it had evolved into a cocktail lounge and delicatessen and eventually a supper club. Inspired by a Polynesian restaurant he had visited in California, George and his wife, Minnie, made trips to Hawaii and the Philippines to purchase canoes, surfboards, wooden tiki gods, lava rocks and other knickknacks that carried out the island theme. He called it George Rudin's Tropics, and clearly it was. As his daughter, Natalie, recalled for writer Benjamin Kline, "Dad was here until 4 a.m. for 40 years. He bought the food, prepared the menus, cut his own steaks. He did everything." That included the remodeling. "Once he built a mother-of-pearl wall around the bar, didn't like how it looked and the next day it was gone." Rudin served Cantonese and American food, along with standard cocktails and tropical drinks in tiki mugs. He also provided entertainment, ranging from major stars such Lucille Ball, Dean Martin & Jerry Lewis and Lester Flatt & Earl Scruggs to local favorites Big Red ("Dayton's one and only Red Hot Mama") and even Vicki & the Rest, an all-girl teenage rock band from suburban Kettering. From the flaming torches in the parking lot to the profusion of bamboo and palm trees, the Tropics was the height of tiki kitsch. And then, in August 1987, Rudin abruptly closed his little corner of paradise.

However, during the 1960s and 1970s, it was a rare city that didn't have some form of half-hearted tiki bar or tiki room. After a few drinks, they all looked pretty much the same anyway.[13]

4
THE STORY OF KAHIKI

It was one of the greatest Tiki temples ever. I remember getting a little weak-kneed. You saw that A-frame building and you're, "Oh, this is going to be good." Then you go in and see the fireplace, and that's everyone's Tiki dream.
—Frank DeCaro

For many people, their first exposure to the Kahiki was a billboard. There was one on Olentangy River Road and another at Hamilton and Livingston Avenues. It featured the face of a "Polynesian Goddess" that would mechanically "wink" at passersby. As a young boy of six or seven, Doug Motz remembered seeing it every Sunday morning on the way to church, which "scared the devil out of me, and I would duck down behind the seat of my parents' station wagon for fear she would see me."

From several blocks away, the Kahiki was as conspicuous as Noah's ark run aground on an asphalt beach. It was surrounded by strip malls, fast-food outlets and an assortment of bars and motels. However, these distractions were offset by an oasis of landscaping. In combination with the striking architecture, the heavy concentration of vegetation, especially along Broad Street, helped to create an exotic atmosphere. This was further enhanced at night by a series of patio lights that outlined the driveway, as well as the red glow of the Kahiki sign, supported on faux bamboo posts. The lettering on this and the few other signs that dotted the property employed an "oriental" font.

When attempting to describe the Kahiki, many patrons found that mere words failed them. They couldn't capture it all. There was just too much to process. Even repeated visits did not suffice. "We already

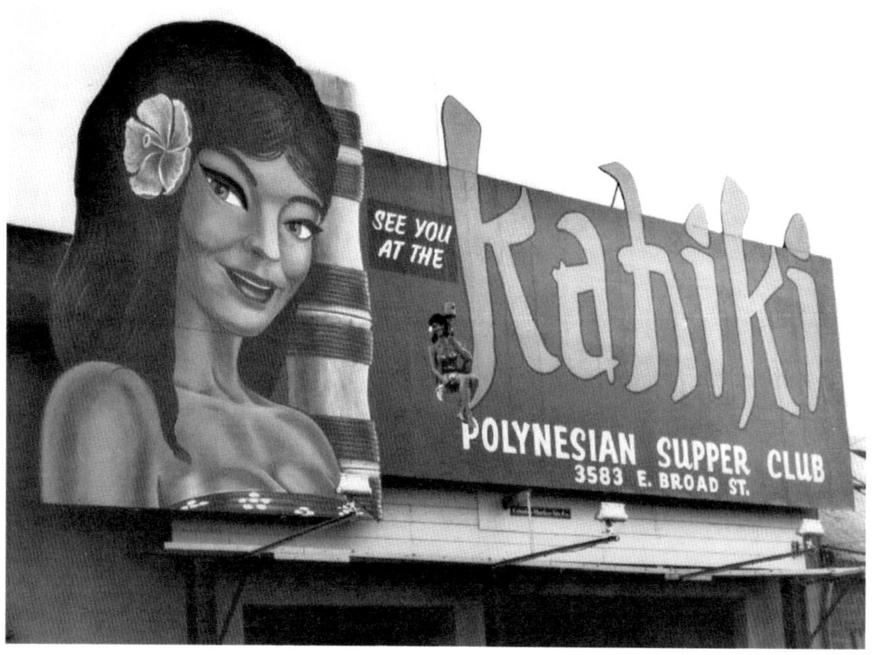

One of the famous Kahiki billboards (note the young lady suspended from a crane just below the "K"). *Courtesy Sapp/Henry.*

overwhelmed the customer as they walk in," Michael Tsao, who later purchased the restaurant, told Renee Montaigne in an interview broadcast on *NPR Morning Edition*. "Then you have to go through the whole experience of dining."

The following marketing piece dates from early in the Kahiki's history, perhaps as far back as the opening, and conveys a sense of what the restaurant was like. It may have been written by Robert F. "Bob" Slatzer, a former reporter who later claimed that he had been secretly married to Marilyn Monroe. He was a friend of Lee's who was a talented copywriter. Or it could have been written by Bill Kite, who also worked on promotional materials for the restaurant. It is entitled "The Story of Kahiki."

> *When the Islanders say "Kahiki" they speak of a joyous voyage filled with laughter and expectation of all that awaits them at their destination…Tahiti. For only here can be found the great heart of the South Sea Islands, which beckons with the timeless enchantment of tradition and promises a fantasy of tropical splendor in every phase.*

It is here, amid the breathtaking beauty of a jungle paradise, that many exotic preparations of food and drink have been originated for festive occasions and for the never-failing approval of gracious Tiki gods.

So, with this most inadequate bit of background...Welcome to your "Kahiki" the fabulous, million-dollar Polynesian supper club, where not one detail has been overlooked in making your trip to Tahiti come true.

And now that your car is in the hands of a capable attendant, let's pause and observe this magnificent structure, as it covers over seventy feet in width, approximately one hundred and fifty feet in length and gracefully arches to a majestic five stories of height. We are reminded of a great gleaming jewel as it reflects the highlights from many flaming luau torches which border the winding drive of the spacious, three acre area.

The spell is surely upon us and we hesitate only long enough to look with wonder at two towering Easter Island Heads whose heights are crowned with fiery halos; and passing between them now, we cross the bamboo bridge which spans a lagoon of sparking waters.

Before us is a huge bronze door, and through this we enter the realm of strangely glowing waterfalls which spill from lofty heights and cascade over frothy cliffs of coral. We are watching the magic action of "black light," an iridescent substance in the rushing waters, which appears to have captured straying tropical moonbeams, for the sole purpose of illuminating this entire area.

Just beyond the waterfalls, and through the massive bronze double doors, we come upon the Grand Foyer or "Giant Hut," as it is so aptly named, and to the left our attention is drawn to a large collection of odd and beautiful shells which are arranged and labeled for easy identification; also in this location are entrances to the "telephone shells"...where you may experience a most delightful way in which to send a message, by simply stepping into a giant shell whose inner contours shape a tunnel-like hallway, which winds into the soundproof center.

Another charming appointment can be found in both guest lounges, where the washbasins are giant shells, presided over by Tiki gods, whose mouths issue forth hot and cold running water. You will note that every effort has been made for comfort and accommodations here in Kahiki, which includes a large six hundred coat checkroom and the spacious downstairs party room which seats two hundred guests.

Directly opposite the shell collections and to our right, is the exclusive "Beachcomber Shop" that features one of the most unusual displays of unique merchandise to be found anywhere. These exotic items have been

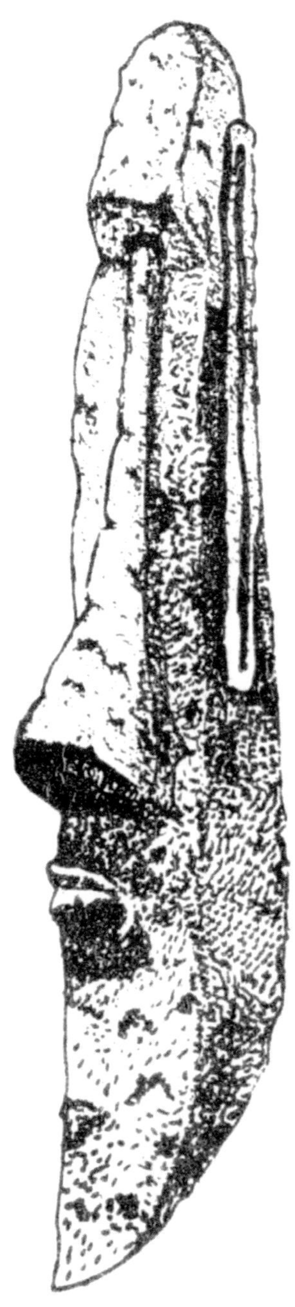

This iconic head was used in various advertising campaigns. *Courtesy Sapp/Henry.*

imported directly from the islands of the South Pacific and include exciting Hawaiian dresses, handsomely tailored shirts and garments for both men and women, smartly styled from original tapa cloth print. There are gaily colored leis, shoes of the popular thong-type, metallic cuff links of Tiki design, a wide selection of earrings, enticing costume jewelry, a complete line of various type dishes, drinking cups and bowls cut and carved from rare woods, sparking glass and all of native origin.

Dominating the "Giant Hut," by its very presence, looms the massive carved head of the sacrificial Tiki god. You are not alone with the impression that nothing escapes notice of this idol's blazing green eyes. Special lighting effects color the flood of red waters which pour from the mouth of this threatening god, as he jealously guards the peaceful, contented way of life in the Quiet Villages.

Beyond this Tiki idol, a golden doorway beckons and we see a lovely fountain in the center of a primitive cocktail lounge. On our left, from the direction of the Hawaiian Bar and nearby piano, rippling notes of soothing melody fill the air and we want to relax in the land of South Sea Island enchantment. While to the right of the fountain is the gleaming "Outrigger Bar," encircled by comfortable Captain's Chairs. We may choose from a wide variety of exotic tropical cocktails in which rare rums, spices and fruit juices go into the making of the most exquisitely refreshing drinks you have ever enjoyed, while cares of the outside world seem far away from this wonderland of music and whispering waters.

We notice Thatched Huts beyond this lounge and approaching them now, we enter the main dining room area or elegant "Quiet Village" where we are welcomed by a gracious Maître d'…nor have we come a victim of our own imagination, for the village street down which we stroll is actually strewn with small shells, pebbles and beach sand that have been mixed and imbedded in a special composition and used for the first time here in Kahiki.

The dining tables of rustic beauty, with mirror-polished tops have been hewn from split trunks of monkey pod[14] *and zebrawood trees; and as we take our places, a raven-haired Polynesian hostess, clad in a stunning sarong, presents a menu which offers an assembly of the finest foods available. We may choose from a tantalizing array of exotic dishes, tempting appetizers, over thirty Cantonese preparations, two dozen American entrees, a variety of refreshing desserts and many delicious tropical drinks.*

While dining in [sic] *our utmost satisfaction, we see the tropical theme again carried out by the attire of our waiters, who are wearing white trousers and contrasting shirts of colorful tapa print cloth, as they move about beneath the towering palm trees which line the village street.*

On the east side of this room there is a lovely glass-enclosed garden of luxuriant plants and exotic ferns, resplendent in their natural setting of authentic island habitat. While on the opposite side of the room, our eyes feast upon the unforgettable beauty of the "Rain Forest" as it re-enacts the equinoctial storms typical of the tropics, complete with lighting and thunder, and through this maze of glistening woodland we follow the flights of brilliantly colored tropical birds as they wing their way to favored spots throughout the bower.

At the far end of the Village, reaching twenty eight feet in height, a mammoth Easter Island Head provides the rare combination of a wood-burning fireplace and a waterfall. As you look beyond the waterfall that curtains a six foot width of the idol's upper lip, a blazing log fire set back in his mouth shines through…and you can almost hear an age-old welcome spoken, as the Tiki god grants shelter from the storm.

When the time has come to leave, our thoughts travel back over the many strange and beautiful sights we have seen. We look again at the beautifully carved native ornaments; the spears and shrunken heads; and on closer examination, one marvels at the artistry displayed in the carved Tiki gods, the crystal ware and in the various designs of rattan and handiwork of bamboo.

As the great bronze door closes behind us, we think of the pleasure that awaits those who will visit here and of the travelers who will come from hundreds of miles away for their first visit to Kahiki…the world's most beautiful Polynesian Restaurant, located on Route #16, East at 3583 East Broad Street, Columbus, Ohio. As we pause on the bamboo

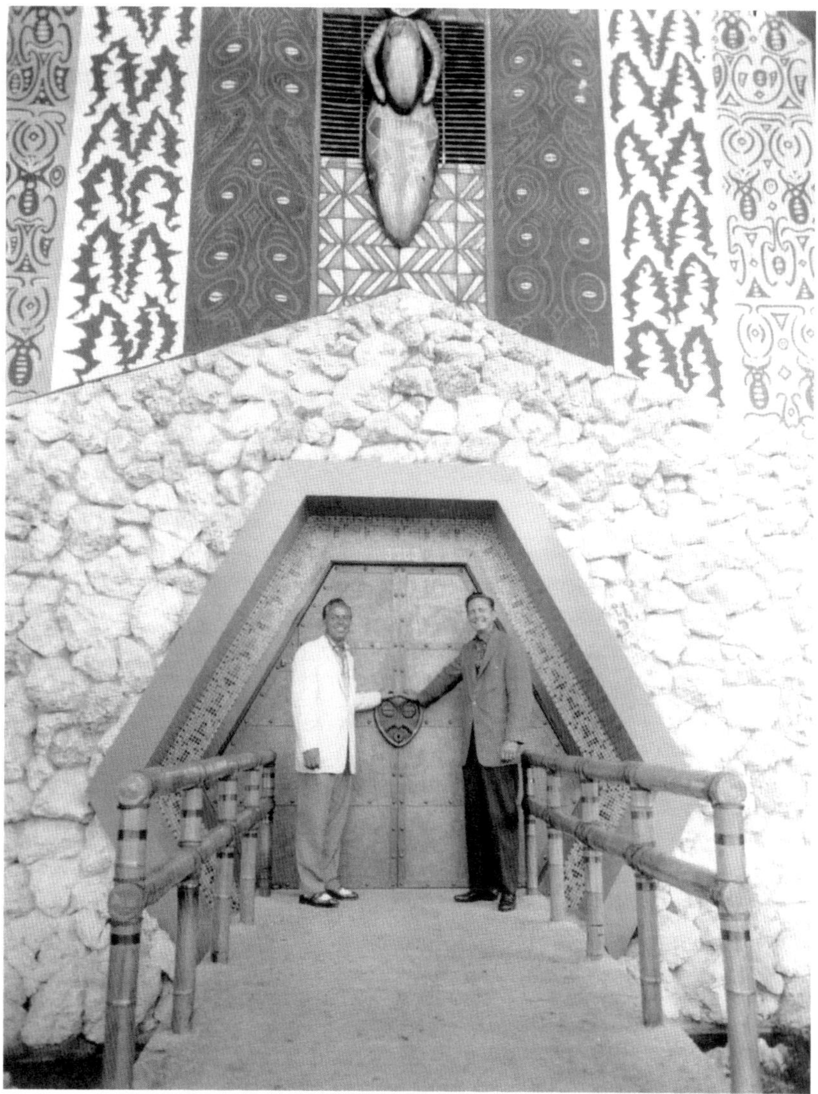

Bill Sapp and Lee Henry prepare to throw open the doors to the Kahiki Supper Club. *Courtesy Sapp/Henry.*

bridge, reluctant to leave a paradise, we toss coins below with a wish. The shimmering waters seem to whisper the answer…Aloha, until we meet again and we know you'll return to Kahiki.

5

SONG OF THE ISLANDS

Hours…I might have found long and lonely, passed quickly and cheerfully by, occupied and soothed by the expression of my thoughts in music.
—Queen Liliuokalani of Hawaii

Just prior to the onset of World War I, Hawaiian music was gaining favor on college campuses throughout the country, and Ohio was no exception. Recordings by Hawaiian-born Frank Ferera, the Waikiki Hawaiian Orchestra and other early recording artists brought the exotic sounds of the islands to the continental United States. In 1911, German-born Leon Berg published his first Hawaiian song, "Beautiful Isle of Love," following it up with "In Honey Honolulu" six years later after he had settled in Dayton. Columbus's own ragtime king Shep Edmonds contributed "Honolulu Lou" in 1920.

The University Boys Company (James R. Frew, A.W. Cubbison and H.S. Billings) entertained audiences on the Ohio Chautauqua circuit with Hawaiian music during the summer of 1916. Frew, who played ten instruments, also signed a contract to record a number of phonograph records using the Hawaiian steel guitar, the ukulele and the Taro Patch (one-string) fiddle. The same year, Goldsmith's Music Store in Columbus was advertising "Genuine Hawaiian Ukuleles," as well as sheet music for popular Hawaiian-themed songs of the day, in the *Ohio State Lantern*.

While interest in this new musical genre declined upon the nation's entrance into the "Great War" in April 1917, the popularity of the ukulele continued. Along with the raccoon coat, it became part of the collegiate uniform during the 1920s. However, the second wave of Hawaiian music

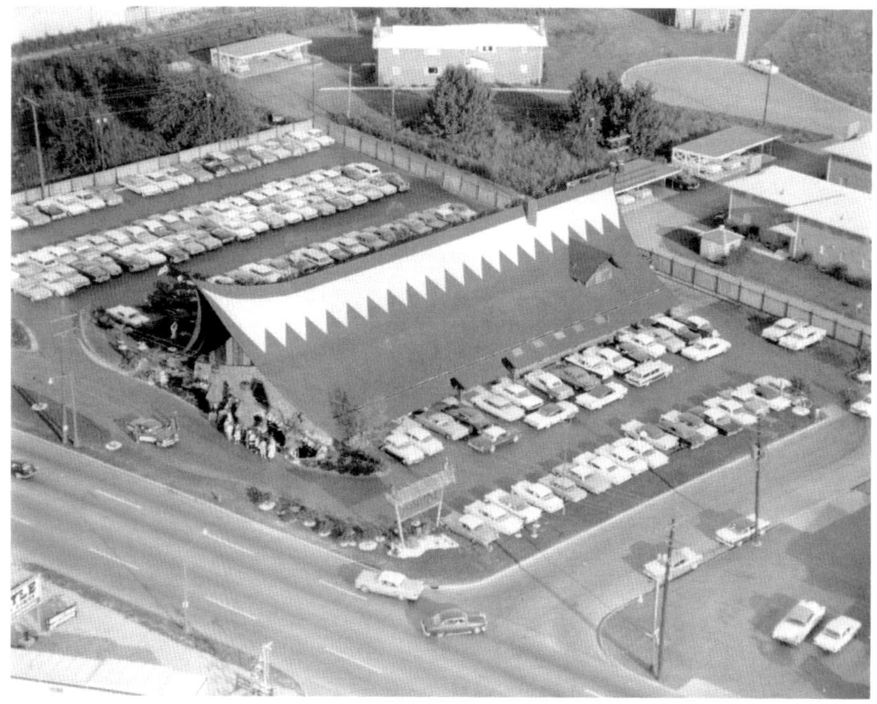

Aerial view of the Kahiki taken not long after it opened in 1961. *Courtesy Sapp/Henry.*

was ushered in by another instrument, the lap steel guitar.[15] San Francisco's Pan-Pacific Exposition introduced the Hawaiian guitar to the mainland in 1915. Over the next decade, the instrument was electrified and picked up many fans, ranging from bandleader Alvino Rey to country musician Jimmy Davis. Soon it was incorporated into big band and country recordings, where it remains ubiquitous.

As early as 1931, Weldon Groves and Herbert A. "Buck" Clark were playing electric (i.e. Hawaiian) guitars along with Harry Taverack on bass at the Airport Restaurant in Columbus. While performing regularly at Port Columbus Airport, Buck was also heard twice weekly on WCAH radio, with Martha DeGood on ukulele and vocals and Charles "Bud" Clark on guitar. They were billed as Theronoid's Hawaiians in honor of their sponsor, the Theronoid Corporation of Cleveland, manufacturer of a sort of electrified belt that was guaranteed to cure whatever ails you.

By 1939, the demand for ukulele music prompted John Jay Calborn of Columbus to start Calborn Music Publishing Company. He issued several dozen sheet music titles, primarily public domain tunes arranged for Hawaiian guitar. Much the same thing was happening in Cleveland at Oahu Publishing. In 1950, entertainer Arthur Godfrey, who had learned to play the uke from a Hawaiian sailor during the 1920s, decided to promote it on television. Although he already had two shows on CBS, he talked the network into giving him another, *Arthur Godfrey and His Ukulele*. The "Old Redhead" caused sales of the instrument to boom.

Enter Ernest Gantt, aka Donn Beach. Gantt unwittingly gave rise to a new musical genre, "exotica," when he hired classical pianist Martin Denny for a two-week engagement at his restaurant in Hawaii. A form of easy listening music, exotica uses various types of percussion instruments and often birdcalls and jungle sounds to convey its sense of mystery and wonder. The arrangements also played a big role in setting up a rich tropical background. Like a good tiki bar filled with grass skirts, puffer fish and other Polynesian pop, the goal was pure escapism.

Attracted by the island lifestyle, Denny had decided to remain in Hawaii after his gig ended. Forming his own group in 1955, he quickly landed a job at the Shell Bar in the Hawaiian Village on Oahu. Although his combo frequently played on the mainland, they returned to their home base every twelve weeks to reunite with their families.

It was while at the Shell Bar that Denny happened on the formula that would become "exotica." His group was playing near a pool of water one night when he noticed that bullfrogs were croaking along with the music. When a tune ended, the frogs would stop. As a joke, several guys in the band began adding in tropical birdcalls. However, the next day someone specifically requested the arrangement with the frogs and birds. At the next rehearsal, Denny had his band play "Quiet Village" with each musician adding in a birdcall, while he reproduced the frog part.

In 1957, Martin Denny released his first album, entitled simply *Exotica*, on Liberty Records. This album not only gave a name to an entire genre of music but also launched the entire exotica movement. Two years later, Denny's album would reach number one on the *Billboard* charts while the song "Quiet Village" peaked at number two on the singles chart. Soon, albums by Arthur Lyman, Robert Drasnin and others flooded the record stores and grocery marts.

The music could place the listener on a beach on a South Sea Island or plunge him/her into the deepest jungles with voodoo drums pounding out a hypnotic beat. Because of the nature of this music, it's not surprising that a vast majority of exotica artists were also film composers, including seasoned professionals Les Baxter, Robert Drasnin and Dominic Frontiere.

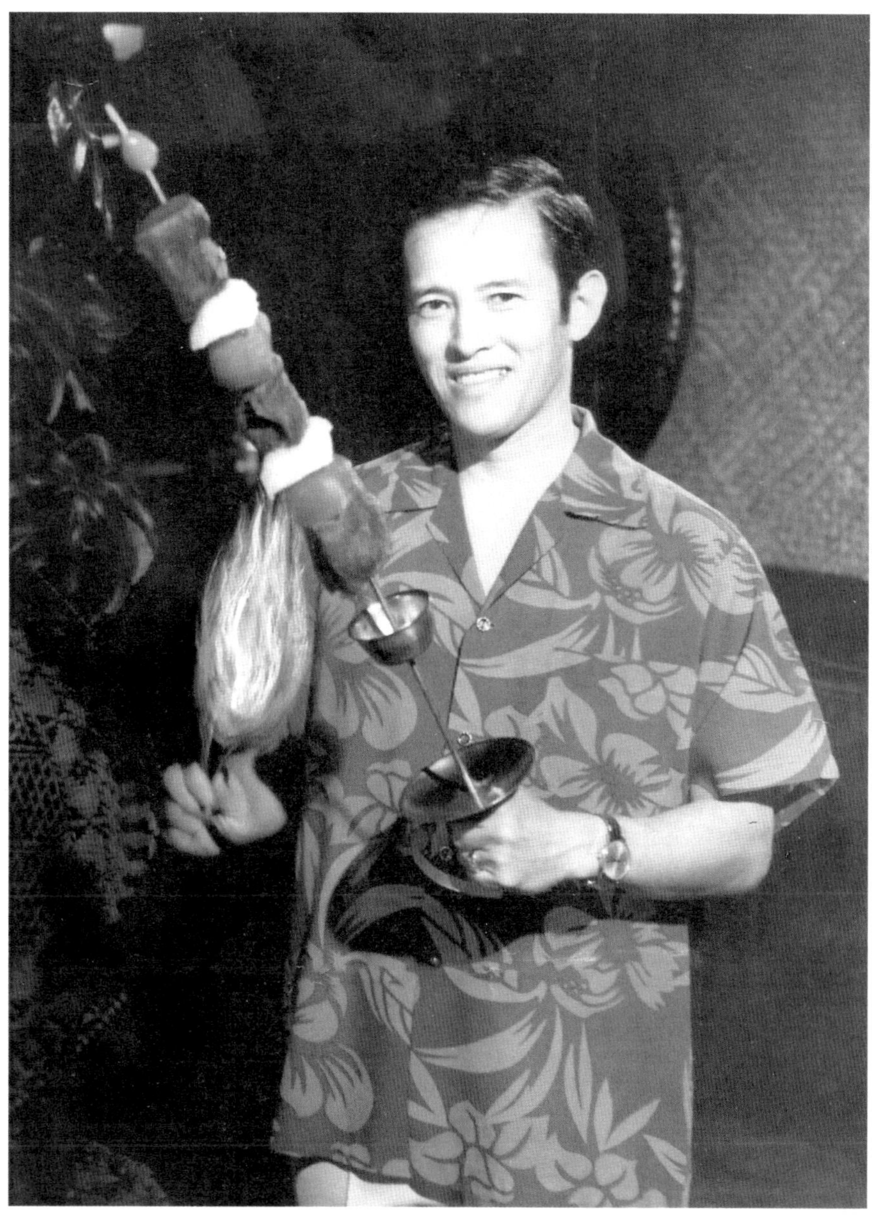

John "Johnny" Yee Gim was one of many Kahiki success stories, working his way up from the kitchen to assistant manager. *Courtesy Sapp/Henry.*

Baxter was somewhat of a musical prodigy. A classically trained musician who studied composition at Pepperdine University in Los Angeles, he had many pop hits in the early 1950s and had full carte blanche at Capitol Records. But for Baxter, creative ideas and original exotic compositions would be his true calling. The seeds were planted when he forged the exotica style with his arrangements for Yma Sumac's debut album, *Voice of the Xtabay*. And his albums *Ritual of the Savage* and *Tamboo* sealed his legacy as the godfather of exotica. Released in 1952, *Ritual of the Savage* contained the first appearance of the song "Quiet Village."

In exotics, the use of colorful titles and inventive liner notes (such as these from *Ritual of the Savage*) became as important as the music itself: "Do the mysteries of native rituals intrigue you…does the haunting beat of savage drums fascinate you? Are you captivated by the forbidden ceremonies of primitive peoples in far-off Africa or deep in the interior of the Belgian Congo?"

At the Kahiki, the Outrigger and Maui bars were located on either side of the foyer, and often the Beachcomber Trio could be found there playing a fusion of Latin jazz and Polynesian melodies. Marcel "Marsh" Padilla was recruited to assemble a house band in 1961 and did not relinquish the job for the next seventeen years. Born in Mexico on January 16, 1918, Marsh came with his family to the United States in the 1920s and began studying the sax and clarinet as a child. He eventually mastered the tenor sax, alto sax, flute, clarinet, guitar, piano, bass guitar, marimba and congas. At fourteen, the Padillas relocated to Topeka, Kansas, and Marsh began jobbing in local combos. He joined Juan Rodrigo's band out of El Paso in 1936, moving with it to Detroit two years later. He subsequently played with many bands throughout the Midwest. During World War II, he served as lead sax for the Camp Roberts Band, backing the likes of Judy Garland, Martha Raye, Bing Crosby and Bob Hope.

After the war, Marsh returned to Detroit to organize the Marcel Padilla Orchestra at the Famous Door and Haig's Supper Club. Then, in 1958, he moved to Columbus. In addition to his regular gig at the Kahiki, he also worked at the Clifford Hotel, Neil House, Deshler Hotel and Valley Dale. For a time, he toured with Bob Crosby's band as a tenor sax player. Besides becoming a barber and operating his own salon with his wife, Nina, he taught woodwinds at Coyle Music. Marsh officially retired in 1998. The following year, he was inducted into the Columbus Senior Musicians Hall of Fame.[16] In 2009, Marsh and his wife settled in Boise, Idaho, to be closer to family. While preparing to move, he discovered three reel-to-reel tapes of performances by the Beachcomber Trio recorded in 1965. Jeff

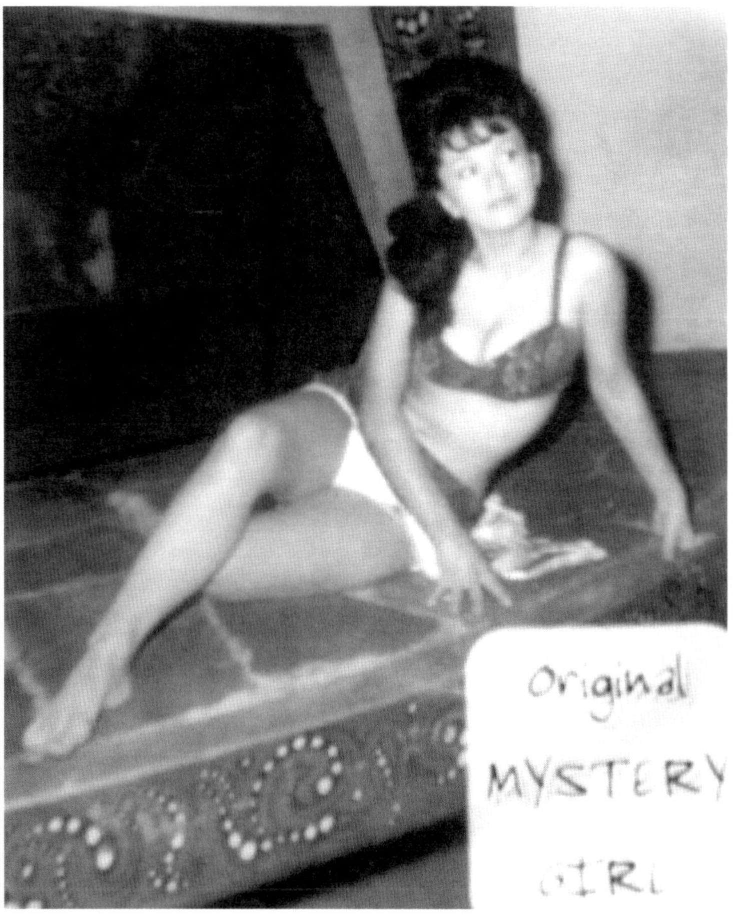

A rare slide of the original Mystery Girl (whose identity remains a mystery). *Authors' collection.*

Chenault and Lee Joseph of Dionysus Records would go on to release the *Beachcomber Trio "Live" at the Kahiki* album in 2010, a few months before Marsh passed away.

Asked whether it was fun playing at the Kahiki, Marsh replied, "Yes it was, when you had the right people. It was hard to keep the right people. The money wasn't there, and the schedule was pretty tight. We could play anything we wanted. The only limitation was the personnel. We got a new man on guitar, got a new man on the bass. We went through a lot of people, but I stayed there and kept the thing going for seventeen years—until finally we got the word they were going to cut out the music." However, he noted they did not play all Hawaiian music. "If you had to play Hawaiian music continuously, you'd go out of your mind."

Over the years, the Beachcomber Trio included Marsh Padilla (flute/percussion/guitar/ piano/bass), Leroy Plymale (guitar), Don Hales (guitar), John Dragu (vibraphone), Bob Chalfant (piano), Henry Burch (vibraphone/conga/bells/trumpet), Don Browne (marimba/timbales), Rod Metz (bass/guitar) and Roger Wolf (drums).

Don Browne, who now resides in Florida, said, "I was fortunate enough to play in the Beachcomber Trio from 1968 to 1969 with Leroy Plymale and leader Marcel Padilla. I was a senior in the music school at Ohio State University and then a music teacher at New Albany High School. The Kahiki was a great place to visit and work. I met lots of great people there, including the staff from around the world and visitors from all over as well."

Both the Joe Weisberg Trio and the Sonia Modes Trio (Weisberg and Modes were also inducted into the Columbus Senior Musicians Hall of Fame) held court at the piano bar until it was removed. They played everything from light jazz to show tunes. There were also several percussion-driven groups, including the Tropics Island Band and Island Breeze.

Unlike the Mai-Kai, the Kahiki never booked big-name acts or had a floor show such as a hula review. The reason, according to Bill Sapp, had to do with a different customer base. "We never really needed to get into a review like they do at the Mai-Kai. We figured that we wanted to attract local customers mostly because the Mai-Kai had a steady stream of visiting customers. In Columbus, Ohio, you really didn't get that."

6
MUGS, BOWLS AND GRAVY BOATS

For years, Polynesians were regarded as a people who had either completely lost, or never engaged in, the art of pottery making. However, post–World War II archaeology soon documented that pottery manufacture had been a common cultural practice through the first millennium BC...before its manufacture ceased in the initial centuries of the first millennium AD.
—Patrick Vinton Kirch and Roger C. Green

From the beginning, Kahiki customers were presented with a multitude of Kahiki tchotchkes for those who wanted them. From matchbooks and swizzle sticks to backscratchers and postcards, a wide range of souvenir items were sold in the Beachcomber Gift Shop. However, not all were satisfied with what they could buy. Some customers also made off with items of tableware. For example, the Kahiki silverware and china were made by Sterling China of East Liverpool, Ohio. These all had the restaurant's logo on them with the plates bearing a small tiki as well. However, it is the ceramic items that attract the most attention now, the provenance of which varied over the years.

The story begins in Mexico, where Bill Sapp and his first wife, Marceline, went to a clay shop. While there, Marcy (as she was known) designed the original Mystery Bowls with the "straw-in-the-mouth" tikis, but when they were shipped back to the United States, all but two were broken. As a result, no further items were ordered from Mexico.

The mother of Linda and Mark, Marcy was originally from Durham, North Carolina, but moved to Walterboro, South Carolina, when she

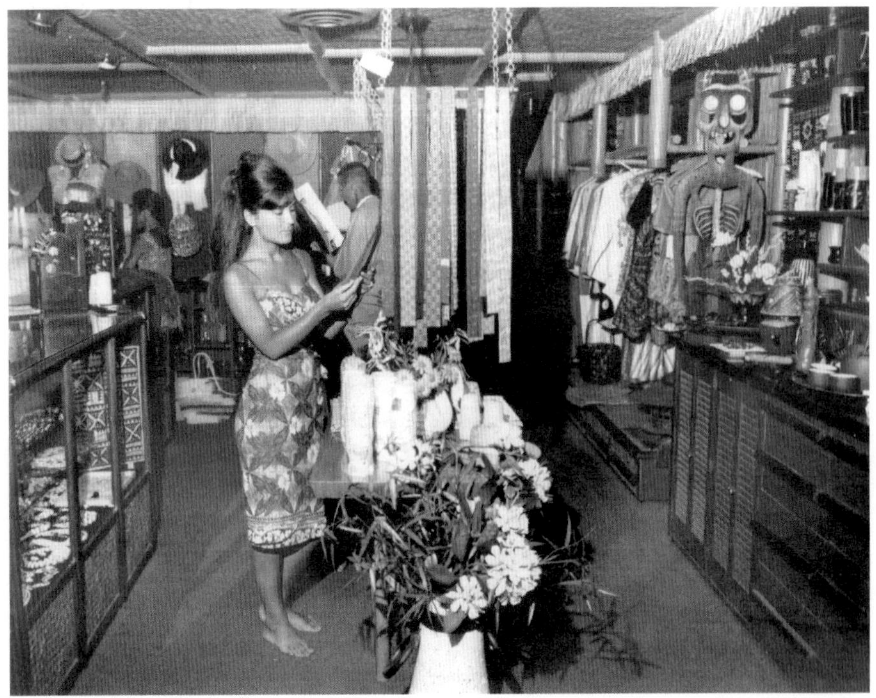

The Beachcomber Gift Shop had something for everyone. *Courtesy Sapp/Henry.*

was little. She became a print model for wedding gowns and moved to Cleveland, then Chicago and finally Columbus, where she modeled for the Noni Agency Finishing and Modeling School, founded by Ivola C. Nonenmaker. One day, Lee had a party and invited a lot of pretty girls, Marcy among them. At the time, she was working as a hostess at the Deshler Hotel. Bill met her at the party, and they began dating. After they married, Marcy took art classes. One of her friends, renowned local artist Emerson Burkhart, encouraged her painting. After the Kahiki opened, she helped with the gift shop.

In the early days, the oil lamps, ashtrays and several of the mugs were all handmade by Marcy. She recruited family members and other volunteers to help make items that were used in the restaurant in the basement of the Kahiki. Some of her creations also included the original Rum Barrel, Zombie mugs, the Headhunter Mug and the Idol's Cast. The face on the Zombie mug was replicated in brass on the original door handles of the main entrance, but they disappeared over the years.

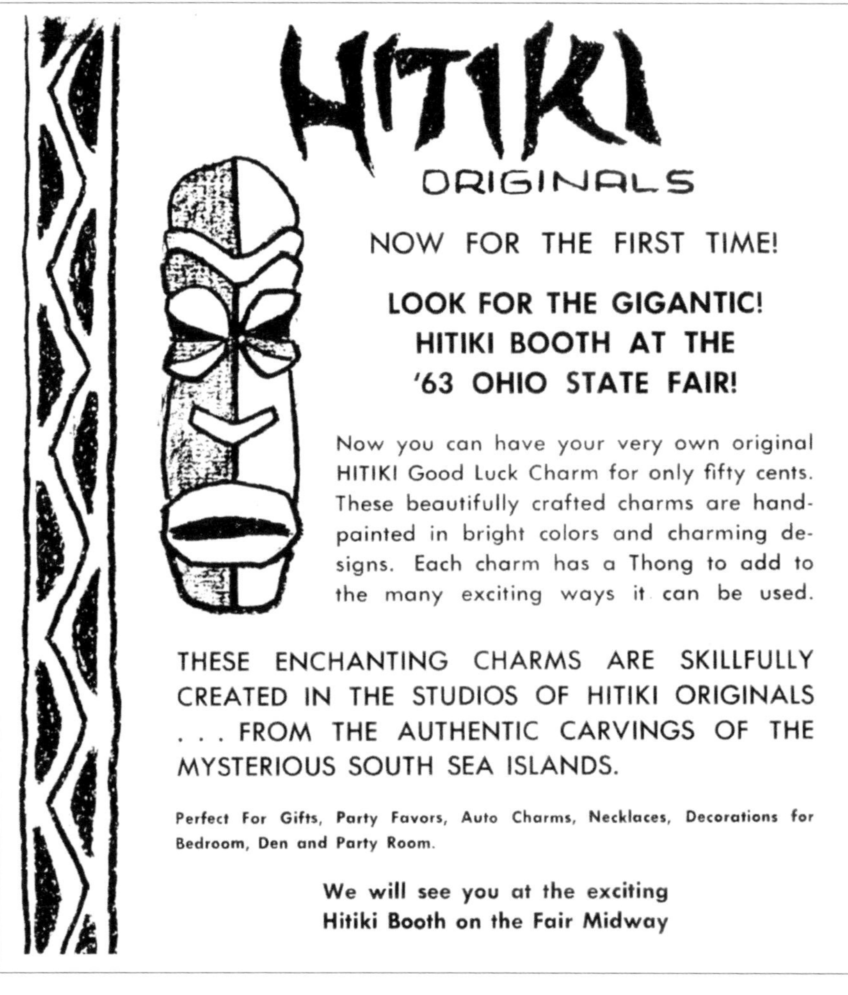

In addition to manufacturing items for the Kahiki, James Hite formed his own company, Hitiki, to market his Polynesian creations. *Authors' collection.*

Another name that regularly turns up in conjunction with Kahiki pottery is James Joseph Hite, a family friend. According to Bill Sapp:

> *He made various ceramic products for the Kahiki.* [Marcy] *was very instrumental in designing and making ceramics…so they worked together on various drink vessels…Almost all of the mugs that were made out of clay were made by my wife and James. These were before Hoffman Pottery. We didn't get into buying that commercial stuff at the time*

> *because there wasn't any, until the Kahiki got really going. The Hoffman stuff came later.*

Hite made tiki items under the name HiTiki (December 1963–78). According to Humuhumu (aka Michelle Trott), "HiTiki items were the earliest handmade collectibles sold by the Kahiki restaurant. These items included masks, ashtrays, small Moai heads and necklaces. He also made the female tiki that was built into the desk of Lee Henry upstairs in the Kahiki offices." In 1963, Hite filed for federal trademark registration on the name HiTiki for "statuary, carvings, novelties and works of art."

A graduate of North High School and an alumnus of the Columbus College of Art and Design, Hite was the first interior designer for the Bell Telephone System. After retiring from Southern Bell in Fort Lauderdale, Florida, he settled in Spruce Pine, North Carolina, and opened Hite Effects, a graphic design service, with his wife.

Because the ceramics operation in the basement of the Kahiki could not keep up with the demand, the mugs, bowls and other items were eventually made by local ceramicist Hoffman Pottery using some of Marcy's original designs as well as designs approved by the Kahiki. Hoffman Pottery was founded in Columbus, Ohio, by Richard P. "Dick" Hoffman in 1946. Hoffman's dream was to do something creative that he could enjoy and be proud of at the same time. Following graduation from Ohio State University in 1941 with a bachelor of science degree in both fine arts and education, he went on to teach an adult class in ceramics for one year. However, he wanted to create something different in the art world, so after his short stint in teaching, he traveled around Ohio looking for ideas. With the help of his wife, Evelyn, he started making his own pottery in the basement of their home. As business grew, he built a small garage to make his wares. Eventually he bought the property at 4295 East Main Street and opened his first Pottery Shop. The place literally was a shed until he added a building onto the back area and two storage rooms for supplies.

Eric Hoffman, Richard's son, fondly recalls the early days: "It was a family operation: Mom worked in the shop while Dad did all the artwork. The Kahiki business really helped my dad through the years. I remember working on mugs and bowls all summer and delivering them to the Kahiki. Sometimes they would even give us coupons for a free dinner after we made a delivery."

Hoffman Pottery would go on to make some of the most prolific lines of Kahiki products ever made. The list consisted of the Mystery Bowl, the

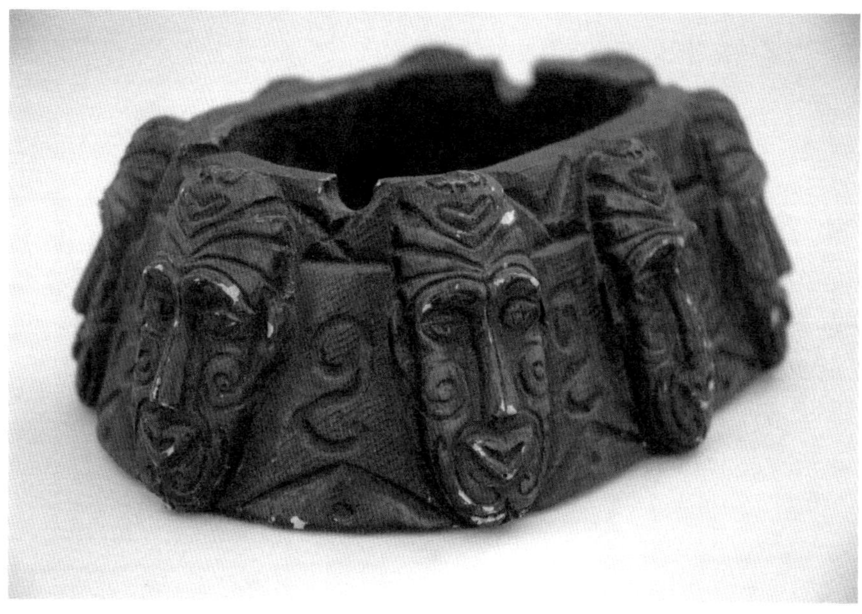

James Hite's Hitiki Maori ashtray. *Courtesy Joe Schuster.*

Idol's Cast, the Headhunter Mug, a Coconut Mug, Candle Holders, salt- and pepper shakers, condiment jars and the Hot Buttered Rum Mug. Both the Kahiki Mystery Bowl and the Idol's Cast featured alternating brown and black triangles supported by three tiki idols. Original owner Bill Sapp said that only twenty-five of the Mystery Bowls were made because they were expensive, broke easily and were prone to being stolen.

In *More Columbus Unforgettables*, local historian Bob Thomas profiled Dick Hoffman. Thomas noted that Hoffman created his fine-textured ceramics using his own recipe, which included "ball clay from Kentucky, kaolin from Florida, feldspar from Canada, talc from the southern United States and flint from Zanesville, Ohio." In addition to his work for the Kahiki, he produced items for Lazarus Department Stores, promotional items for First National Bank and the fez salt- and pepper shakers for the Shriners. He also made thousands of personalized birth and wedding plates.

Being a commercial potter, Hoffman used various marks to identify his work. This can be seen on some of his creations for the restaurant. For example, most pieces are imprinted with the word "KAHIKI." Some will then have the words "HOFFMAN POTTERY" forming the upper and lower arcs of a circle, with "Col's HP Ohio" dividing it in half horizontally. Others

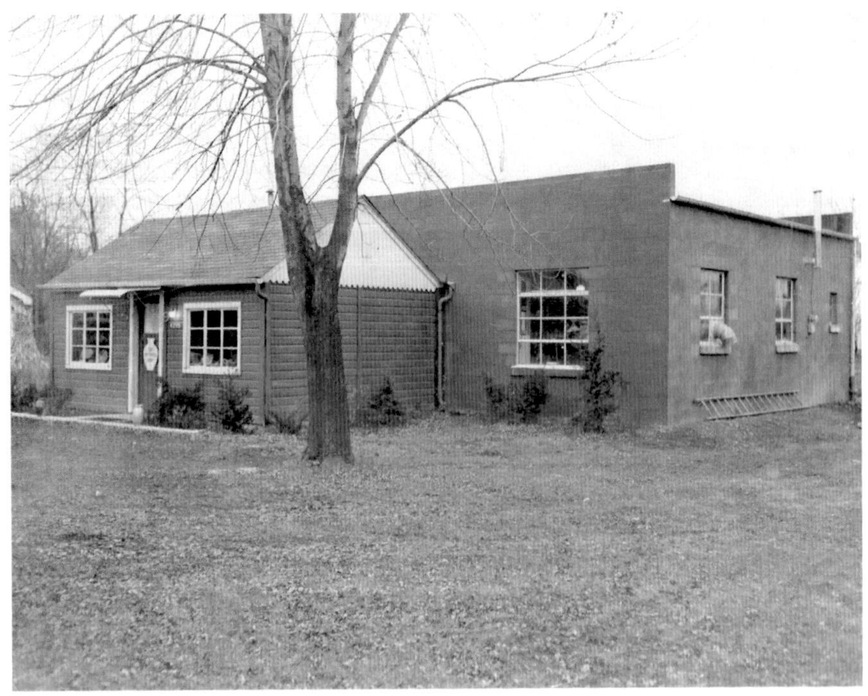

will have "Ceramics by Hoffman" in script. There are also some marked "RH HANDCRAFT" over a loop or "HANDCRAFT BY HOFFMAN," with each word connected by a curvy line. According to Eric Hoffman, the molds for all the Hoffman Pottery stuff were all in a garage, which sustained a lot of water damage, and were subsequently destroyed.

During the last few years of the Kahiki, the Headhunter Mugs were made by another local ceramicist named Mario Torres. These mugs varied widely in quality, with most of them taking on a, for lack of a better term, "globby" appearance. Usually these can be found with just a handwritten Kahiki logo on the bottom. Other mugs followed, such as the Fountain Mug and Candle Holder, another mug with the tri-footed tiki. The Mystery Bowls at this time were still being ordered from Orchids of Hawaii, but some were made by Mario with the Kahiki hand logo on the bottom. Even after the Kahiki was razed, a gift shop located in the same building as the Kahiki frozen foods offices continued to sell these mugs. Eventually the gift shop closed, and the mug production stopped.

In 2005, the Fraternal Order of Moai was formed in Columbus, Ohio. Its two core values are good works and preservation. Similar to the Shriners, it is a

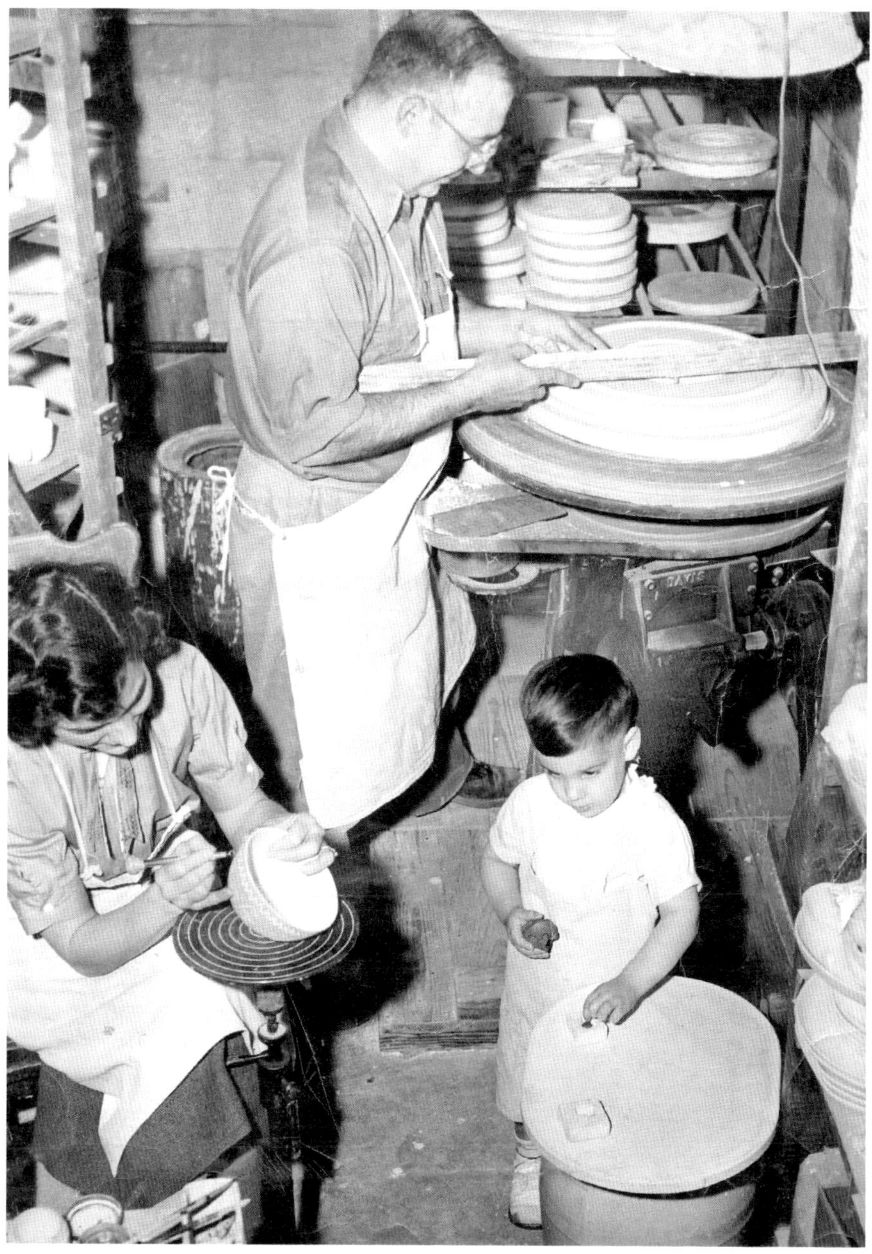

Above: For Richard "Dick" Hoffman, manufacturing pottery was a family affair. *Courtesy Eric Hoffman.*

Opposite: The Hoffman Pottery was located on Main Street in Columbus. *Courtesy Eric Hoffman.*

fraternal organization with a Polynesian twist. Its logo is the Kahiki fireplace. From its humble beginnings with the Kahiki Chapter, the order has grown to a national entity with various chapters operating all over the United States. It has commissioned a handful of mugs dedicated to the remembrance of the Kahiki. One such mug was produced for the 2007 Hot Rod Hula Hop. It was a re-creation of the Kahiki fireplace and was manufactured in a limited edition of one hundred. In 2013, the order commissioned a mug based on the "fire fish" that lined the roof of the Kahiki.

For the benefit of collectors, here is a list of Kahiki pottery by manufacturer, including descriptions:

Handmade by the Sapp Family

- Zombie Mug: held a glass and had a zombie face on the mug.
- Rum Barrel: large brown barrel with raised Rum Barrel lettering.
- Ashtrays: round with face and small circular indentations.
- Oil Lamps: large reddish/brown tiki Base.

Hoffman Pottery

The earliest are marked "Ceramics by Hoffman." The later items are marked "Hoffman Pottery."

- Mystery Bowl: alternating brown and black triangles supported by three tikis.
- Idol's Cast: alternating brown and black triangles supported by three tikis.
- Headhunter Mug: brown with green interior; various Hoffman stamps with some having a carved Kahiki on the bottom.
- Coconut Mug: brown with Hoffman Pottery logo on bottom.
- Candle Holders: very rare and might not have been used in the restaurant.
- Salt- and Pepper Shakers: moai heads with Hoffman Pottery printed on the bottom; both green and brown colors exist with green being the most popular.

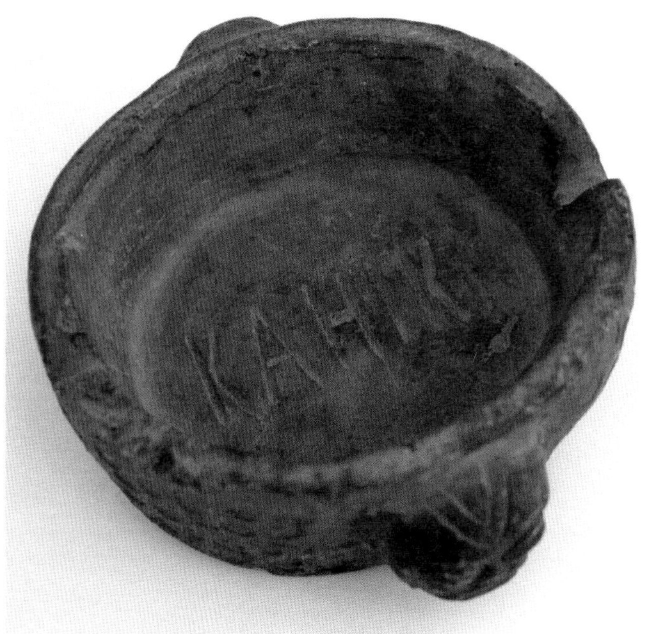

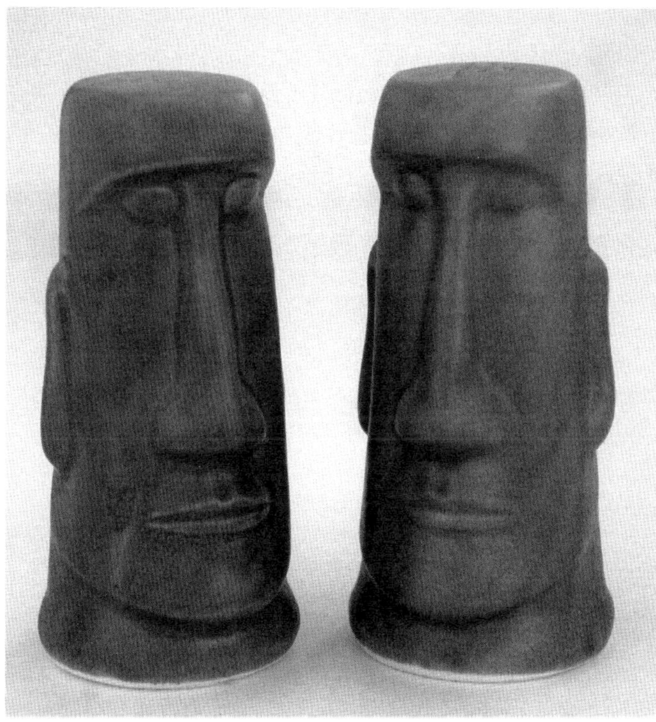

Top: The "dimpled" appearance of the ashtray was made by Marcy Sapp using a pencil eraser to create texture. *Courtesy Eric Hoffman.*

Left: Kahiki salt- and pepper shakers manufactured by Hoffman Pottery (later produced in Japan). *Courtesy Joe Schuster.*

- Condiment Jar: brown coconut shape with Kahiki in raised white lettering.
- Hot Buttered Rum Mug: brown with cartoonish face.

ORCHIDS OF HAWAII

- Headhunter Mug #1: brown color with raised imprint on bottom.
- Skull Mug #2: white with shading and a handle, as well as raised imprint on bottom.
- Coconut Mug: brown with white dots.
- Volcano Bowl: used as the Mystery Bowl.
- Scorpion Bowl: small version of the volcano bowl minus the volcano.

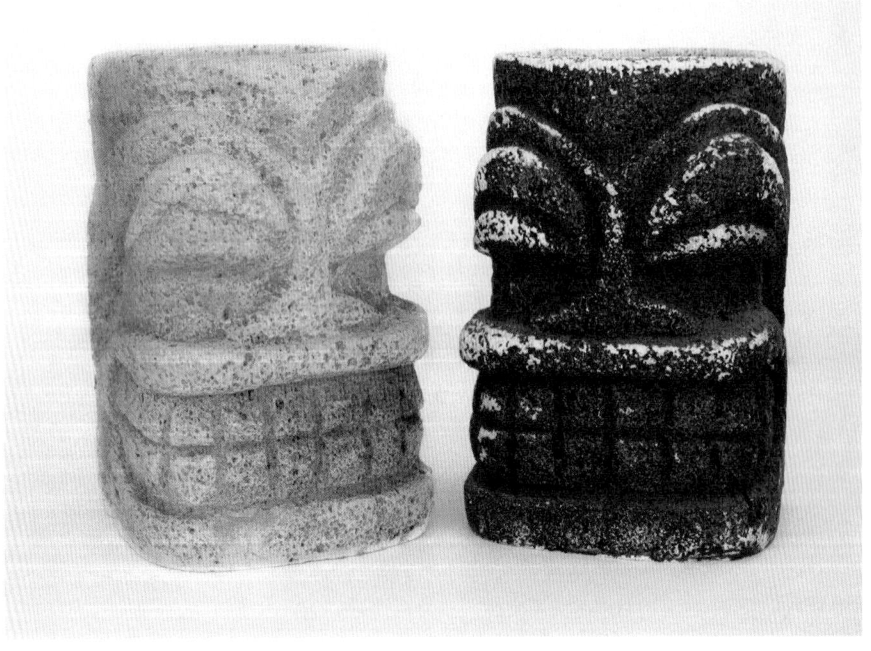

A couple of commercial artist James Hite's Hitiki planters. *Courtesy Joe Schuster.*

7

THE MAKER OF THE MOAI

In a piece of experimental archaeology, a team of local and U.S. researchers showed that the massive statues, known as moai, can be moved from side to side by a small number of people, just as one might move a fridge.
—Rossella Lorenzi

They are called moai (or mo'ai). They are the massive stone figures carved by the Rapa Nui people of Easter Island between AD 1250 and 1500 (or from roughly the time of the Mongol Empire to Columbus's discovery of America). Apart from the magnificent building itself, the feature of the Kahiki that is best remembered are the two sixteen-foot-tall concrete moai out in front of the restaurant and the twenty-eight-foot-tall fireplace moai inside. The latter was so impressive that some people estimated it was actually fifty to eighty feet tall.

The creator of the moai was Philip E. Kientz. Born in 1924 to a family of stonecutters, Kientz was a man who left his mark wherever he went. Both he and his father, also named Philip, were avid collectors of Native American relics and contributed some of their best finds to the Ohio Historical Society. After graduating from South High School in 1942, Kientz saw combat while serving in the U.S. Coast Guard during World War II. Upon his discharge in 1945, he enrolled in the Columbus College of Art and Design (CCAD). With degree in hand, he found work as an artist and stonemason, eventually opening Kientz Custom Studio. Among the artists he studied with were such local greats as potter Chester Nicodemus, one-time dean of CCAD, and watercolorist Byron Kohn.

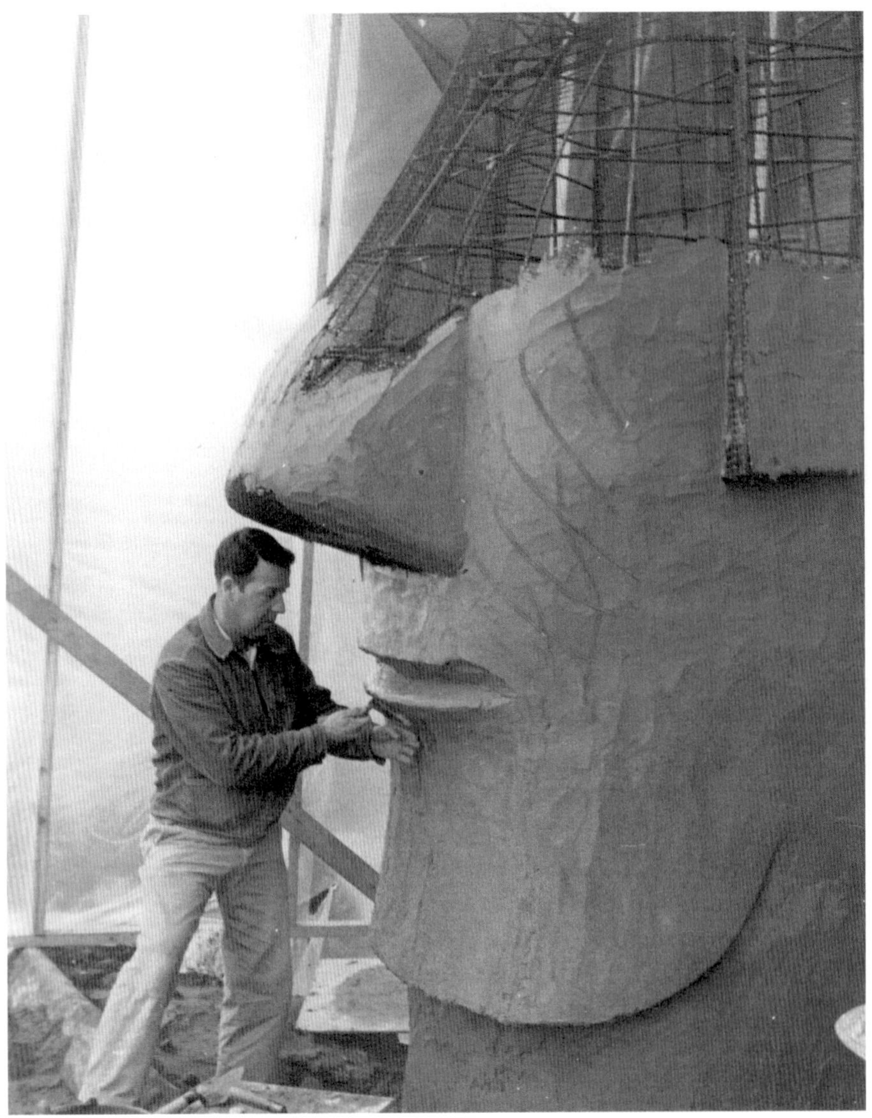

Above: Sculptor Phil Kientz fabricates one of the twin moai that guard the entrance to the Kahiki. *Courtesy Shirley Kientz.*

Opposite: Kientz's towering fireplace moai dominated the center of the restaurant. *Courtesy Shirley Kientz.*

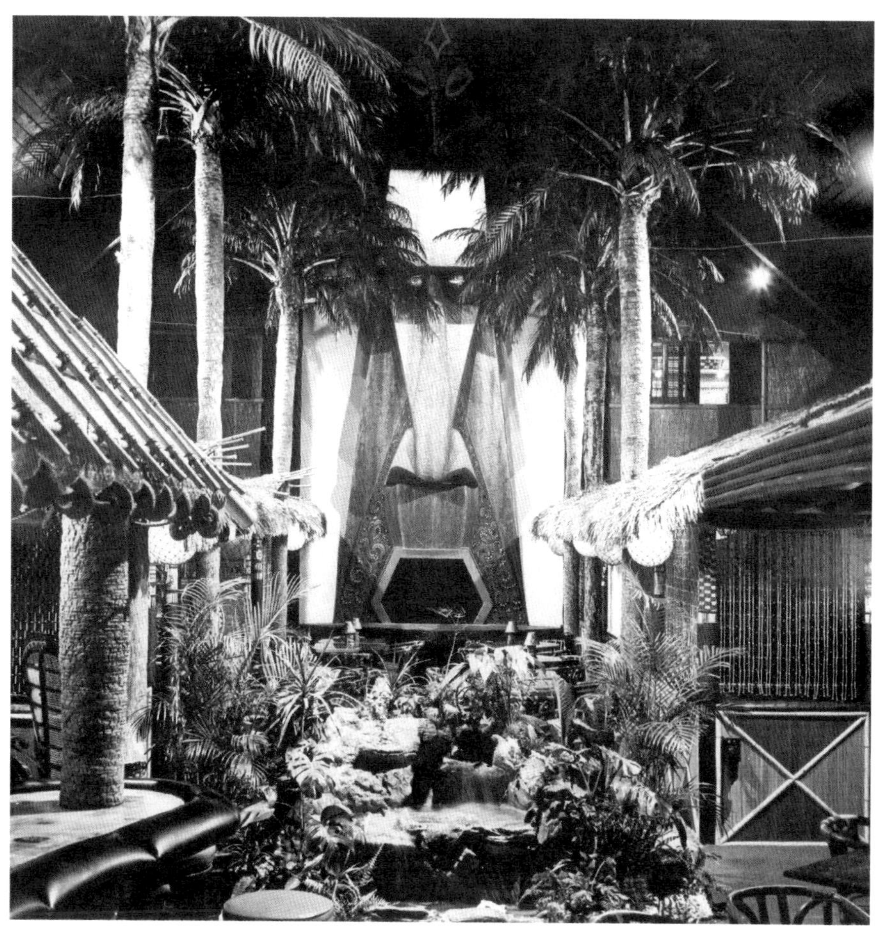

A lifelong resident of German Village, where he built two homes, Kientz and his wife, Shirley, were among the original founders of the German Village Society in the 1960s. Their home was one of the ten opened to the public for the first Haus und Garten Tour. (Shirley purportedly asked tour creator Frank Fetch, "Lord, Frank, who is going to pay a dollar to see these old houses?") Kientz also designed the organization's emblem.

Over the years, Kientz held a variety of jobs. His granddaughter, Stephanie Yochem, noted that "one was for Anchor Hocking Glass, and while there, [he] drew many designs which are on many vases and glass ware. He designed the horse head on the Rolling Rock label. I was always asking why we don't get free beer, but he would laugh and say, 'I don't know.'" Other projects were the Nativity scene at the downtown State Auto

Insurance building, the Durrell Street of Yesteryear at the original Center of Science and Industry (COSI), the famous Lazarus Christmas windows and even the store's talking Mr. Tree. Kientz also contributed to the look of the Wine Cellar and Desert Inn restaurants. Called upon to design the officers' quarters at Lockbourne Air Force Base, he then was asked to do the same for a military base in New England. According to Stephanie, he even drew the image of "the German beer guy" for Plank's restaurant in German Village (which may have gotten him a free beer or two). Kientz died on November 9, 2006, at the age of eighty-two.

Stephanie said that her grandfather was especially proud of his work on the Kahiki. "I'm not sure why, considering all that he had done, but he would always talk of this and make sure we would go and eat dinner there every now and then." True to the Easter Island heads, Kientz's moai are minimalist sculptures, composed primarily of large, flat planes, which he cast in concrete. The original Easter Island figures were intended by the Rapa Nui people to represent power and authority. At the Kahiki, the exterior moai, which flanked the main doorway, spouted flames from their crowned heads while the fireplace moai, naturally, had a large flaming, hexagonal mouth that emulated the shape of the front door.

"The fireplace and the two giant moai outside were a combination of Bernie, Coburn and myself," Bill said. "Everybody always seemed to come up with an idea, and if it sounded good, we went with it." Using Coburn's design, Kientz was also responsible for sculpting the iconic stone head that graced the fountain in the foyer of the restaurant. Interestingly, Bill Sapp and Lee Henry refer to it as the "Pig" or "Pete." However, during Michael Tsao's ownership of the restaurant, it came to be called "George" and the "Monkey."

When it was announced that the Kahiki might close, columnist Joe Blundo of the *Columbus Dispatch* invited readers to share their memories. One of those readers was Phil Kientz. "It was a highlight of my life," Kientz said. "I got to do artwork and stonemasonry." However, he noted that, along with the Kahiki, the original COSI, the Wine Cellar restaurant and Desert Inn have all been razed. "They keep tearing down everything I did."

Kientz's moai became the ultimate Kahiki collectible.[17] Not only were they bigger than the other souvenirs, but they were also considerably rarer. However, Michael Tsao, the restaurant's last owner, decided to hang onto them when the Kahiki was razed in 2000. He put the moai in storage and installed the "Pig" in the lobby of Kahiki Foods, his frozen food operation. His hope was that the statues would find a new home, possibly along the downtown riverfront if he succeeded with his plans to open a new restaurant there.

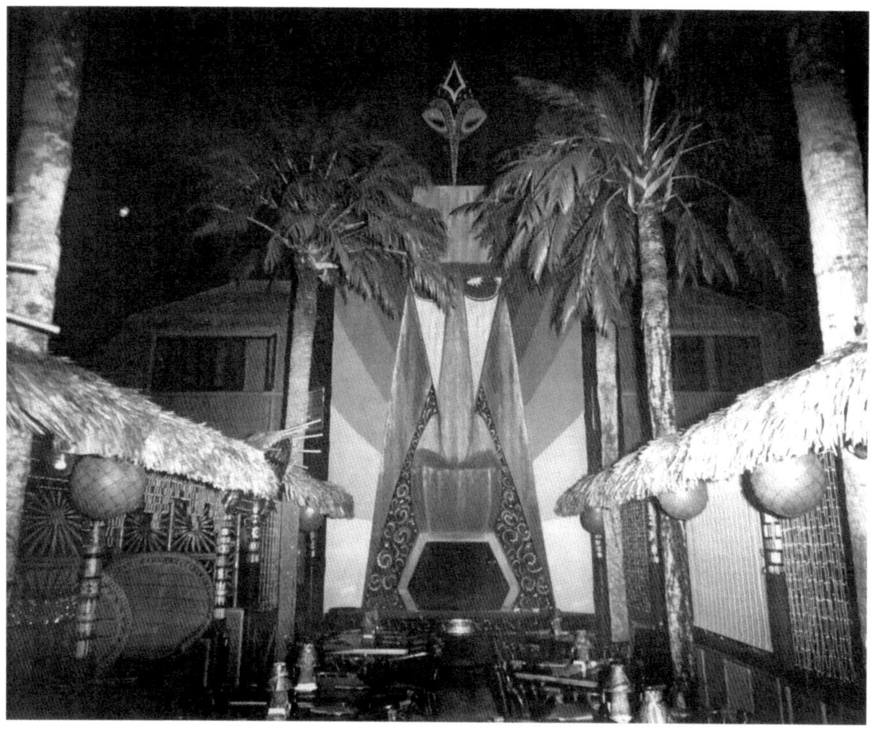

The palm trees, fabricated from real trees, were even taller than the fireplace moai. *Courtesy Shirley Kientz.*

In 2006, following the death of their patriarch, the Tsao family decided to dispose of the Kahiki items they had been storing in a downtown warehouse. Coincidentally, Melissa Andrews was interviewing Linda Tsao for a book she was working on. Melissa and her husband, Greg ("Hulacat"), struck a deal with Linda to buy the items, including the twin moai that had stood outside the restaurant and the giant fireplace moai that had been the centerpiece inside. Melissa borrowed all the money she could and put the rest on credit cards to buy everything in the warehouse.

Jeff Chenault spent an afternoon helping load things onto a large semi-trailer truck. He can attest to the fact that it was completely packed with Kahiki artifacts, so much so that there was not enough room for one of the twin moai. John "tikiskip" Holt, a friend of Greg and Melissa's, was told he could have it for free as long as he could supply his own transportation and a crane to off-load it, which he did. It is now resting forlornly in his backyard, waiting for the call that might never come to return to service. The other one and the fireplace moai were transported to New England.

> [A]*s the driver and I* [Hulacat] *were strapping the fireplace down, I was excitedly babbling about how great it felt to rescue this symbol of tiki/poly pop culture and waxing about how many thousands had been to the Kahiki, how this, above all things Kahiki, was the most impressive. In my bloated glee I didn't notice that Merle (the driver) was intent on my blather with some concern knitting across his forehead. I mentioned how the mystery drink was presented to the fireplace moai before serving. Merle asked if the fireplace was ever used in actual worship (as in religious)...Whoa!...realizing that I was treading on sensitive ground (for him) I tried to spin to more benign turf...but just as I was beginning damage control...SOMEONE...my friend and true blue rock of tikidom...said, "Oh Yeah, they had pagan rites and DEVIL WORSHIP every night at the Kahiki."*

TikiGreg (real name unknown) picks up the story:

> *The truck driver didn't want any part of the fireplace and moai, since he somehow deduced through conversation that they were used for some pagan ritual. This went against his religious beliefs, so he was refusing to move them. But Hulacat and Tikiskip convinced him they were just artifacts from a restaurant, and no bad things were associated with them.*

Andrews stored the fireplace under a tarp in his backyard in Brattleboro, Vermont, while the second of the twin moai wound up in Hampton Beach, New Hampshire.

Then, in November 2013, many of the remaining Kahiki artifacts held by the Tsao family were sold in an online auction. The most significant of the items was the fountainhead—George, or the "Pig." In an emergency meeting of the Fraternal Order of Moai, it was agreed that it needed to purchase it to ensure that this important piece of restaurant history remained in Columbus. But it would not be cheap. The successful bidder also had to pay to remove a window and rent a forklift to remove the statue from the lobby of Kahiki Foods. Nevertheless, the FOM members pooled their cash. As one of them later related:

> *In the final bidding minutes, we were here, in a tiki bar, drinking real Zombies with the owners of the Grass Skirt. And when the bidding went*

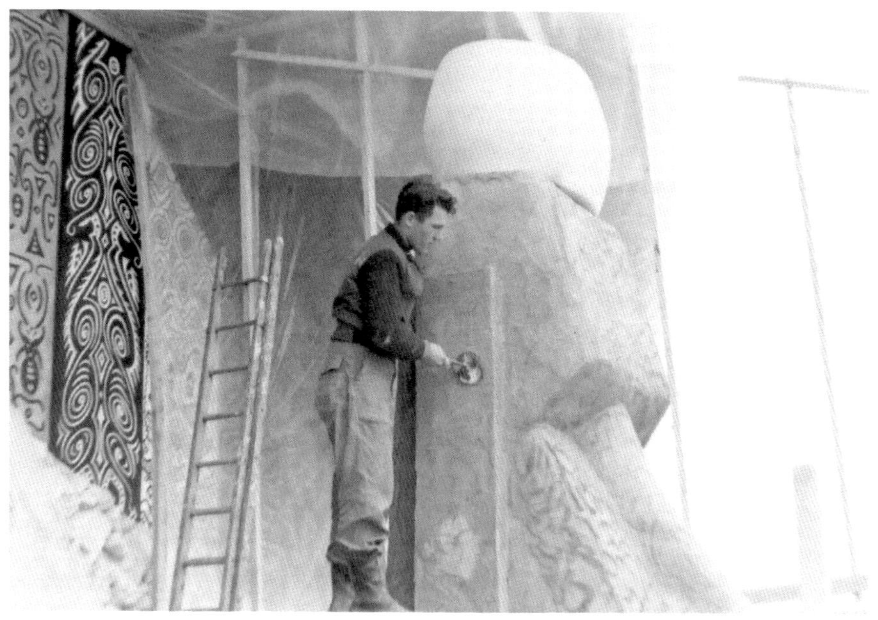

Unlike the Rapa Nui people, Phil Kientz had to construct the moai in place. *Courtesy Shirley Kientz.*

just above the FOM's limit, the Grass Skirt owners, Amy and Carmen, said, "We will cover it. Win it." And so we did. So tonight, tiki fans won. This historic artifact will stay in its hometown, and be on display for the public in a tiki bar. And that is what matters…Ahu.

8
MYSTERY GIRLS AND MYSTERY DRINKS

The first love, the first sunrise, the first South Sea Island, are memories apart.
—Robert Louis Stevenson

From the beginning, the Kahiki Supper Club was known for its attractive female staff, or *wahines* (the Maori and Hawaiian word for woman). According to the original advertising brochure, "Most of the cocktail waitresses are the wives of servicemen or ex-servicemen and all are from Japan or Korea. Although none of them had experience in this type of work, they were all trained rigidly for a two-month period prior to the Kahiki opening in February." Costumed in bikini tops, displaying bare midriffs, and sarongs, they cut quite the figures, especially during the cold Columbus winters.

In an interview with Renee Montaigne on NPR, Michael Tsao gave his take on the popularity of the Kahiki. "You have to understand to start with, you have to go back into the '40s and the '50s. During that time, our military boys have R&R and going into the islands, and experience a phenomenon, which is drinks, relaxation, naked women. When they come back to the mainland, they started restaurants and copied that phenomenon. And that's how actually Polynesian restaurant is the granddaddy of the theme restaurants."

A highlight of any trip to the Kahiki was the appearance of the beautiful Mystery Girl, Kalua (her official name). When summoned by a large brass gong struck by the bartender, the Mystery Girl would appear bearing a massive ceramic bowl with a smoking volcano in the center.[18] She would then sashay up to the main tiki god and, after bowing to the idol, deliver the

KAHIKI APPLICATION FOR EMPLOYMENT

NAME ________________ (Please Print) ________________ Date of Birth ________________

ADDRESS ________________ Phone ________________

Person to call in case of emergency ________________ Phone ________________

Height ________ Weight ________ (Male) Shirt Size ________ Trousers ________
(Female) Dress Sige ________

EMPLOYMENT RECORD (List last, or present, employer first)

Date From	To	Name of Co	Address	Position	Pay Rate	Duties-use other side

Marital Status Single ____ Married ____ Divorced ____ No. of Dependents ____
Circle Last year of education completed 1 2 3 4 5 6 7 8 9 10 11 12 13 14 15 16

How did you learn of our restaurant ? Paper ( ) Friend ( ) Other ( ) ________

May we contact previous employers for reference (except present employer) Yes ____ No ____

I certify the above information is true to the best of my knowledge.

Signature ________________

The Kahiki had an enlightened employment policy, offering many immigrants their first American jobs. *Courtesy Sapp/Henry.*

drink to the appropriate table. Removing a lei of orchids from her own neck, she would place it over the head of the honored guest (originally, the orchids were flown in two to three times a week from Hilo, Hawaii).

Naturally, the drink came with a backstory. Supposedly, it symbolized an ancient sacrificial ritual that could quiet a volcano that was in danger of erupting. "According to legend, the maiden chosen for the sacrifice was usually the Chieftain's daughter. After several days of ceremony, feasting and luaus, the young lady would climb the volcano and fling herself into its crater." To further play up the "sacred ritual" aspect of the ceremony, Mystery Drink orders were spaced at least twenty minutes apart. The Mystery Drink itself was a heady concoction containing eight ounces of rum and brandy and intended to serve four people. It should be noted that in the forty-year history of the Kahiki, there were no recorded volcanic eruptions in Columbus.[19]

When Linda Sapp was thirteen, she was assigned the job of going through thousands of Kahiki brochures and coloring over the face of one wahine with a black marker. It was not because the young woman was underage, as has been rumored. Rather, she had been advised not to sign the photo release by Arthur Godfrey, a popular radio and television personality, who had taken a shine to her.

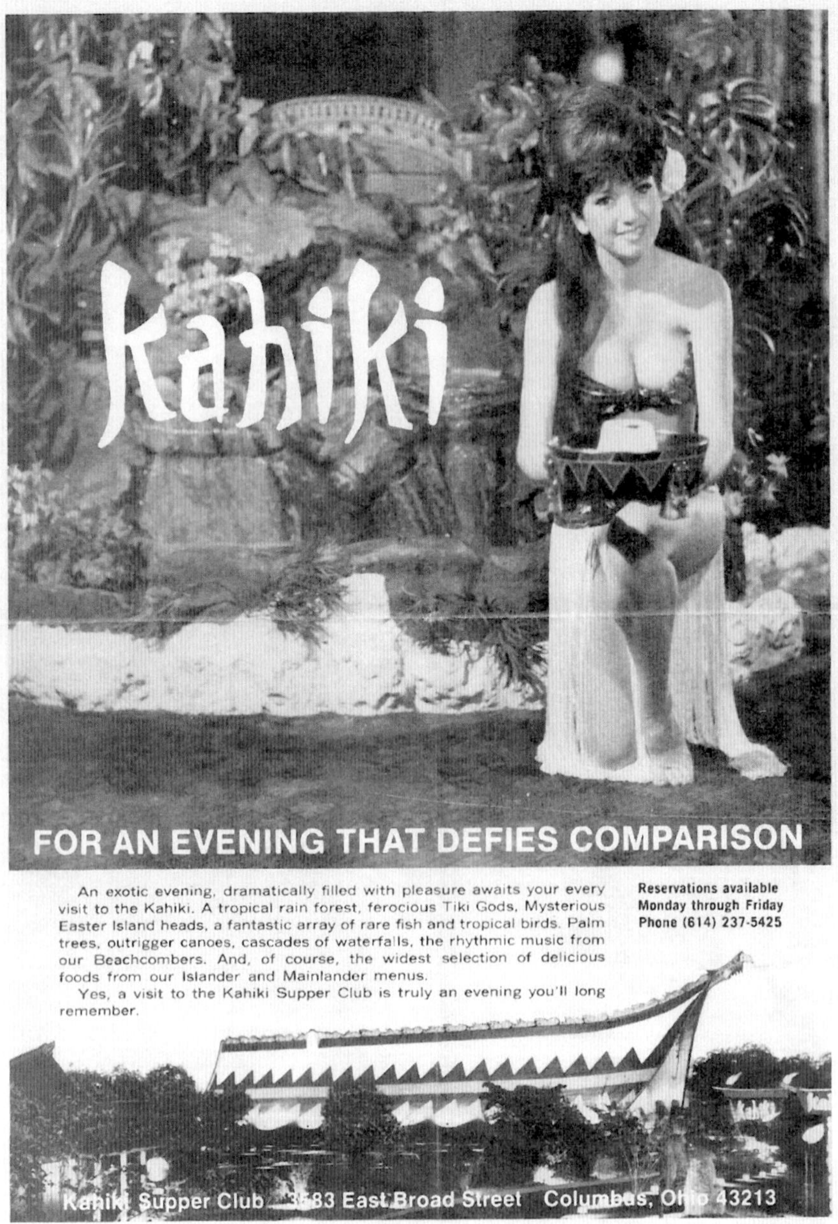

Advertisements for the Kahiki appeared in a number of magazines, including *Life*. *Authors' collection.*

Arguably (some would say inexplicably), Godfrey was the most popular television personality of the 1950s and a major booster of Hawaii. When he sang "My Little Grass Shack" and other hapa-haole tunes while accompanying himself on the ukulele, he spurred a revival of interest in the instrument, driving up sales on the mainland and a consequent demand for ukulele teachers.

According to Lee, Godfrey had visited the Kahiki once while in town and had been served a smoking drink by Tina Butts, Mystery Girl du jour. Lee later received a call from her. Godfrey, who flew his own plane, wanted her to accompany him back to California for the weekend and said he would talk about the Kahiki on his radio program. Lee didn't object. She wound up staying at Pierre Salinger's house,[20] and for a long time, Godfrey continued to plug the restaurant on his show. In fact, people began asking them, "What do you guys have on Arthur Godfrey?" Eventually, Tina settled in West Virginia, where she passed away a few years ago.

Another Mystery Girl was Toshiko Shirley Jane Davis, who, like Marcy Sapp, was a model with the Noni Modeling Agency and a recent Ohio State graduate. Her mother, Hisako Mary Miyamoto Davis, was a supervisor at the Kahiki. Toshiko became a media favorite when she began dating Donald "Buz" Lukens, a representative in the Ohio State Senate. When they subsequently married in 1973 (he was forty-two, and she was half his age), Governor James Rhodes was one of the guests, and entertainment was provided by vocalist Bob Braun of WLW-TV's 50-50 Club. The couple quietly divorced ten years later, before Lukens became embroiled in several scandals for which he later was sentenced to thirty months in federal prison. Toshiko relocated to Chicago.

In 2010, Jeff Chenault interviewed Gerline Lude, a one-time Mystery Girl, after he was contacted by her daughter, Tracy. She had seen her mother's photo on the cover of *The Beachcomber Trio* album. He was invited to visit with Geri at the home she shares with her husband, Jack. The first thing he noticed was that the entire backyard garden area was decorated like a Polynesian village. There were fountains, a swimming pool, banana plants, tropical flowers and a Japanese-style gazebo that doubled as a cocktail bar. He later learned that it had won multiple awards from the Columbus Home and Garden Show and was featured in various magazines. Geri was also a fancier of exotic birds (she had nine) with two macaws, a couple cockatoos and many parrots.

"I started working [at the Kahiki] in 1962," she said. "I was twenty when I started there and wasn't old enough to serve drinks. I started as a hostess, then became a waitress. I was also a Mystery Girl for a couple years…All the waitresses had to wear [dark-colored] wigs. Back in those days, the poofier the better. Originally, I tried darkening my hair, but it wasn't dark enough. They were always on me about my hair, and I thought, I'm getting tired of wearing these stupid wigs!" (Note: Not all wore wigs. Some of the young women got their hair done at Joe Florio's Beauty Parlor on the Hilltop, a neighborhood on the far west side of Columbus.)

"Oh, it was a lot of fun, so many good memories…I remember the gong used for the Mystery Girl was so huge it would just echo, echo, echo constantly. It would never stop ringing. The tables were all numbered, and they had little huts you would go into. The Rainforest Room was on the right and the fish tanks were on the left. Down the middle, behind the big waterfall, you came to an area with a big round table. I'll never forget the name, Table #51. That's where all the Kenley Players, a summer theater troupe, used to dine. Oh my, I had so many pictures taken with so many stars back then. I just loved Robert Stack, from *The Untouchables*. George Hamilton was really nice, also Robert Goulet, Ray Milland and Zsa Zsa Gabor was there a lot.

"When you walked past the *maître d'* stand, the piano bar was on the left. On the other side of the piano bar there was a hallway where the Mystery Girl would come out. Just before you entered that area, back towards the service bar, the big gong was hanging on the wall. Everybody stopped and looked when that gong went off because it was a big deal when that Mystery Girl came out.

"When we would serve the Mystery Drink, we would carry the drink out and we would walk in front of Table #51 and we would first present the drink to the big tiki god fireplace, kneel down on one knee and then back up again, then bring the drink to the customer. We also had a lei that we would place over their head, and if it was a man, I would usually kiss him on the forehead.

Charles Moore was the photographer who shot the image used on *The Beachcomber Trio* album. Although Geri didn't remember him, she thought the session took place in 1963 or 1964. "They just set everything up and told us what to do and where to stand," Geri said. "I had my big wig on for that shot."

As far as Marsh Padilla, leader of the band, was concerned, "Everybody loved Marsh. He was so talented and could play so many different instruments…There was always music playing. The band usually played from 8:00 p.m. to 1:00 a.m. After that, the music was pumped in from a big reel to reel that I think was upstairs in the office. The controls were over by the *maître d'* stand. It was mostly Hawaiian style music.

"I remember they had a big toucan bird upstairs in the offices named George, and every day, I would come up and bring some fruit for him. He would come up to the cage and let me rub his beak. He was a great bird. I also remember they had a little pottery shop downstairs in the basement. They would make things like ashtrays and stuff down there and sell them in the Beachcomber Shop. Back then, they sold some really nice stuff. Quality stuff that you didn't see later on. It was just a fun place to work. Some of the best years of my life!"

The influence of the Kahiki has touched on many different aspects of Geri's life. Each year, she holds a luau in her backyard to celebrate everything that the Kahiki embodied: friends, food, drink and a true love for the famous restaurant.

When her mother took her to the Kahiki for her sixteenth birthday, Autumn Shah was "so enthralled" with the place that she "asked for an application on the way out."

> *I was not a waitress; I was a hostess. I wore the green floral, polyester sarong (which I still have!) usually, but on Sundays, I wore the Mystery Girl outfit. I was not allowed to be the Mystery Girl, of course, because I was only sixteen…I did have an embarrassing experience while I was there! My grass skirt got caught on the bamboo wall and whisked it off of me. Still probably the most embarrassed I've ever been in my life!*

What Autumn liked best was being around so many different cultures. She thinks she and the manager, Lisa, were the only native-born Americans working there at the time. She was especially in awe of Michael Tsao, who use to come in just before the dinner crowd.

> *I remember him being a large man, larger than life in my eyes. I was somewhat in awe of him. He usually came in with a keen eye on how things looked and started giving instructions right away, but never in a rude or bossy way. He was stern but still quite charming and had a wonderful, huge smile. I was often the only hostess there at the time and he asked me questions about working there, about school, just to be nice (after all, I wasn't anyone in charge, so he could be more friendly with me). He would sometimes pat me on the shoulder as he left.*

9
STARRY, STARRY NIGHTS

There is nothing more miserable in the world than to arrive in paradise and look like your passport photo.
—Erma Bombeck

In 1966, Sally Wheeler, a North High School student, won first prize in a contest sponsored by Dan Dee Potato Chips: dinner at the Kahiki with the Dantes, a teenage rock band from Worthington. Although they might not have been as popular as the Beatles, the Dantes had the advantage of being available. Bill Spencer, general manager at Dan Dee, came up with the idea for the contest. According to his daughter, Candi, her father was a singer who wanted to become part of the music scene when they moved to Columbus in March 1966. Aligning himself with "the hottest band in Columbus" would provide him with an entrée and help to promote the sale of Dan Dee products.

Many celebrities dined (and drank) at the Kahiki, especially those who were appearing in various Kenley Players summer stock productions at Veteran's Memorial.[21] Producer John Kenley[22] made the cast members available on Tuesday nights, and according to David Cohen,[23] "People used to line up for two or three hours outside the Kahiki just to see them." Jack Carson, "Slapsie" Maxie Rosenbloom, Andy Williams, Robert Goulet, Gordon and Sheila McRae, Hugh O'Brian, Raymond Burr, Barbara Eden, Gig Young, Betsy Palmer, Betty White, Laurel Lea Schaefer (Miss America 1972) and Gypsy Rose Lee all stopped by while performing in Columbus.

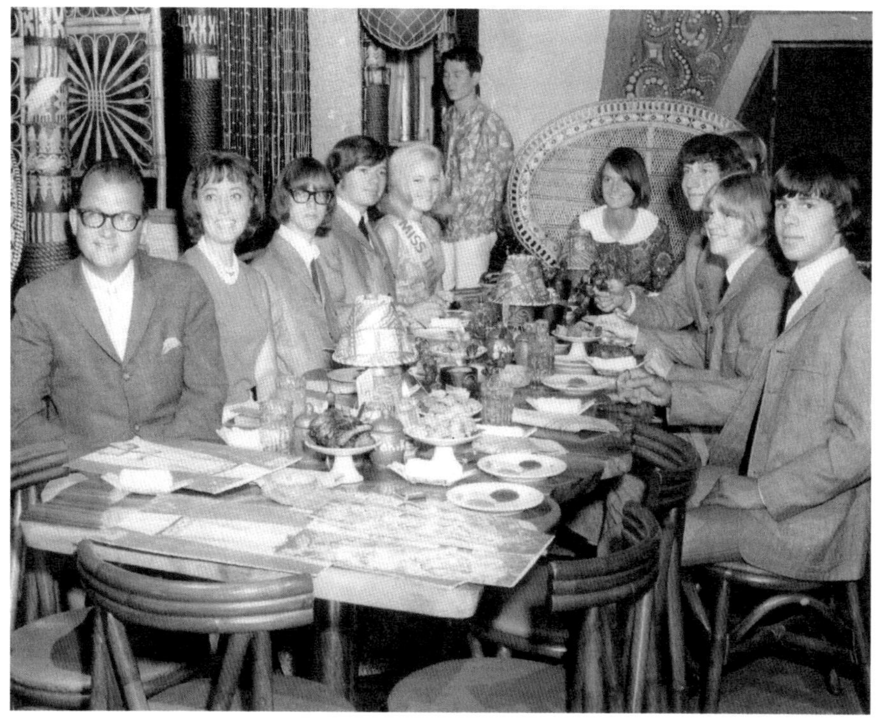

The Dantes and guests (clockwise from left): Bill Spencer, Jane Spencer, Dave Workman (lead guitar), Carter Holliday (bass), Shana McCabe (Miss Dan Dee), unknown waiter, Sally Wheeler Ruault, Lynn Wehr (rhythm guitar), Barry Hayden (vocals) and Joe Hinton (drums). *Courtesy Lynn Wehr.*

Zsa Zsa Gabor is said to have looked over the vast drink menu and ordered milk. Milton Berle is rumored to have barged into the restaurant one night after closing, entered the kitchen and started fixing himself something to eat. Johnny Gim was tapped to be the official photographer and handed a four- by five-inch press camera. The photos were then hung on the wall in the Outrigger Bar.

An autographed photo of Paul Lynde was one of these. Born up the road in Mount Vernon, Ohio, Lynde was far and away the most popular actor to ever appear with Kenley Players, having developed a near fanatical following among housewives with his mama's boy persona. Known for his frequent TV appearances, including his role as Uncle Arthur on *Bewitched* and being the center square on *Hollywood Squares*, he mugged his way through *The Impossible Years*, *Plaza Suite*, *Don't Drink the Water* and other farces on a near annual basis—nine shows altogether, for which he was paid as much as $50,000 a week. Such was his popularity that Governor Rhodes declared May 17, 1980, Paul Lynde Day, no doubt hoping some of the adoration would rub off on him.

On a double date in 1961, Lewis Schottenstein saw Kenley's production of *West Side Story*. When they went backstage to get autographs, one of the stars, Carla Alberghetti, was "very snobbish," he said. "We then went on to the Kahiki. Our dates went to the restroom, and my date said to her friend, 'Wasn't Carla Alberghetti a big snob?' And then they saw Miss Alberghetti come out of [a] stall." Carla was the younger sister of Anna Maria Alberghetti (also a Kenley actress) and had replaced her in the role of Lili in the Broadway musical *Carnival*.

During a family gathering at the Kahiki, Ann Hentz recalled that her four-year-old granddaughter wandered away. "We were all talking and enjoying the evening and did not see Jennifer slip over to a booth by the aquarium. She was sitting with a beautiful lady and a gentleman and having a wonderful time when I spotted her…The lady said how much they had enjoyed talking to Jennifer and how very nice it was to see such a lovely family out together. It was such a warm, sincere compliment—and the lady was Sheila MacRae, who was in town for a performance with the Kenley Players."

Andy Williams and his new bride, Claudine Longet, stopped by the Kahiki in 1962 while he was appearing in the Kenley Players production of *Bye Bye, Birdie* with Selma Diamond. The popular singer had met the young woman, who was fifteen years his junior, in Las Vegas, where she was a dancer in the Folies Bergère. Although they would remain married for nearly fourteen years, anyone who saw the two of them arguing at their table that night wouldn't have been surprised if it didn't last until their first anniversary. A year after Williams and Longet parted company, she was charged with the shooting death of her boyfriend, Spider Sabich, at their Aspen home.

Governor Rhodes was a regular at the Kahiki, always accompanied by a highway patrol major. One evening, he came in after seeing a Kenley Players show, and Bobby Joseph, the head bartender, grabbed two handfuls of napkins and threw them at him, saying, "Get that bum outta here." The major immediately went for his gun, but the governor, who was used to Bobby's shenanigans, got a big laugh out of it and calmed his bodyguard down. Bobby was also an accomplished singer who packed them in at the Outrigger Bar.

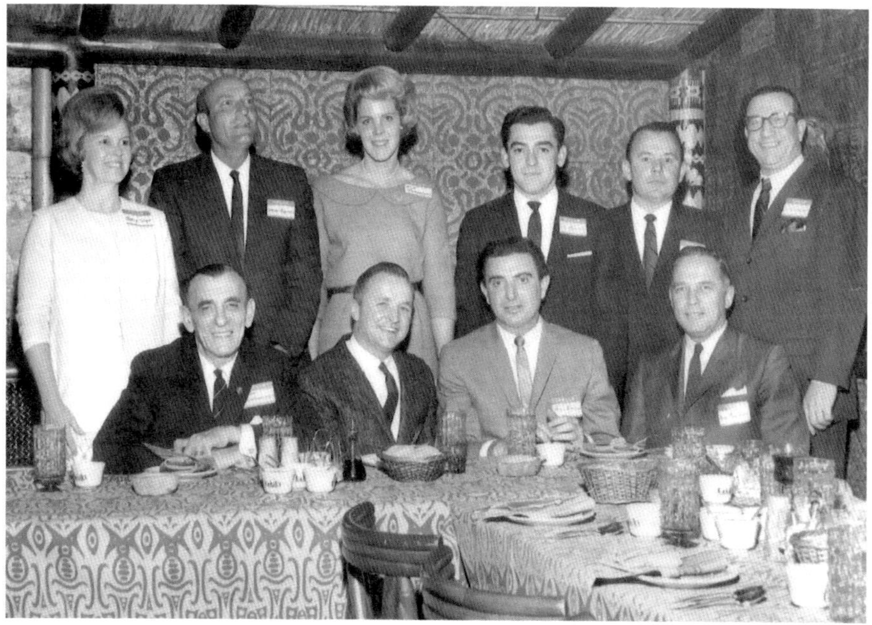

Politicians such as Mayor Maynard Sensenbrenner (front row, far left) often gathered at the Kahiki. *Courtesy Sapp/Henry.*

Bill Sapp recalled that of all the stars he met

> *the one that really impressed me was the guy that played in* The Lost Weekend, *Ray Milland. He was really a down-to-earth, nice guy. I was sitting in the office doing some bookwork, and he just wandered upstairs and was looking all around and my door was open. He just walked in and says, "Hey, how you doing?" I said, "Fine, how are you?" He says, "Oh, I'm doing great. You know you really got a nice place here. I really enjoyed it." I said, "Well, sit down and let's talk about it." He sat down, and we talked for two hours. I never did know who he was until he started to leave, and I said, "By the way, what's your name?" He said Ray Milland. He was really a big star back then.*

The Academy Award–winning actor was known for not taking himself too seriously. He appeared as Professor Henry Higgins in *My Fair Lady*.

Most of the celebrities who visited the Kahiki enjoyed themselves and were a joy to be around. "Ann Margaret and I got along famously," Bill said. "Joey Heatherton not so much." Zsa Zsa Gabor slipped Lee her phone

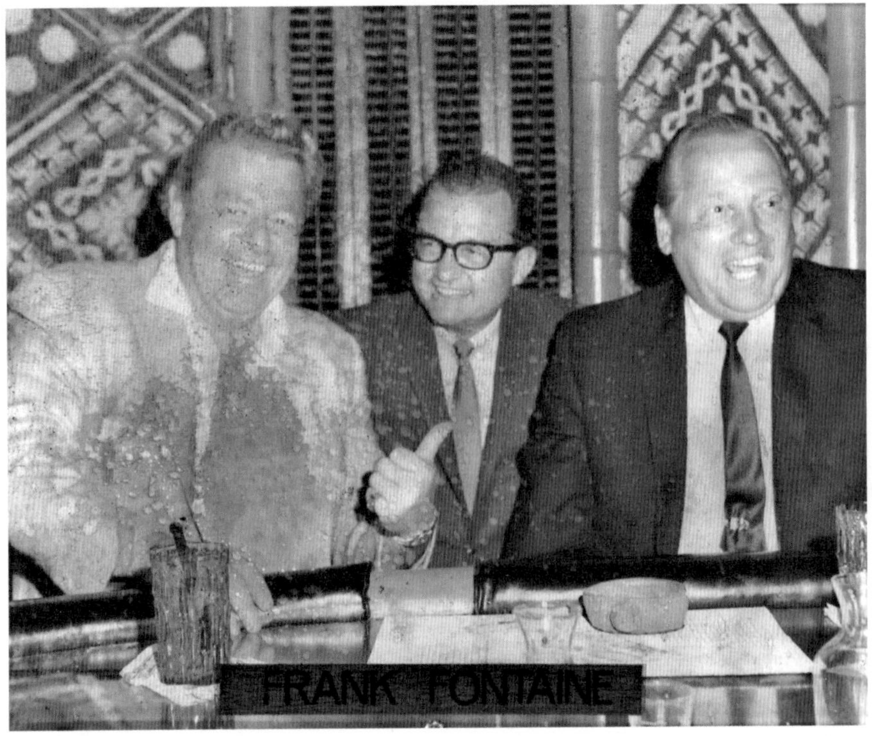

From left: Frank Fontaine, Bill Spencer and "Spook" Beckman in a photo salvaged from the Outrigger Bar wall. *Courtesy Candi Spencer.*

number and invited him to call her up the next time he was in California. He didn't.

When the bar was remodeled in 1992 or 1993, Candi Spencer was able to retrieve the photo of Frank "Crazy Guggeheim" Fontaine. A break-out star from *The Jackie Gleason Show*, his goofy, bug-eyed character was featured in the "Joe, the Bartender" sketches, which would conclude with him demonstrating his surprisingly good singing voice. Joining Fontaine in the picture were her father, Bill Spencer, and his frequent drinking buddy, local radio and TV personality "Spook" Beckman. Unfortunately, the photograph is faded from years of smoke and accumulated grime.

One person who dined at the Kahiki before he became a celebrity was Michael Eisener, future CEO of Disney. A 1995 article in *Fortune* revealed that when he was attending nearby Denison University in Granville, he sometimes ate at the Kahiki when he came into Columbus for entertainment. As writer Wayne Curtis put it, "If there's a better contemporary version of

'George Washington slept here,' I don't know what it is." However, most people nowadays would be more likely to ask, "Michael who?"

Of course, many writers stopped by the Kahiki, some on assignment, some not. Most probably passed through the doors unrecognized. Writer and talk show host Frank DeCaro, author of *The Dead Celebrity Cookbook*, *A Boy Named Phyllis: A Suburban Memoir* and other humorous works, was one. When he heard it was closing, he flew in from New York. As he told Elizabeth Gibson of the *Columbus Dispatch*, "At the point when the last great tiki bar closes, someone will open a new one and everyone will say these are great. It's a shame we always seem to realize too late how much things mean to us."

Robert Ward described in *Renegades: My Wild Trip from Professor to New Journalist with Outrageous Visits from Clint Eastwood, Reggie Jackson, Larry Flynt, and other American Icons* a lunch he once had with publisher Larry Flynt and his girlfriend (later wife), Althea Leasure. The Kahiki was the place to go for celebration when John Hannigan was in graduate school in the mid-1970s, as he related in *Fantasy City: Pleasure and Profit in the Postmodern Metropolis.* It was his touchstone for writing about themed eateries.

In *Unveiling Claudia: A True Story of Serial Murder*, Daniel Keyes quoted Claudia Yasko as saying that she went to dinner at the Kahiki with her friends "Pigman" (Lenny White) and "Ginger" just after overhearing Gary Lewingdon talking about the three murders he and his brother, Thadeus, had committed. The Lewingdons are better known as the 22-Caliber Killers. *Sports Illustrated* reported that the Columbus police tried to catch former Ohio State quarterback Art Schlichter in an illegal gambling "sting" operation at the Kahiki when he was a sophomore in college. However, he failed to meet up with a police informant who was posing as a bookie.

10

THE ROAST BEEF WARS AND OTHER CAMPAIGNS

The feeling of friendship is like that of being comfortably filled with a roast beef.
—Samuel Johnson

An often overlooked chapter in the story of Bill Sapp and Lee Henry was their involvement in the Roast Beef Wars. It was an uncharacteristic endeavor, given their reputation for creating some of the most highly regarded restaurants in Columbus history. However, it does speak to their restless spirit and their emphasis on quality, even in the fast-food arena. That they eventually lost out to Arby's does not diminish the fact that they fought the good fight.

During the 1960s, the Roast Beef Wars raged throughout the United States, and Ohio, for some reason, was the site of some of the bloodiest skirmishes. The opening salvo was fired in Boardman, Ohio, in 1964, when Forrest and Leroy Raffel entered the fast-food business but decided to serve roast beef sandwiches rather than hamburgers. They called their restaurants "Arby's," which was the phonetic spelling of the initials "RB" for Raffel brothers, not "roast beef" as many believe. For a time, the siblings had the market to themselves, but then in 1967, Jack Roschman of Springfield, Ohio, started JAX Roast Beef. After he sold his small chain to General Foods two years later, it was renamed RIX and later reverted to JAX. But by 1982, it became RAX.

Around 1967, former Ohio State University basketball star Jerry Lucas (from Middletown, Ohio) thought he would found a chain of roast beef restaurants. A five-year member of the Cincinnati Royals professional basketball team, he was determined to build a financial empire. Instead,

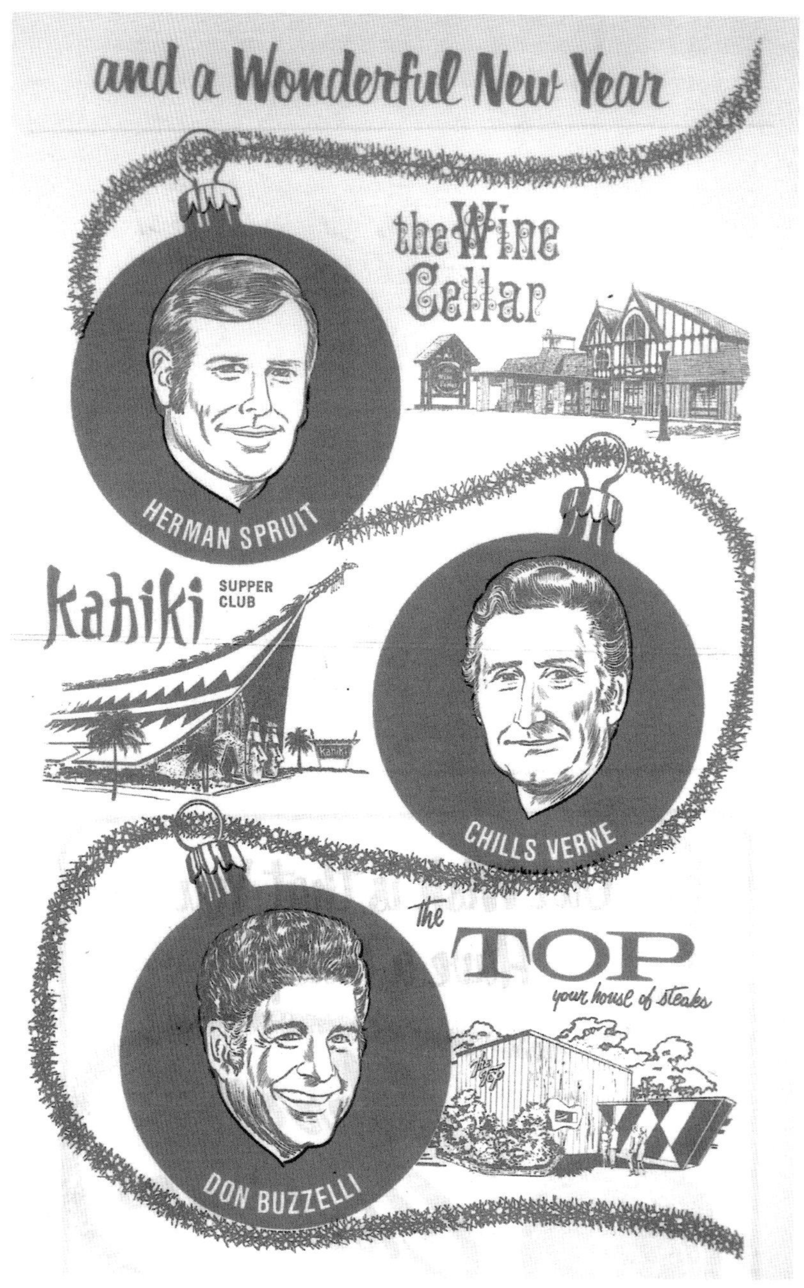

Christmas advertisement for Bill and Lee's "trifecta" of restaurants: the Wine Cellar, the Kahiki and the Top. *Courtesy Sapp/Henry.*

Jerry Lucas Beef-N-Shakes went bankrupt in concert with three of his other companies in 1969. The restaurant business is a harsh mistress.

Finally, in 1968, the Marriott Corporation licensed the image of Ohio-born cowboy star Roy Rogers for a chain of fast-food restaurants. Based in Fall Church, Virginia, the Roy Rogers Restaurants were unique for the time in that they offered hamburgers, chicken and roast beef sandwiches, going head to head with McDonald's, Kentucky Fried Chicken and Arby's, respectively.

It was in 1967 or so that Bill and Lee, fresh off the success of the Kahiki, opened Saxon's Sandwich Shoppe. "When Arby's first started," Lee explained, "they used inside round [steak]. We tried to buy a Columbus franchise, but it was already purchased. So we decided to start our own." Bill had become enamored of not only the sandwiches but also the mocha shakes. They hired Coburn Morgan to design the old English-style timber frame buildings, which were quite substantial for a fast-food chain. At a restaurant show in Chicago, they discovered everyone was getting into the business from Jerry Lewis to Herkie Styles. "Who's ever heard of Herkie Styles?" Lee asked.[24]

Unlike the competition, which tended to serve thin slices of a processed roast beef deli loaf, Saxon's offered the real thing, freshly sliced and heated by a jet of steam. The North High store "took off like a rocket," Lee said, which presented a problem. To quote Bill, "How the hell were we going to run it? Lee had a friend and put the lad in as president. Built like crazy." Over the next few years, they opened fourteen restaurants from Columbus to Florida.

From time to time, Bill and Lee noticed there was a guy who was taking photographs and counting cars at their North High outlet. By 1969, they had been looking to sell the chain for various reasons (including the advice of their attorney), so when they received an offer from Indiana, they took it. The buyer was a man who was already operating a restaurant chain in discount stores and wanted to expand. Within a year, he was bankrupt, but Bill and Lee were far from done.

After touring Europe with Morgan, the partners returned home to build the Wine Cellar in 1971. Located on a three-acre plot along East Dublin–Granville Road, it was designed by architect Frederick C. Williams and Morgan at a cost of $2.1 million, twice what they had spent on the Kahiki only ten years earlier. Using a Shakespearean theme, they created a five-hundred-seat restaurant that could accommodate another one hundred at the bar. The Knight's Hall, the main room, was modeled after the Merchant Adventurer's Hall in York, England. Rubber molds were made of the ceiling beams, which were then cast in fiberglass before being shipped to Ohio. For

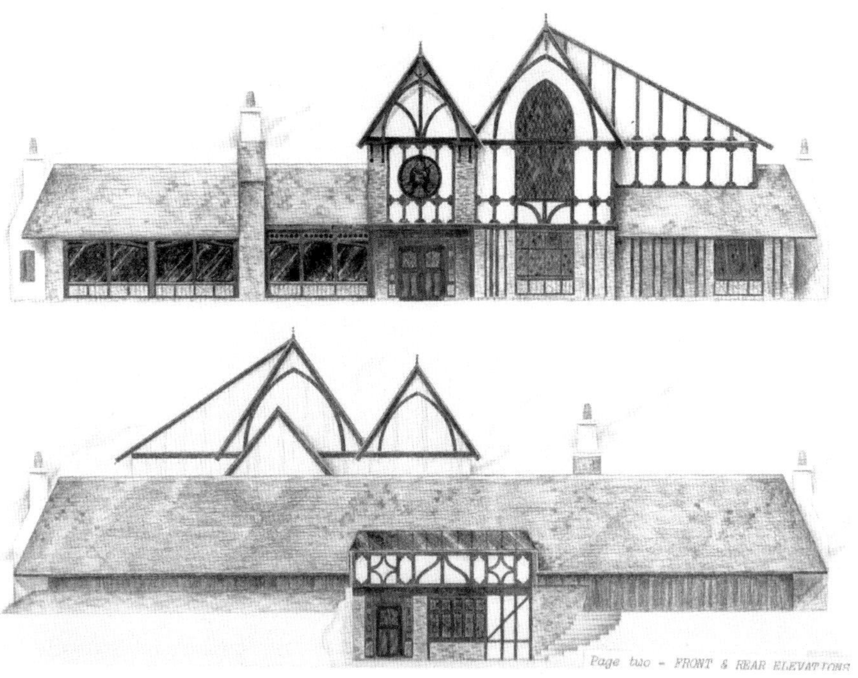

In many respects, the Wine Cellar was the polar opposite of the Kahiki in concept. *Courtesy Sapp/Henry.*

the sake of authenticity, these were supplemented with wood pilings from the Thames River in London. Various other architectural pieces were salvaged from throughout Great Britain. The completed structure featured wrought-iron fences, earthen-red roofing tiles, oak timbers, buttressed chimneys and herring bone–pattern brick work.

Patrons of the Wine Cellar were greeted by waitstaff in Elizabethan costumes and wine stewards in monk's garb. The restaurant was further divided up into the Cockney Pub (with an Inglenook fireplace), Chateau Room, Black Swan Bar (where the piano was inlayed with a stained-glass depiction of a griffin) and the Wine Cellar Grotto. Intended to showcase Bill's vast wine collection, it was unique for the period. "Wine was the rage at the time," Bill says. "Couldn't get a decent bottle in Columbus." Customers could select from thousands of bottles to complement the prime rib and seafood dinners. The Wine Cellar quickly became the largest seller of wines in the entire restaurant industry, dispensing fifty gallons a day. A garden room was subsequently added to the restaurant; it was so far from the

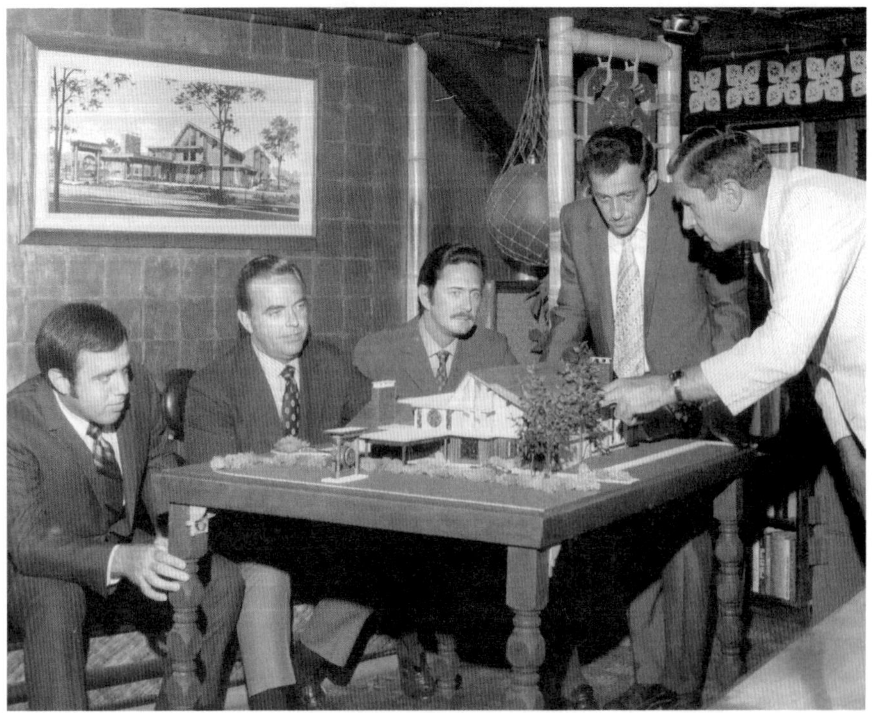

A planning session for the Wine Cellar. *Courtesy Sapp/Henry.*

kitchen that the waitstaff called it the "Morse Road" station, in reference to the road nearly two miles distant.

The Wine Cellar featured live music by pianists Charlie Pickens, Dave Powers, Janet O'Brien (with balladeer Ernest Solomon) and Norm Tyack (who played there for eighteen years until it closed), as well as strolling troubadours Hilda Doyle and Shannon Baughman, a former Disneyland mermaid. When Lee decided he wanted out of the restaurant business in 1980, Bill bought his interests in the Top and the Wine Cellar, continuing to operate both establishments. However, the Wine Cellar had cost so much to build that it required $17,000 a month just to keep it going. In 1985, Bill, who needed money to pay off debts incurred in another restaurant deal, asked John Khoury to speak to businessman Mitch Boich about buying it, and he did.

Like he did with the Kahiki, Boich leased the restaurant to Michael Tsao. This time, Bill kept the inventory—he had started the restaurant with his wine collection, and he walked away with another one. By 1989, the Wine Cellar had closed its doors. Two years later, Boich asked Bill how much it would cost to reopen it. When he told him, he opted to tear it down instead. As restaurant historian Jan Whitaker noted, "16 tall carved knight's chairs" and a "grand piano bar with winged dragon" were among the items auctioned off. Like the Kahiki, it deserved better.

The Wine Cellar marked the end of Bill and Lee's partnership, although they remained good friends. Curiously, they also continued in the restaurant business, following parallel paths. During the mid-1970s, Lebanon, Ohio, became the birthplace of Duff's Famous Smorgasbord when Homer Duff added a sandwich bar to his mom-and-pop grocery. Homer had noticed that a lot of meat had to be tossed out at his deli counter because it became discolored after sitting in the deli case all day. Although there was nothing wrong with it, he couldn't sell it to his customers. So he began using it in a sandwich bar, offering an entire meal for ninety-nine cents. Soon, Homer sold his grocery to open a "one meal for one price," all-buffet restaurant.

Duff's Famous Smorgasbord featured a circling buffet line, designed and patented by Homer. Customers stood in one place while the food came to them directly from the kitchen. The idea caught on quickly, and both Bill and Lee hopped aboard the Duff's bandwagon, although separately. "Got the big idea to move to Florida and build restaurants just after the break with Lee," Bill said. Along with his partners, Bob Isley and Grover Schmidt, Bill built his first Duff's in Fort Lauderdale in 1979. "We made so much money so fast it made your head swim." Before long, they had added five more.

However, just a year later, Bill and his partners ran into financial trouble as the economy "went south." Despite having 150 restaurants nationwide, Homer also had money woes and, in 1983, sold Duff's to a company that promptly went bankrupt.

Lee had also invested in a Duff's franchise, becoming a silent partner with Hal Field, Bruce Allan and Don Levy. They opened a total of three buffets in the Columbus area, but Lee declined to personally sign any of the leases. As a result, his partners gave him a baseball with "Lee plays hardball" inscribed on it. Unlike Bill, he got out before the whole thing "went belly up."

Bloodied but unbowed, Bill opened the Café Martinique in 1988. "It was the best restaurant I ever had," he asserted. He invited John Wolfe of the Dispatch Printing Company and others to join him. Located on the site of the former Ciro's, it was directly across the street from the Top. Like the Wine Cellar, it offered an extensive wine selection, matched with the best in cuisine and service. Taking a cue from New York's 21 Club, the restaurant provided a number of wine lockers for lease. However, there apparently were

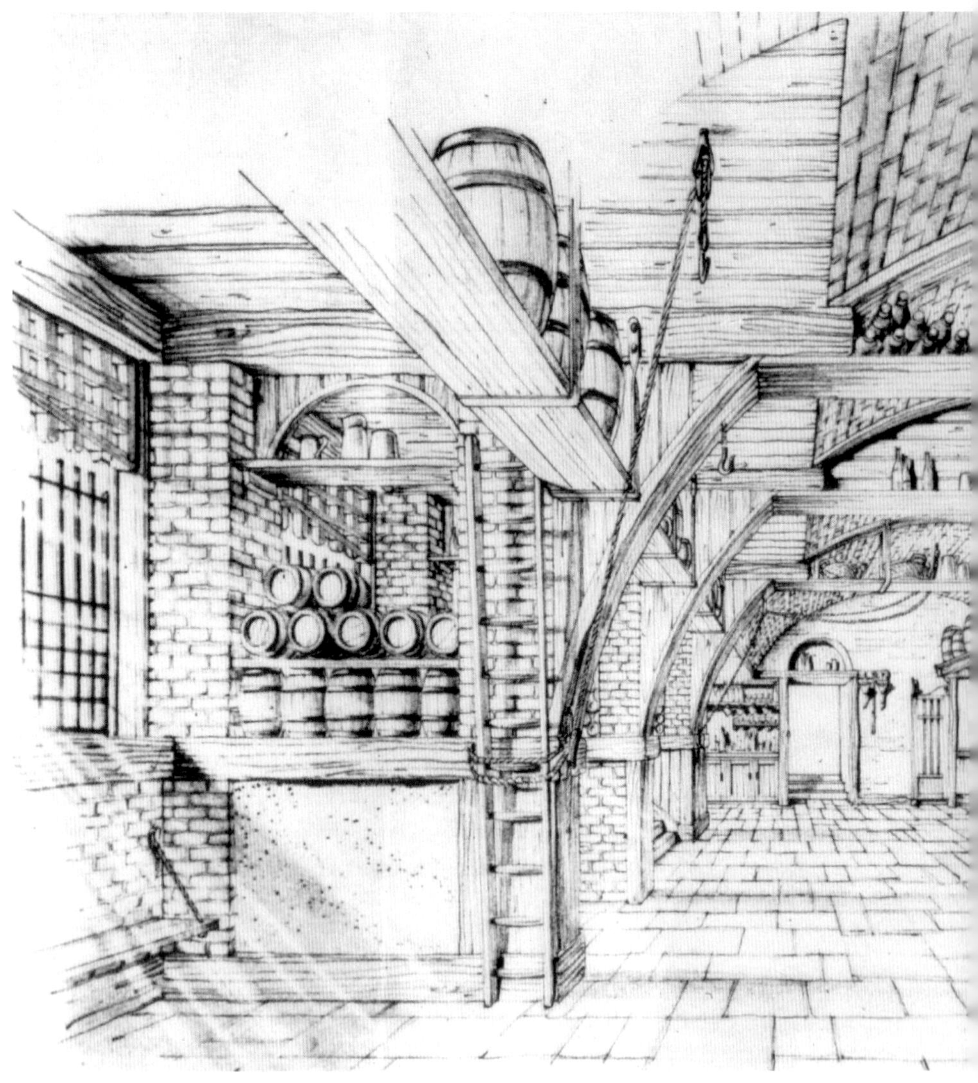

The basement of the Wine Cellar featured vaulted ceilings. *Courtesy Sapp/Henry.*

not enough, for all of them were immediately snapped up (mostly by the original investors). "It did great for five years," Bill said. "Then people didn't want to pay French restaurant prices." Perhaps, the fact that the menu was in French (with English translation) discouraged some midwestern diners. In August 1991, Bill et al. were looking to sell it. A little over a year later, it was out of business.

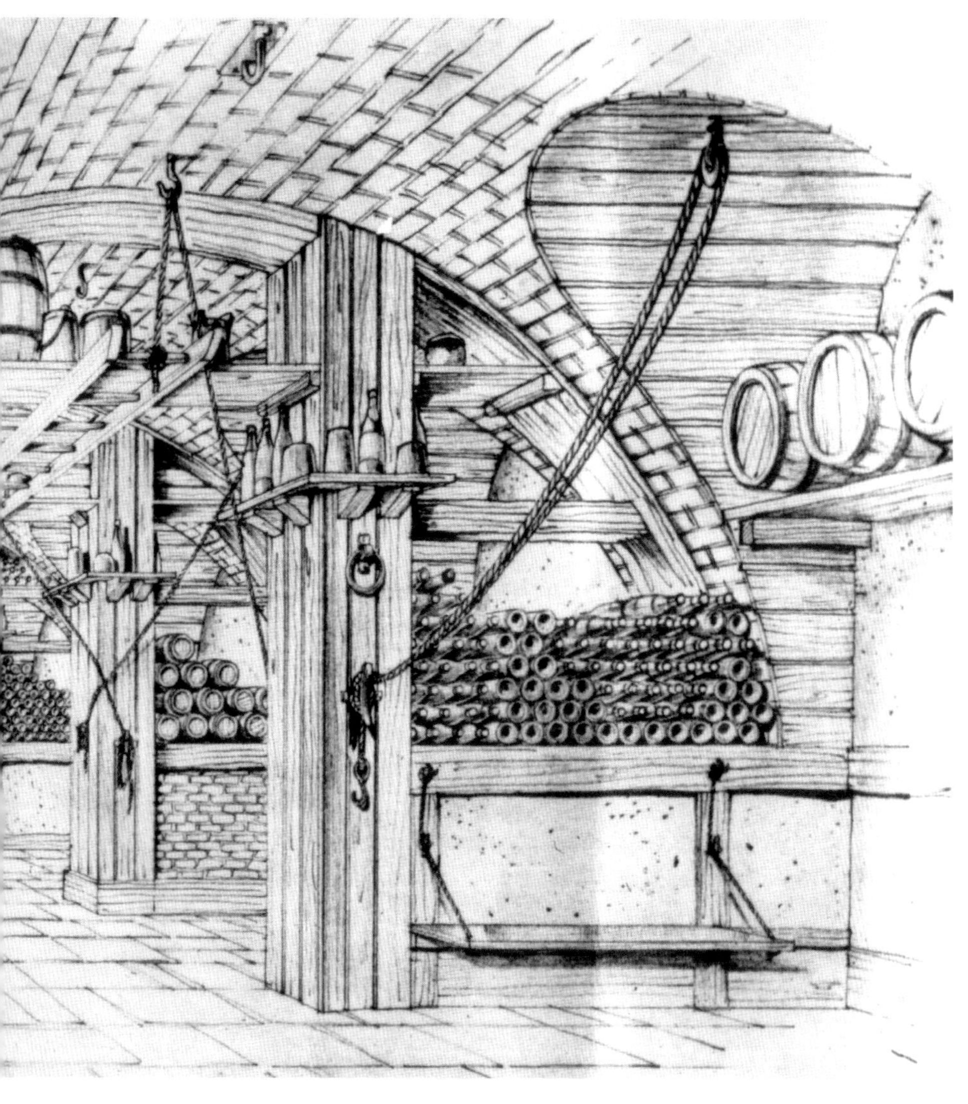

Years later, architect Keith DeVoe III praised both the Kahiki and the Wine Cellar as pioneering restaurants in creating "a sense of place" through their innovative architecture. Unfortunately, most people will have to take his word for it since neither one of these unique buildings remains standing.

11

THE MAN WHO PUT THE TIKI IN THE KAHIKI

People who turn snooty amidst the Kahiki's faux-Polynesia probably haven't experienced the faux-Polynesia of Hawaii itself.
—Steve Stephens

When Coburn Morgan was hired to work on the Kahiki project in 1960, he was head of the design division for Tectum Corporation, supplier of many of the building materials used in the construction of the restaurant. With degrees in electrical engineering and architecture, he was an accomplished painter, sculptor and decorator. In addition to designing the interior and portions of the exterior, Morgan designed many of the artifacts and fountains as well. And he recommended to Bill and Lee that they hire Design Associates as the architectural firm.

According to Jan Whitaker, his "flamboyant design of the Kahiki" may well have launched his career as a designer of themed restaurants and related structures. He soon moved onto

> *the Aztec-themed Thunderbird Restaurant (Lima), a red-fronted prototype for the Bob Evans chain (Chillicothe), McGarvey's Nautical Restaurant (Vermillion), the Wine Cellar (Columbus), Jack Bowman's Steak House (Columbus), the Brown Derby (Columbus), the 18th-century-themed Old Market House Inn (Zanesville), the Tangier Restaurant (Akron), Mawby's (Cleveland), and the "Western Victorian–style" Judd's (Cleveland).*

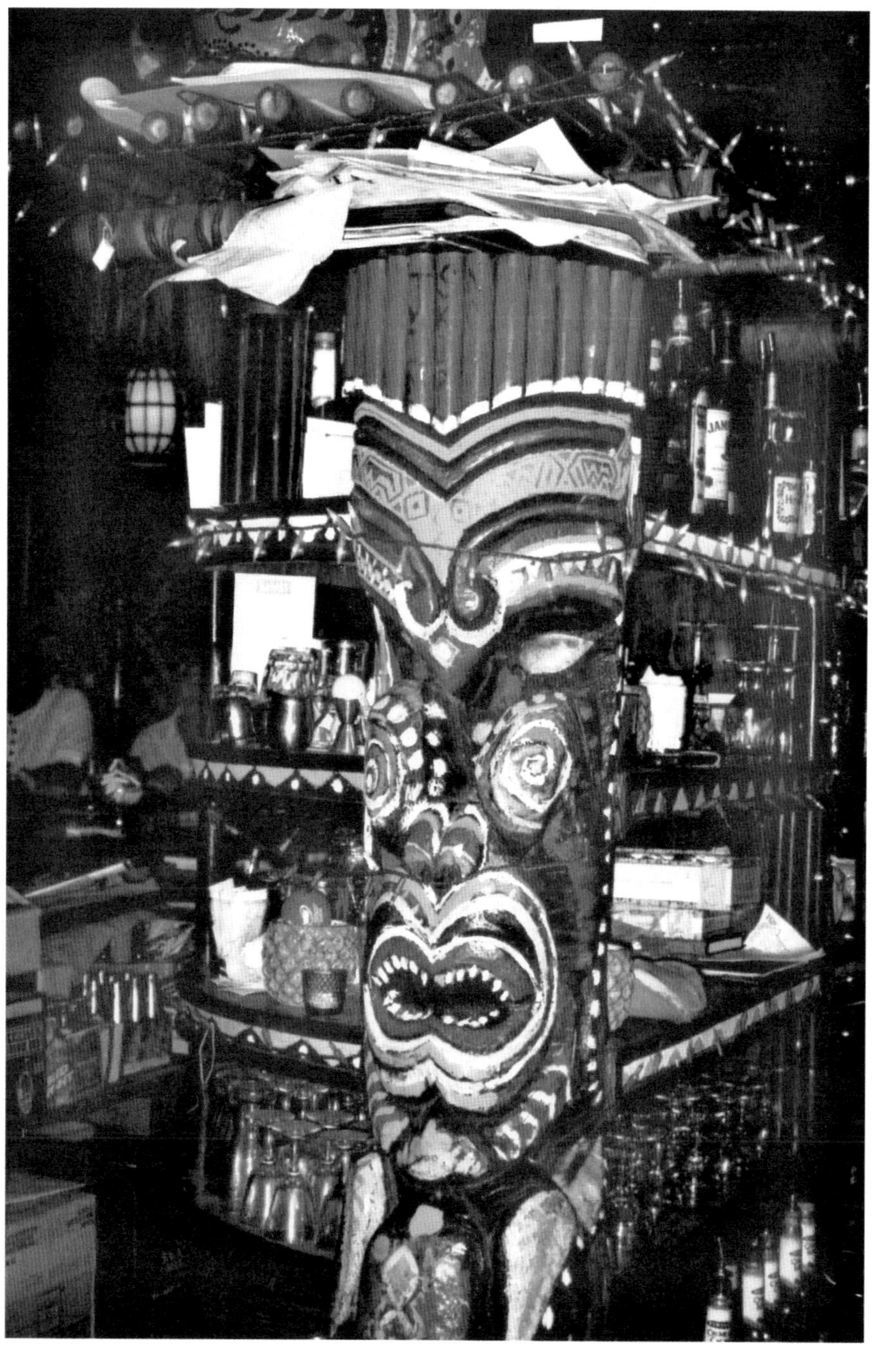

One of several tiki statues incorporated into the décor of the Kahiki. *Courtesy Sapp/Henry.*

He also worked on other Columbus restaurants, including the Jai Lai and Sands Supper Club, as well as the original Bob Evans and Casa Lupita chains.

Lee Stratton of the *Columbus Dispatch* wrote about Bernard Gerson's home overlooking a ravine on the far east side of Columbus. Designed by Morgan in 1964, the 2,800-square-foot ranch house was considered ultra-contemporary at the time of its construction:

> *Stepping through the orange front door is akin to stepping back four decades. The original travertine tile floor, sculptured ceramic tile wall and gold foil wallpaper highlight the foyer. A variety of definitely 1960s light fixtures and grass-cloth wall-coverings remain throughout the home. The original parquet floors are there, as are the pocket doors with acrylic panels sporting red, lime and yellow circles. The kitchen cabinets are red, avocado and orange. The Formica counters are red. The dining and living areas feature brighter tones of the same colors in bold stripes. The guest bath has blue foil wall-coverings and a distinctive geometric pattern in ceramic tile.*

They hired Columbus architect Leon Seligson, a follower of Frank Lloyd Wright, and Morgan, a personal friend. An abstract sculpture of an embracing couple—the Gersons—carved in feather stone (a porous volcanic rock) is mounted on the front of the home. Volcanic rock was also used in the construction of the fireplace and a desk in Gerson's African-themed office. Morgan painted two murals, one of an elephant herd and the other of a Spanish bullfight, as well as a portrait of Marion Gerson, although he changed her black hair to brown for artistic reasons.

Owing to his work on the Kahiki, Morgan suddenly found his services as a restaurant designer much in demand. Just a year later, Bob Susi opened a quality restaurant and steak house in Graceland Shopping Center at a time when all the best fine-dining establishments (the Kahiki excepted) were downtown. "People told me it would never work," he told restaurant reviewer Doral Chenoweth of the *Columbus Dispatch*. Susi called it the Fontanelle Restaurant, and to many people's surprise, it succeeded. He was already running a little bar at the corner of Hudson Street and McGuffey Road, but he felt that the new strip mall would be just the place for an upscale eatery and bar. To make it stand out from the other storefronts, Susi hired Morgan, who transformed it into a landmark with the addition of a distinctive yellow brick front, blue mansard roof, white shutters and fancy ironwork.

According to Barnet D. Wolf (also of the *Dispatch*), Bob Evans came calling a few years later. Evans, the "Sausage King" from Gallipolis, Ohio, worked with Morgan to design the prototype for a proposed chain of Bob Evans Farm Restaurants. The first, built in Chillicothe in 1968, became the ubiquitous red-and-white barn "with Western accents, including the keyhole cutout at the top." It was a countrified version of the Fontanelle.

Originally known as the Linden Party House, Joe Asmo rechristened the East Fifth Avenue restaurant Yolanda's, after his sister, when he purchased it in 1956. A dozen years later, he hired Morgan to redo the interior. Although it was ornate, Morgan managed to keep it tasteful as well, which no doubt contributed to its popularity. It finally closed in 1995, after a thirty-nine-year run.

In 1974, Morgan was hired by James L. Adornetto to remodel a former farmers' market in Zanesville, Ohio. Using the oldest riverfront pub in London, England, as inspiration, he undertook an extensive nine-month renovation of the historic building to create the Old Market House Inn. The same year, Morgan completely redesigned the former Betty Crocker Tree House at 1321 Morse Road in Columbus, transforming it into the thirty-fifth entry in a nationwide chain of Brown Derby restaurants. The total cost of the project was $2 million.

When *Hustler* magazine publisher Larry Flynt bought a house in Bexley in 1976, it was big news. It wasn't so much for the fact that the Columbus-based pornographer was moving into a $375,000 mansion in one of city's toniest suburbs but that the location was directly across the street from the Columbus School for Girls. "Flynt will be out in front of the school handing out lollipops," one local resident joked. Only a year earlier, he had made headlines by publishing nude photographs of Jacqueline Kennedy Onassis. Flynt and his magazine had come a long way with monthly sales soaring to 1.5 million from 160,000 less than two years earlier. His fledgling publication was already third behind *Playboy* and *Penthouse*.

However, Flynt did not intend to create a midwestern version of the Playboy Mansion. Rather, he wanted only to provide a home for his fiancée, four daughters and himself. So he turned to Coburn Morgan of Functional Planning, Inc., to undertake $1 million in renovations. Since the house already had a projection room, library, wine cellar, six bedrooms and numerous bathrooms, Morgan's focus was to be on a courtyard and an indoor-outdoor swimming pool. Presumably, he had nothing to do with the publisher's remarkably tasteless bedroom apartment on the second floor of the downtown Hustler Club.

The village of Kensborough is an eighteenth-century English village just north of the Columbus suburb of Mount Air on State Route 315. Modeled after Groombridge Place, a castle in Kent, England, Kensborough features a gatehouse, a cobblestone street and gaslights, all concealed behind a mounded stone wall. This upscale housing development, which opened in 1990, was drawn up by architect John Reagan with interior design by Morgan. Just three years later, on June 23, 1993, Morgan passed away of liver failure at the age of seventy-one.

12
PASSING THE TIKI TORCH

Company cultures are like country cultures. Never try to change one. Try, instead, to work with what you've got.
—Peter Drucker

Of the two partners, Lee was more interested in building restaurants than running them. In 1978, he persuaded Bill to accept an offer from Michael "Mitch" Boich to buy the Kahiki. Boich was the founder of the Boich Companies, a privately held coal mining and marketing company headquartered in Columbus. "He was a good customer of ours," Lee said. Bill agreed, "Mitch was a great guy." One of Boich's favorite pastimes was playing backgammon. During 1977–78, a backgammon club met in the basement of the Kahiki.[25] In the 1970s, Oswald Jacoby, author of *The Backgammon Book*, hired Marcy, Bill's wife, to travel around to shopping malls, teaching people how to play the game.

A native of Steubenville, Ohio, Mitch Boich had attended Ohio State before entering into construction, coal mining and related industries in the late 1940s. When he passed away on August 25, 2000, Representative Robert W. Ney of Ohio eulogized him on the floor of the U.S. House of Representatives as "a man of tremendous vision who never lost his sense of tradition" and "a man known for his pizzazz and his strength." What Ney left unsaid was Boich's role as a kingmaker. Boich and his family were contributors to the campaigns of many politicians on both sides of the aisle, including Governor (later senator) George Voinovich and Governor Richard Celeste. In exchange, he expected them to support legislation that would benefit his financial interests.

Margaret Newkirk of the *Akron Beacon Journal* wrote about an incident that occurred in 1988 when state representative Jerry Krupinski of Steubenville ran into Boich at the Galleria restaurant in Columbus. At the time, Celeste and New York governor Mario Cuomo had recently proposed a national tax to assist Ohio with the cost of cleaning up its coal-fueled power plants. However, Boich and other coal mine owners didn't support it. So he told Krupinski he was about to head "across the street to the Statehouse to 'kick [Governor] Dick Celeste's ass.' Krupinski said, 'I was pretty impressed.'"

"Mitch got around to every place," Lee said. "He saw [Michael] Tsao at Trader Vic's." They hit it off so well that Boich thought that if he bought the Kahiki, he could bring Tsao in to run it. He would then lease the restaurant to him with a buy option. However, the sale nearly didn't happen. The partners had agreed to sell the Kahiki's inventory to Tsao for $100,000. On the day of the closing, Tsao told them he didn't have the money. Bill wanted to walk away from the deal, but Lee didn't. So they let him have the inventory for free. "We were sorry within two weeks that we sold it," Bill said. "We had this great big gong, like four to five feet across, that went *bong*, and right after we sold it, they replaced it with this little thing that went *ting*."

Michael Tsao was a product of the American Dream. Born in Shanghai, China, he moved to Hong Kong as a youth. At the age of eighteen, he immigrated to the United States with $100 in his pocket and no prospects. Landing a job as a dishwasher, he set about working his way up in the restaurant business until he became general manager of the Beverly Hilton Trader Vic's. During his tenure, it was rated one of the top five restaurants in the Los Angeles area. Declining the opportunity to become vice-president of the San Francisco operation (the most successful of all the company's restaurants), Tsao decided to strike out on his own. "I'm not corporate material," he said. "I'm a maverick."

After eleven years of managing Trader Vic's, Tsao took Boich up on his offer. Packing up his family, chefs and managers, he moved to Columbus, Ohio. "I didn't even know where Ohio was," he said. "All I knew was Ohio State beat UCLA every year they played them in the Rose Bowl."

A graduate of Pasadena City College with a degree in business administration, Tsao was nothing if not ambitious. Over the next decade, he became president and general manager of the four-hundred-room Columbus Sheraton Plaza hotel. He also built upon the success of the Kahiki by introducing a chain of five Chinese fast-food restaurants and a steak house. One of the challenges he had to deal with was standardizing operations. According to Tsao, this was not unusual in ethnic restaurants. "Each person

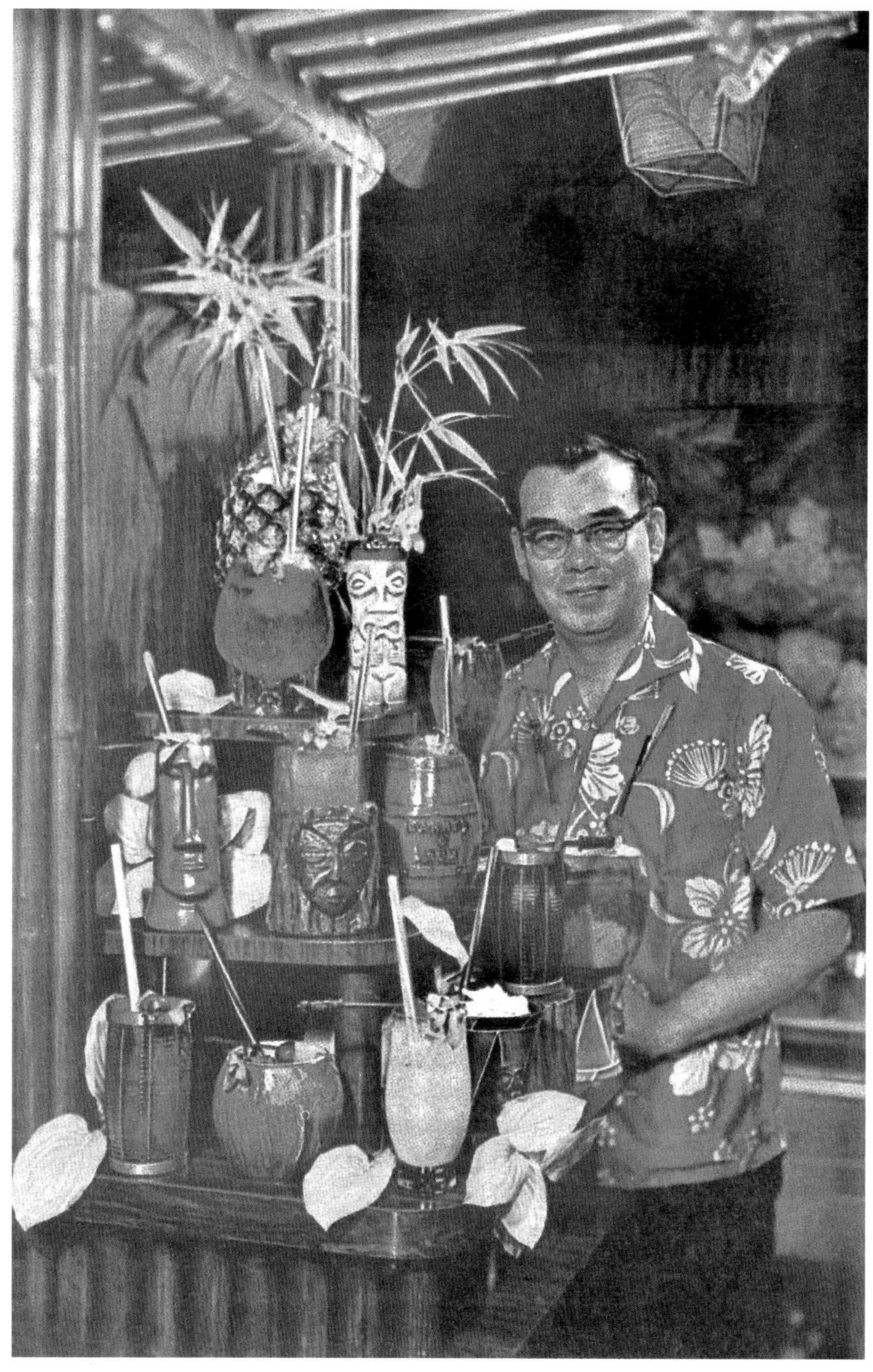

George Ono was also a bar manager at the Kahiki. *Courtesy Sapp/Henry.*

who is Chinese has their own version of how the food is flavored," he said. "There's no standard recipe." Complicating matters further was the fact that tastes varied from Chinese students at Ohio State to patrons at suburban shopping malls.

Rather than engaging in opening more restaurants, Tsao turned his attention to manufacturing foods. He began packaging and freezing egg rolls, stir-fry meals and other Kahiki favorites. "In those days," he told Martha Leonard of *Business First*, "we had a lot of immigrants coming from Asia, like Vietnam and China. The husband and wife can't get a job because they don't speak English, so I thought, 'Why not let them come in and make egg rolls.' So we began to sell egg rolls wholesale." (Much to Bill and Lee's annoyance, he sold them out of a freezer case in the restaurant's lobby, diluting the ambiance they had worked so hard to create.)

In 1989, a year after Tsao bought out Boich to become sole owner of the Kahiki, the "Son of Heaven" exhibition came to Columbus. Housed in the former Central High School, the exhibition of Chinese art and culture was expected to be a major tourist attraction and a boon to the local economy during its run.[26] Working out of the basement of the Kahiki, Tsao had already begun supplying frozen food items to Kroger groceries. But when Columbus-based Wendy's Hamburgers won the catering contract for "Son of Heaven," it turned to him to provide the egg rolls.

During the exhibit's six-month run, Wendy's sold a quarter of a million Kahiki egg rolls. What Tsao took away from that was that there was a wholesale market for his products, but he didn't know how big a market. In 1991, the restaurant won a contract to provide food for state institutions, including colleges and hospitals. A year later, the Kahiki Supper Club was nominated as one of the top fifty restaurants in the country and awarded a Five-Star Diamond rating from the American Academy of Restaurant Sciences.

Having decided to incorporate the Kahiki, Tsao formed a board of directors, chose a president and issued publicly traded stock shares. With the funds raised, construction began in 1995 on a $1 million, seven-thousand-square-foot frozen food processing plant immediately behind the restaurant. Soon Kahiki Frozen Foods began turning out products under the "General Tsao" label. During the next two years, the frozen food operation signed distribution agreements with Walmart, tripling its wholesale business, and 7-Eleven stores, adding perhaps five thousand or so more outlets. By 1997, its frozen food sales, branded and unbranded, approached its restaurant sales. The following year, they began to outpace them. As a strategic planning consultant put it, "With Kahiki, they found the soul was not in

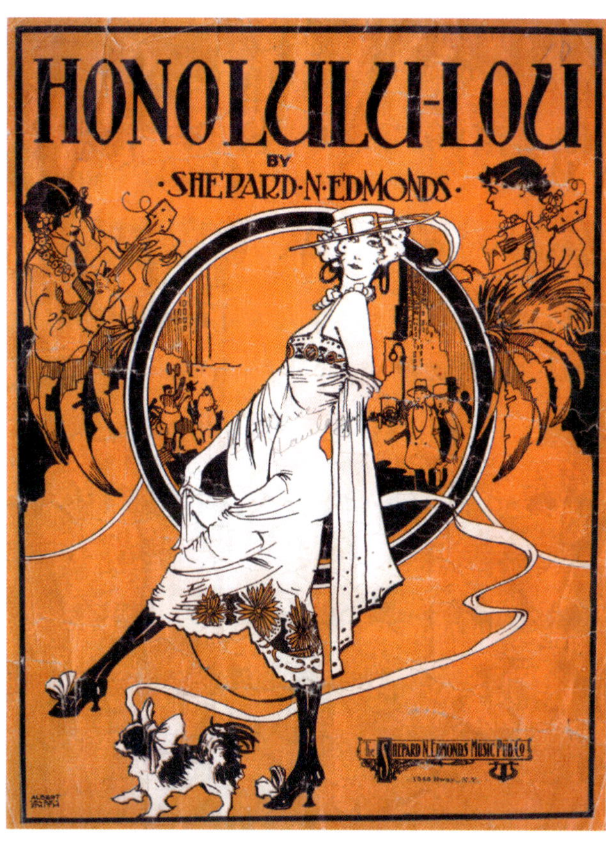

Left: Composed by Columbus's own Shep Edmonds in 1920, "Honolulu Lou" was just one of hundreds of pop songs written about the Polynesian islands. *Authors' collection.*

Below: Both internally and externally, the Kahiki was one of the most visually striking restaurants to be found anywhere. *Courtesy Sapp/Henry.*

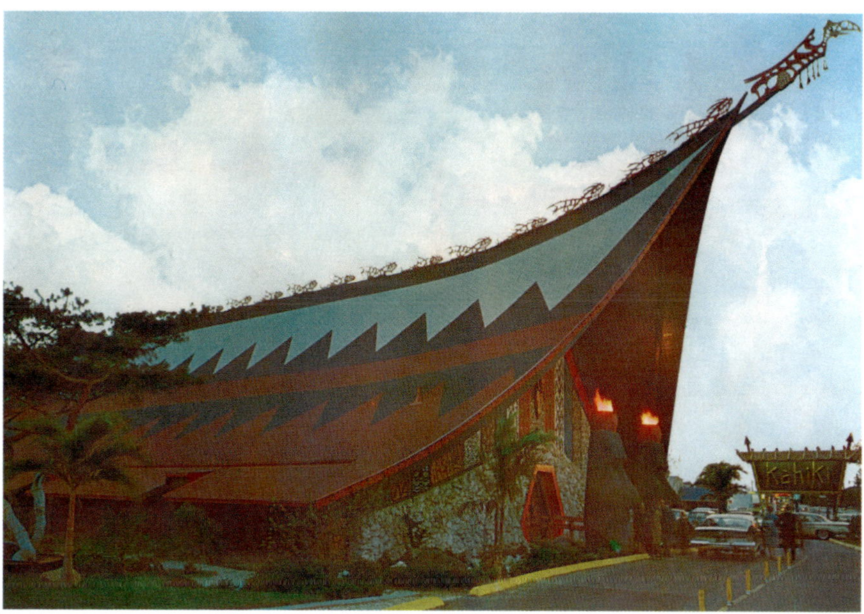

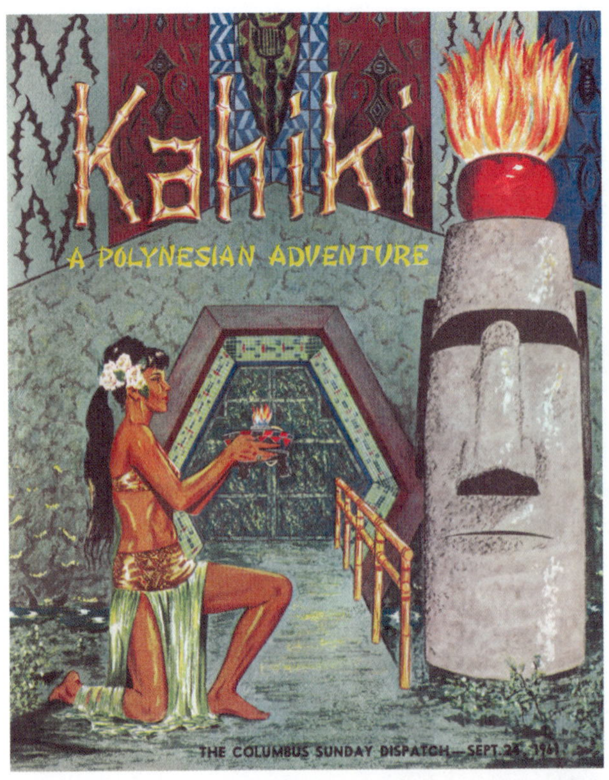

Left: The Mystery Girl kneels to one of the twin moai guarding the entrance to the Kahiki on the cover of this advertising supplement. *Courtesy Sapp/Henry.*

Below: When the Kahiki opened, the wall of aquariums was an unusual feature for its time. *Courtesy Sapp/Henry.*

Opposite, top: In this advertising supplement from the *Columbus Dispatch*, the Mystery Girl raises her bowl to the fireplace moai. *Courtesy Sapp/Henry.*

Opposite, bottom: A visit to the Kahiki was at its magical best at night, when it was easier to pretend it was a tropical oasis. *Courtesy Sapp/Henry.*

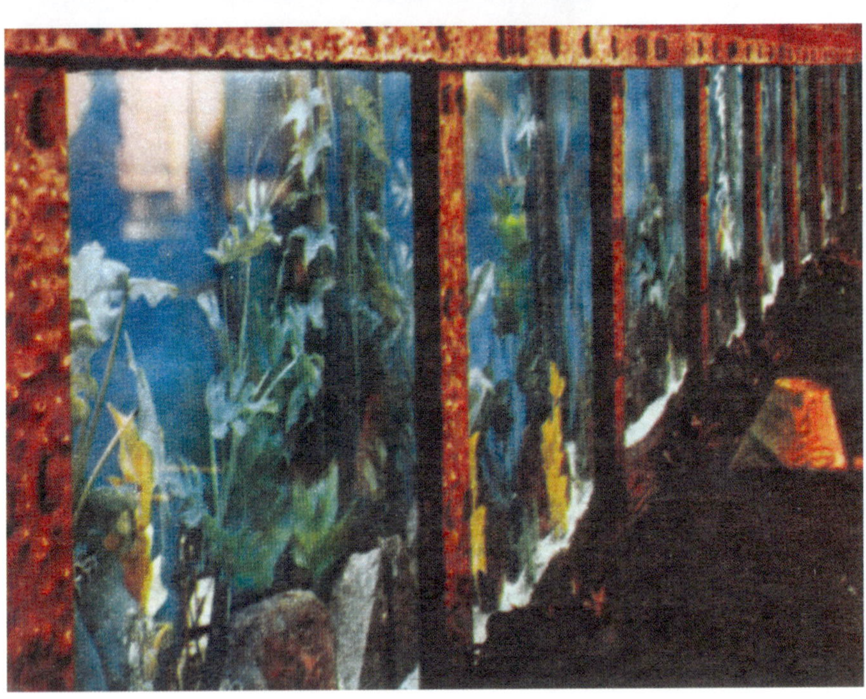

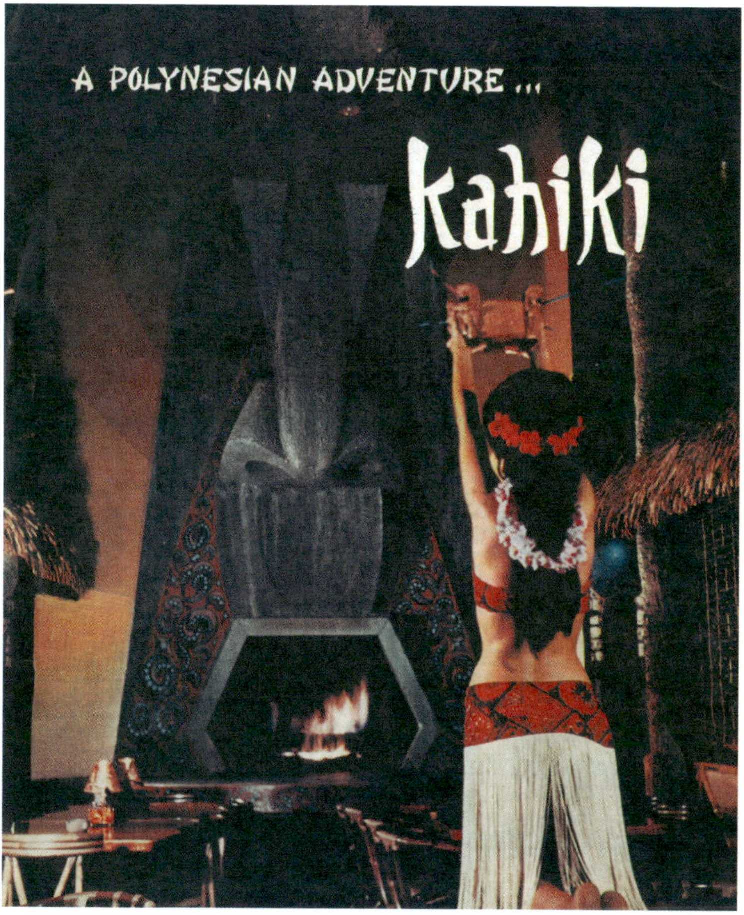

A POLYNESIAN ADVENTURE ...

Kahiki

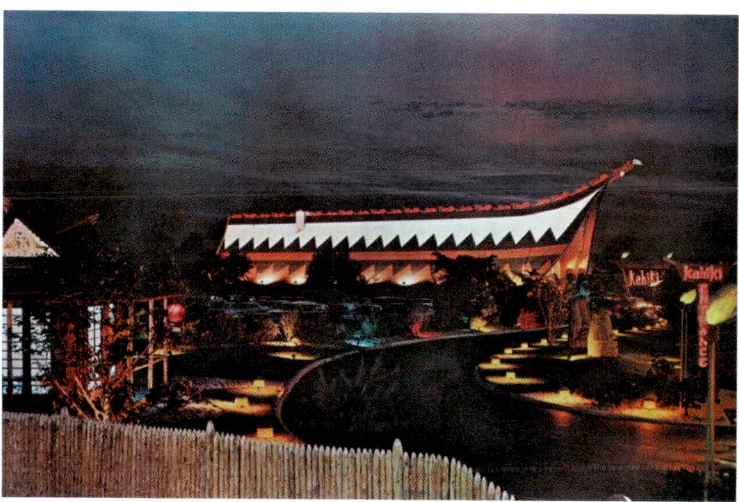

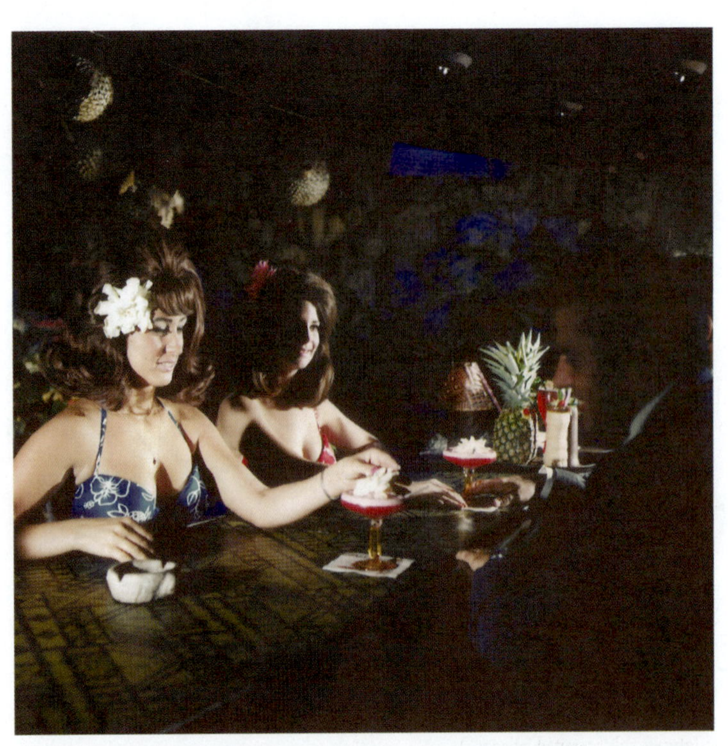

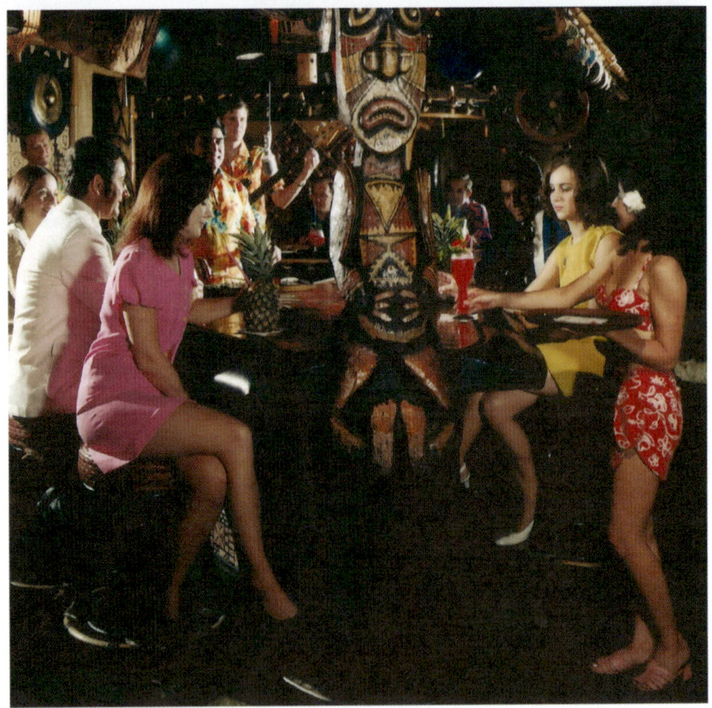

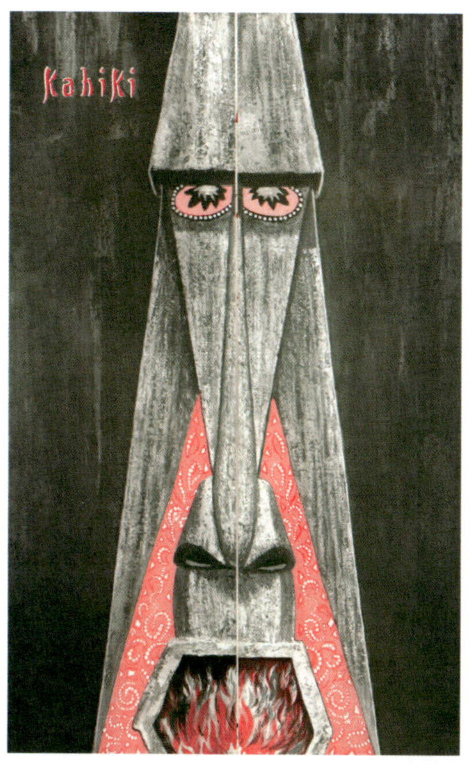

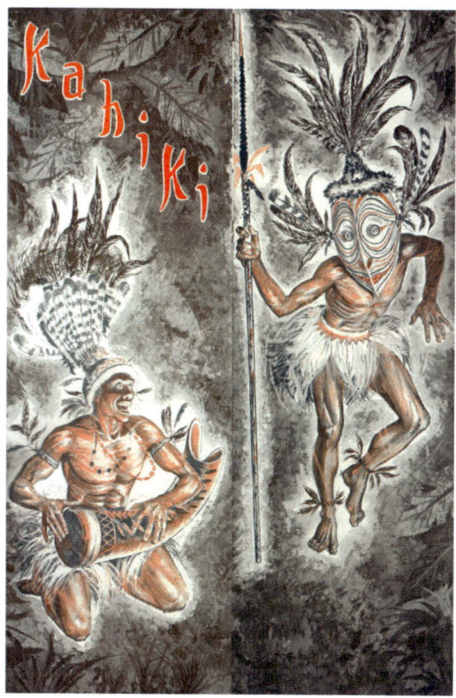

Opposite, top: This photograph by Charles Moore of a couple "wahines" was later used as the cover of *The Beachcomber Trio* album. *Authors' collection.*

Opposite, bottom: Wahines and customers surround Marsh Padilla in the Music Bar. *Authors' collection.*

Top: The enormous fireplace moai with its flaming mouth and eyes graced the front of the dining menu. *Courtesy Sapp/Henry.*

Bottom: Tribal dancers are depicted on the cover of the Kahiki drink menu, which was produced by a firm in Chicago. *Courtesy Sapp/Henry.*

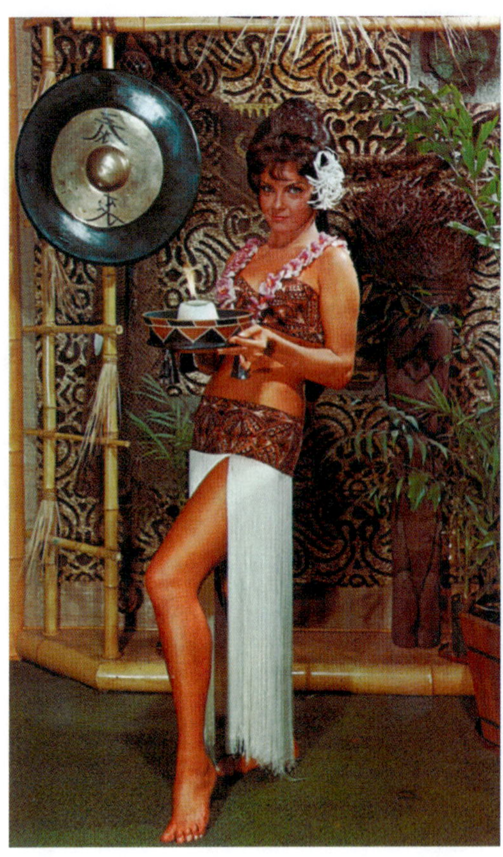

Left: Summoned by a gong, the Mystery Girl delivered the Mystery Drink to the table with much ceremony. *Courtesy Sapp/Henry.*

Below: An illustration of the celebrated four-person Mystery Drink taken from the menu. *Courtesy Sapp/Henry.*

Opposite, top: The advertising supplements included photos of "People You're Apt to Meet at Kahiki." *Courtesy Sapp/Henry.*

Opposite, bottom: Many celebrities visited the Kahiki more than once, especially those who performed in several Kenley Players productions. *Courtesy Sapp/Henry.*

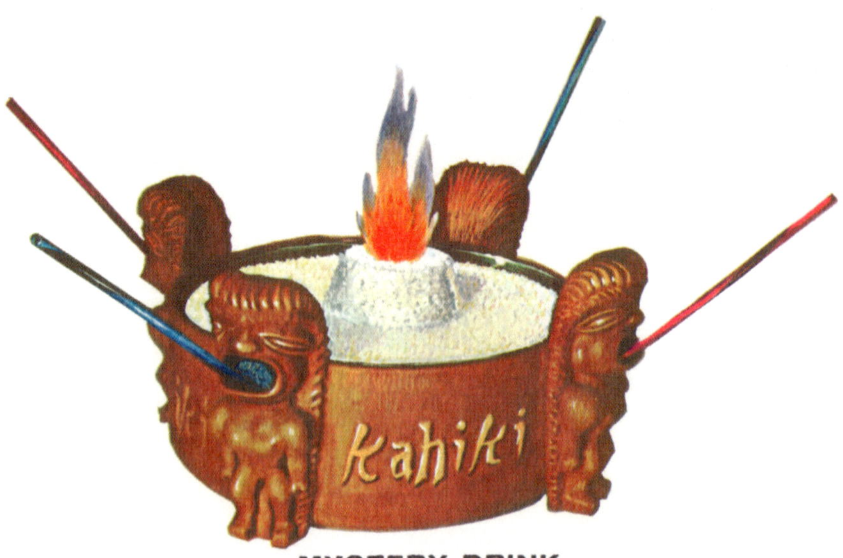

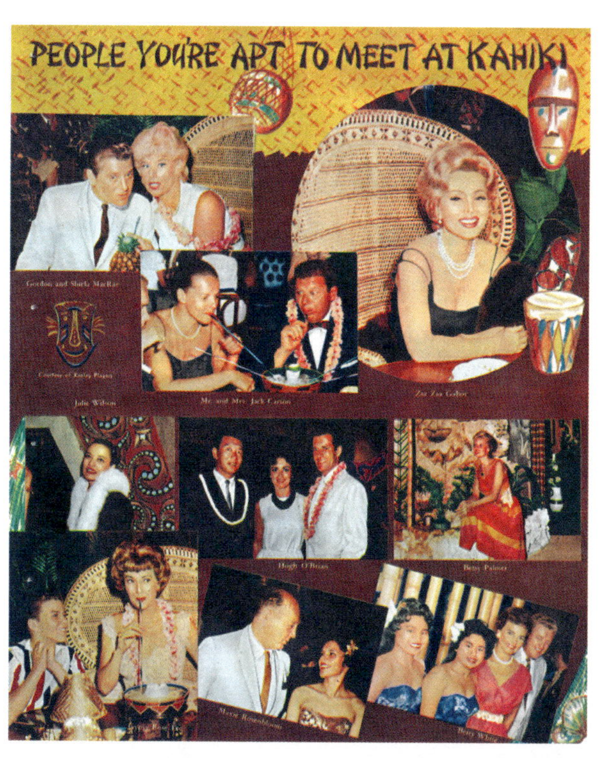
PEOPLE YOU'RE APT TO MEET AT KAHIKI
Gordon and Sheila MacRae
Julie Wilson
Mr. and Mrs. Jack Carson
Zsa Zsa Gabor
Hugh O'Brian
Betsy Palmer
Betty White

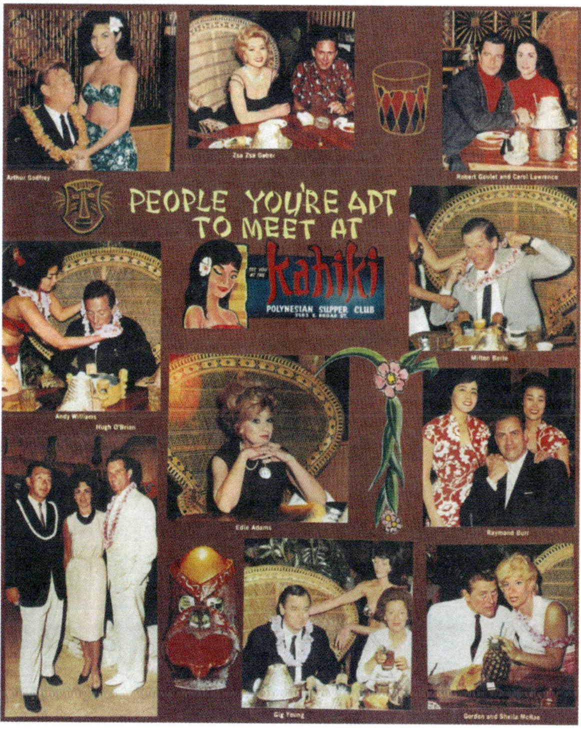
Arthur Godfrey
Zsa Zsa Gabor
Robert Goulet and Carol Lawrence
PEOPLE YOU'RE APT TO MEET AT
Kahiki
POLYNESIAN SUPPER CLUB
Milton Berle
Andy Williams
Hugh O'Brian
Edie Adams
Raymond Burr
Gig Young
Gordon and Sheila McRae

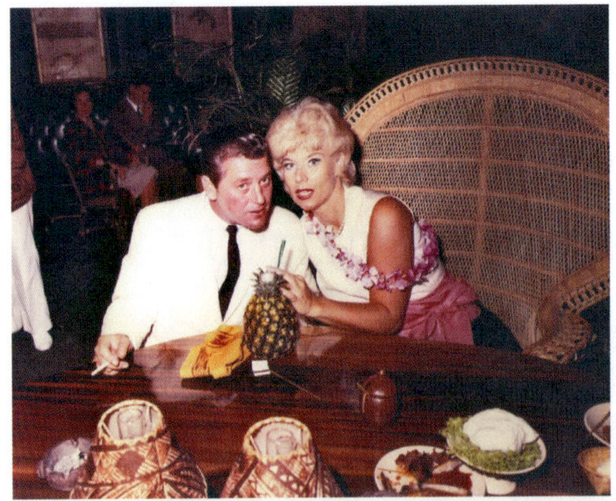

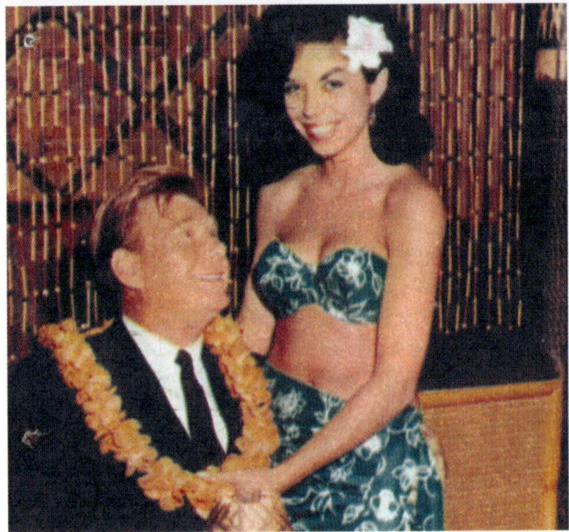

Top: Gordon and Sheila McRae, stars of stage and screen, were just a couple of the many celebrities who had their photos taken by Johnny Gim. *Courtesy Sapp/Henry.*

Left: Arthur Godfrey, the "Old Red Head," photographed with his favorite Mystery Girl, Tina Butts. *Courtesy Sapp/Henry.*

Below: While appearing in a Kenley Players production with actress Betty White, actor Jack Carson visited the Outrigger Bar. *Courtesy Sapp/Henry.*

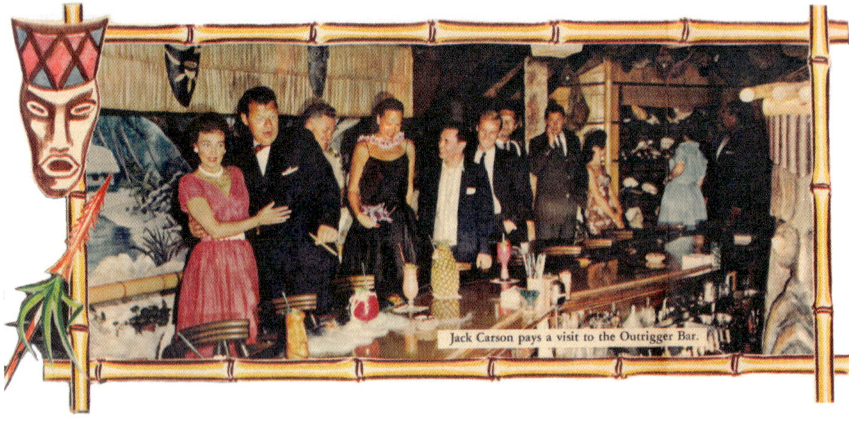

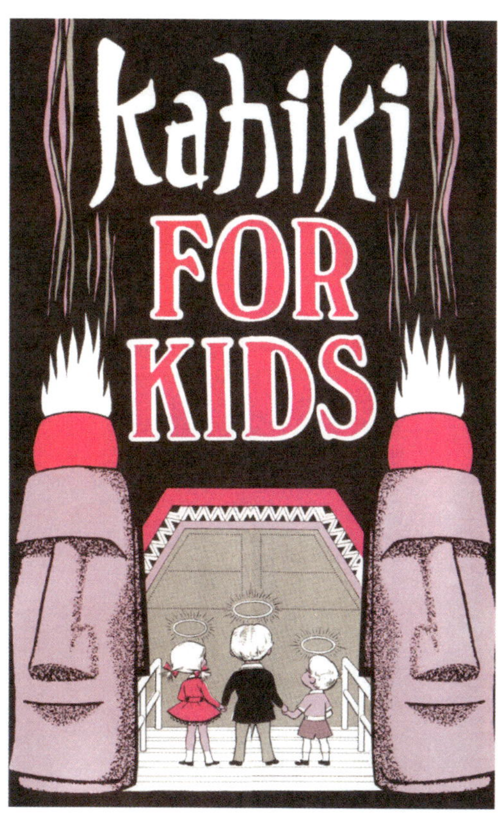

Left: Children were also welcome at the Kahiki, as evidenced by this Kids' Menu with the twin moai. *Courtesy Candi Spencer.*

Below: Celebrating a birthday with "smoking" drinks (from left): Leah Delcamp, Andrew Cloyes and Elise Meyers. *Authors' collection.*

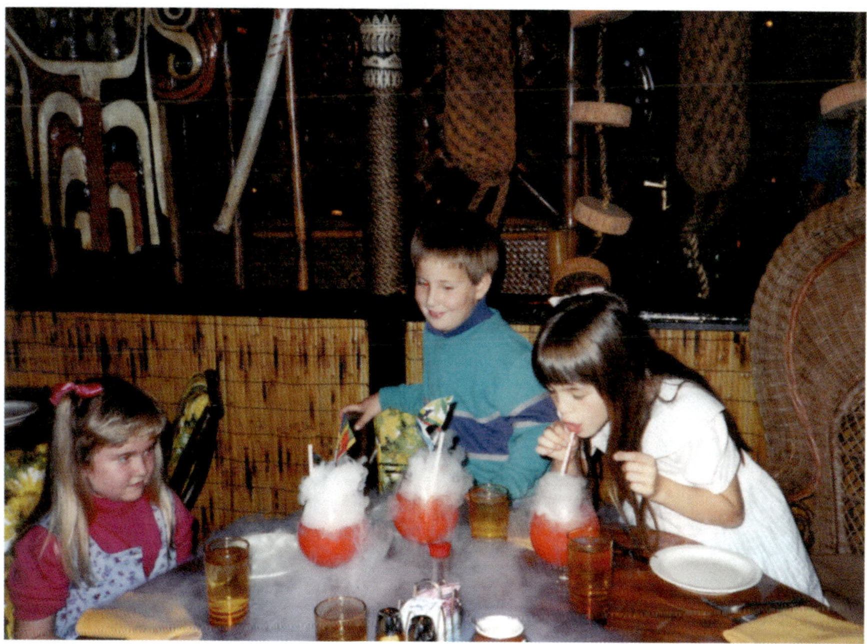

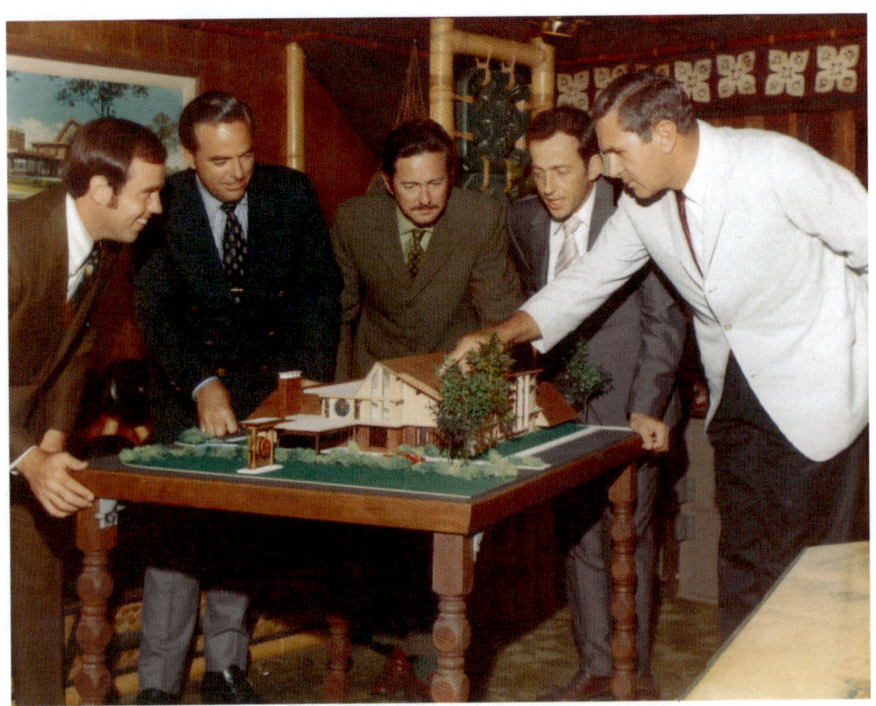

Planning sessions for the Wine Cellar, Bill and Lee's third restaurant venture, were held at the Kahiki. *Courtesy Sapp/Henry.*

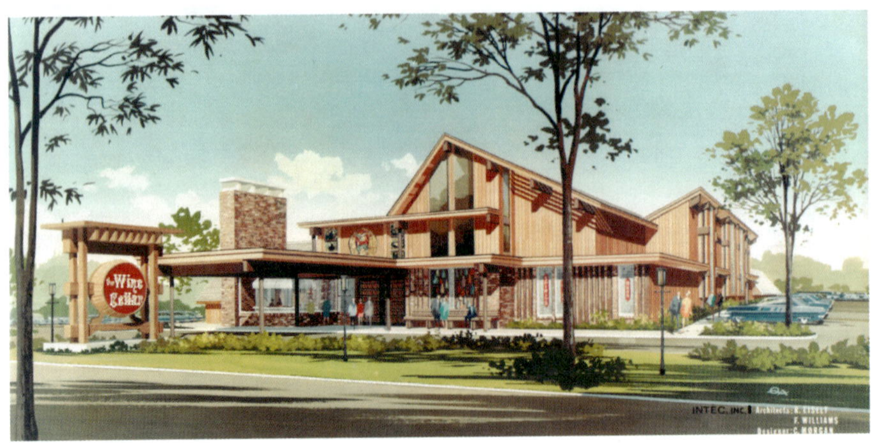

A conceptual painting of the Wine Cellar, Bill and Lee's acclaimed follow-up to the Kahiki. *Courtesy Sapp/Henry.*

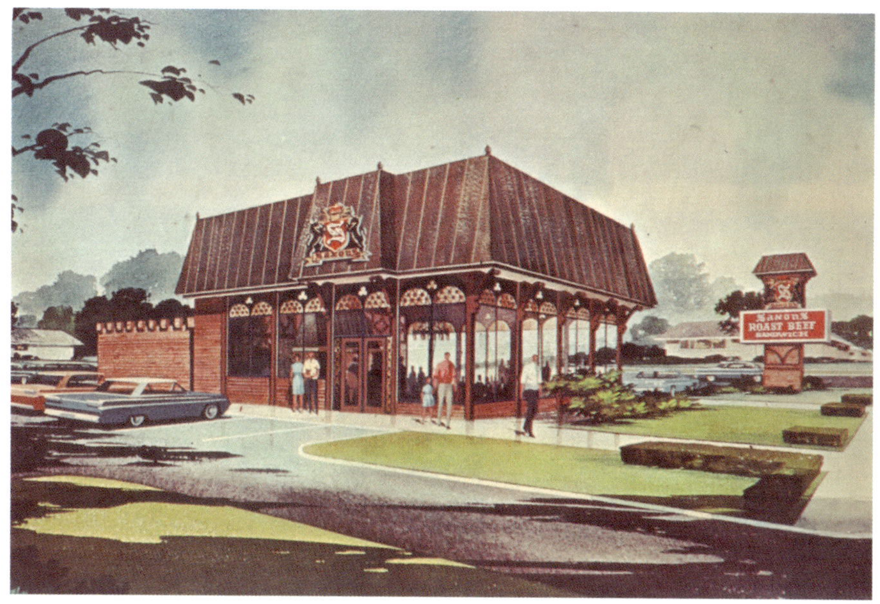

The design for Saxon's Sandwich Shoppes benefited from the Corban Morgan touch. *Courtesy Sapp/Lee.*

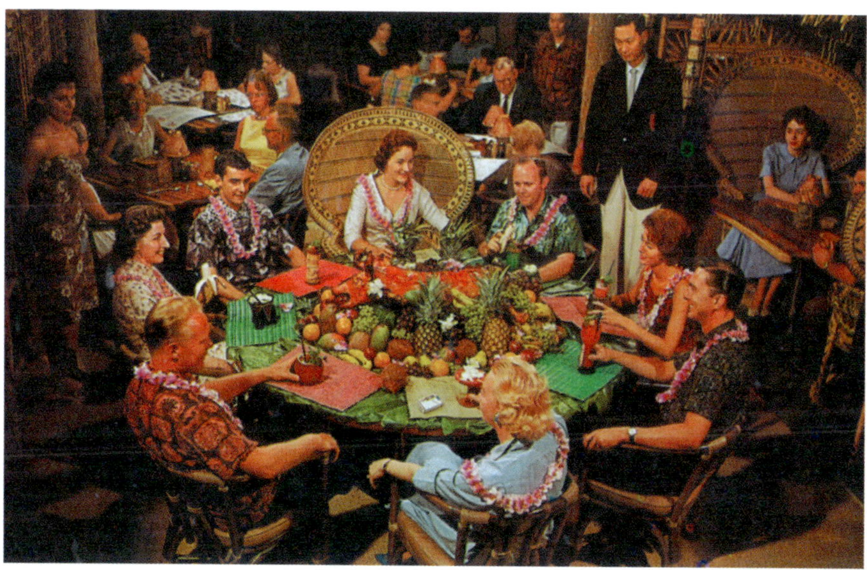

When Bill Sapp and Lee Henry took their wives out to dinner, they had a choice of three outstanding restaurants. *Courtesy Sapp/Henry.*

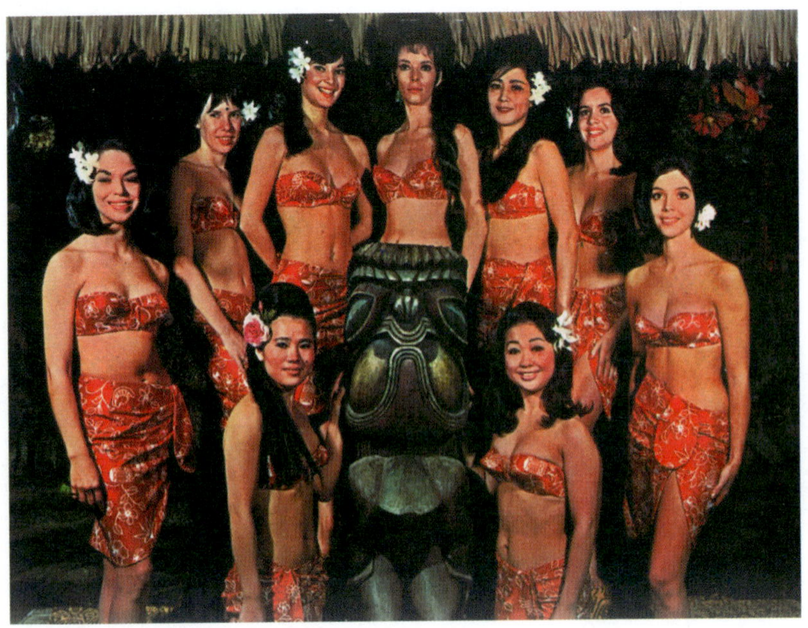

The Maui Lounge wahines are gathered around one of several tiki statues to be found in the restaurant. *Courtesy Sapp/Henry.*

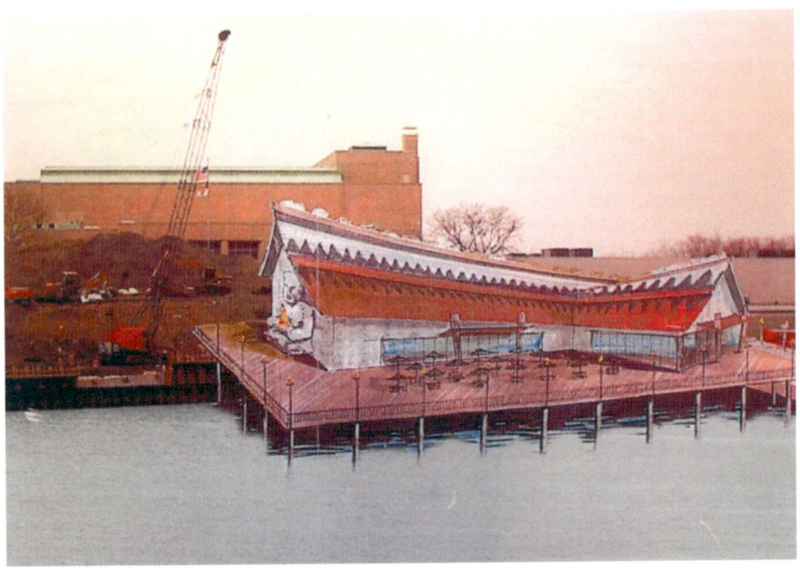

An illustration of Michael Tsao's proposed Riverfront Kahiki in front of Veterans Memorial Auditorium. *Authors' collection.*

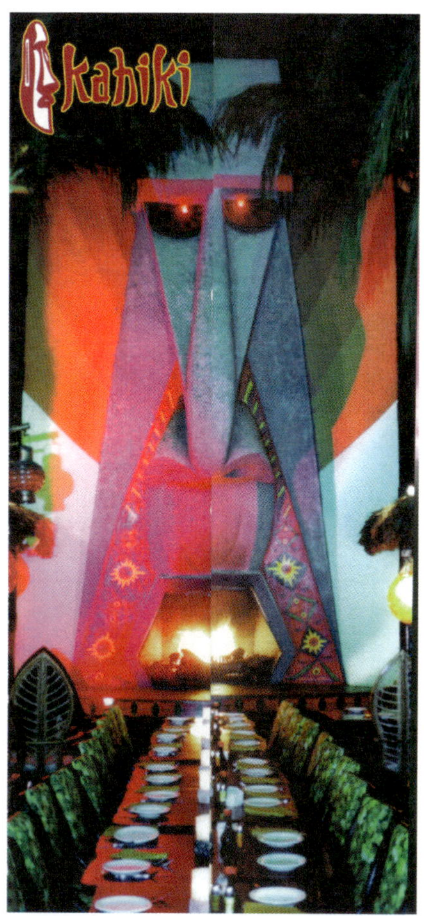

Left: A brochure depicting the enormous fireplace moai with flaming mouth and eyes. *Courtesy Sapp/Henry.*

Below: This postcard shows the restaurant's distinctive logo. *Authors' collection.*

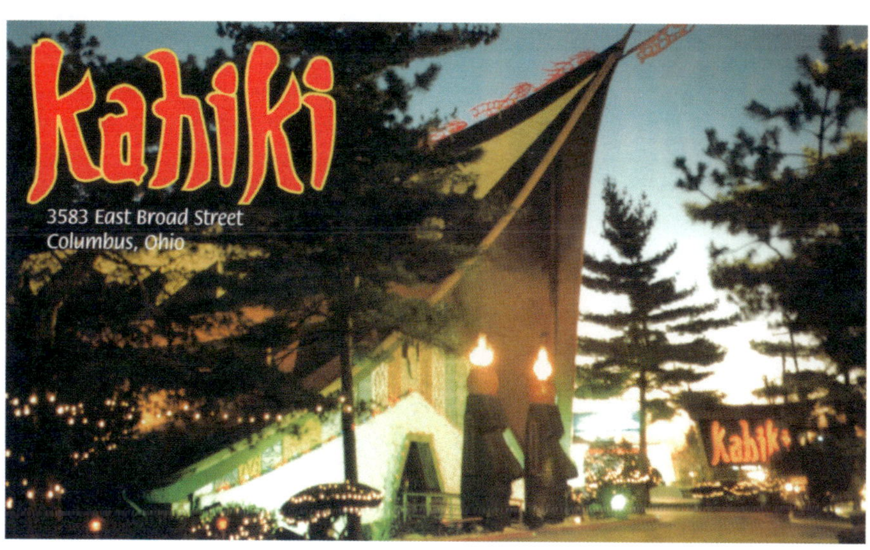

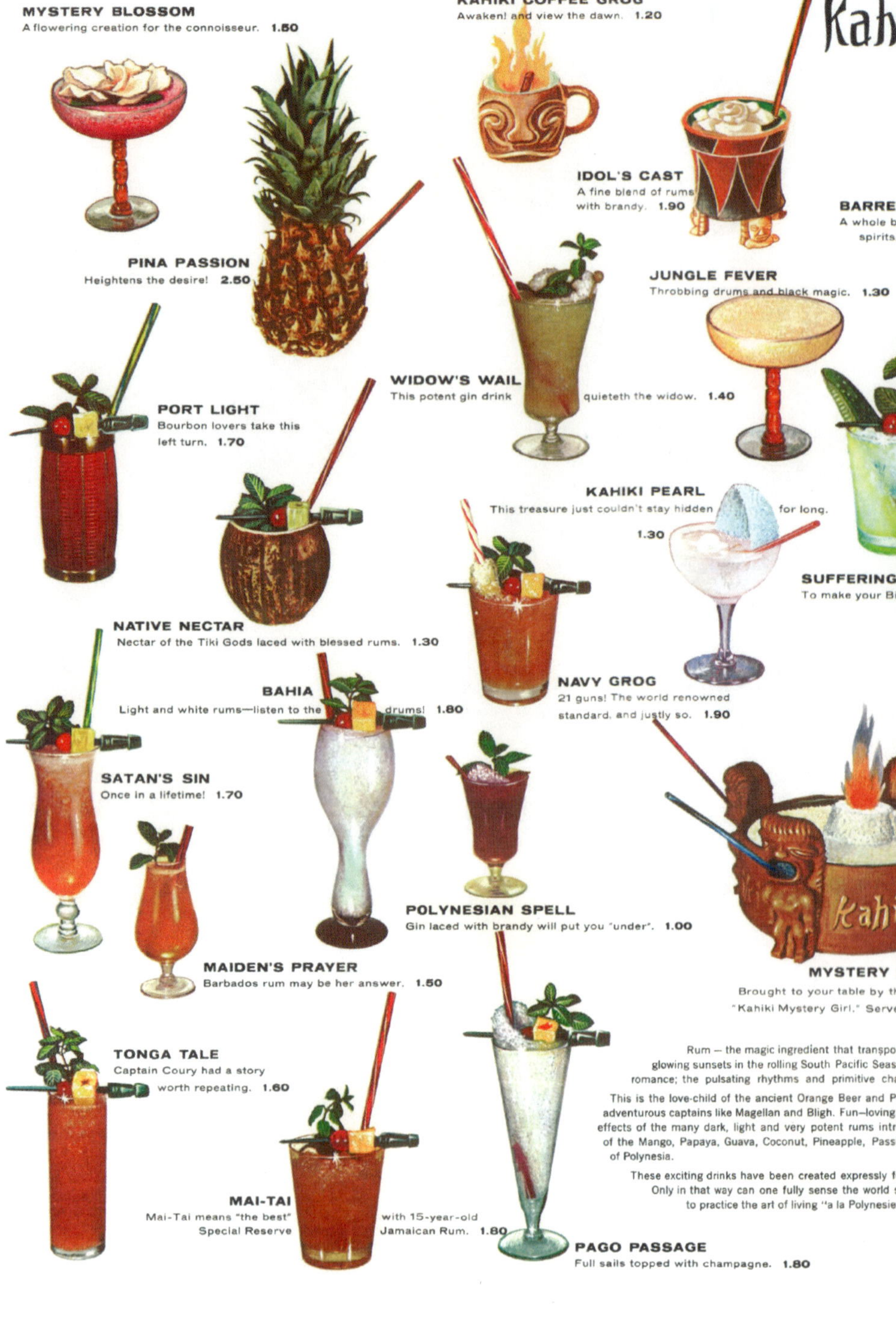

Kahi
MYSTERY BLOSSOM
A flowering creation for the connoisseur. 1.50
KAHIKI COFFEE GROG
Awaken! and view the dawn. 1.20
IDOL'S CAST
A fine blend of rums with brandy. 1.90
BARRELI
A whole bar spirits.
PINA PASSION
Heightens the desire! 2.50
JUNGLE FEVER
Throbbing drums and black magic. 1.30
PORT LIGHT
Bourbon lovers take this left turn. 1.70
WIDOW'S WAIL
This potent gin drink quieteth the widow. 1.40
KAHIKI PEARL
This treasure just couldn't stay hidden for long. 1.30
SUFFERING
To make your Big
NATIVE NECTAR
Nectar of the Tiki Gods laced with blessed rums. 1.30
NAVY GROG
21 guns! The world renowned standard, and justly so. 1.90
BAHIA
Light and white rums—listen to the drums! 1.80
SATAN'S SIN
Once in a lifetime! 1.70
POLYNESIAN SPELL
Gin laced with brandy will put you 'under'. 1.00
Kahi
MAIDEN'S PRAYER
Barbados rum may be her answer. 1.50
MYSTERY D
Brought to your table by the "Kahiki Mystery Girl." Serves
TONGA TALE
Captain Coury had a story worth repeating. 1.60
Rum – the magic ingredient that transports glowing sunsets in the rolling South Pacific Seas; romance; the pulsating rhythms and primitive cha
This is the love-child of the ancient Orange Beer and Pal adventurous captains like Magellan and Bligh. Fun-loving a effects of the many dark, light and very potent rums intro of the Mango, Papaya, Guava, Coconut, Pineapple, Passio of Polynesia.
These exciting drinks have been created expressly for Only in that way can one fully sense the world so to practice the art of living "a la Polynesien
MAI-TAI
Mai-Tai means "the best" with 15-year-old Special Reserve Jamaican Rum. 1.80
PAGO PASSAGE
Full sails topped with champagne. 1.80

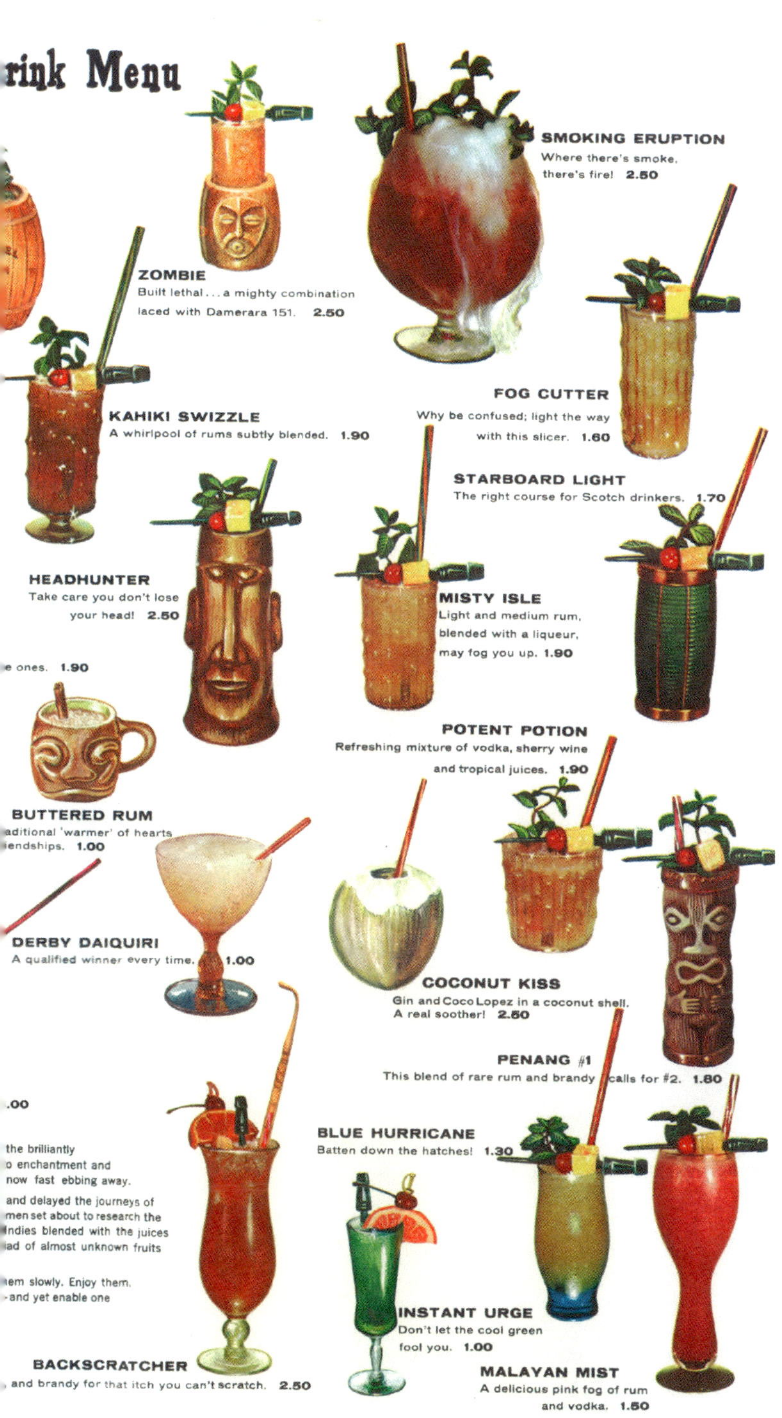

At any one time, the Kahiki listed nearly forty "tropical" drinks on its menu. *Courtesy Sapp/Henry.*

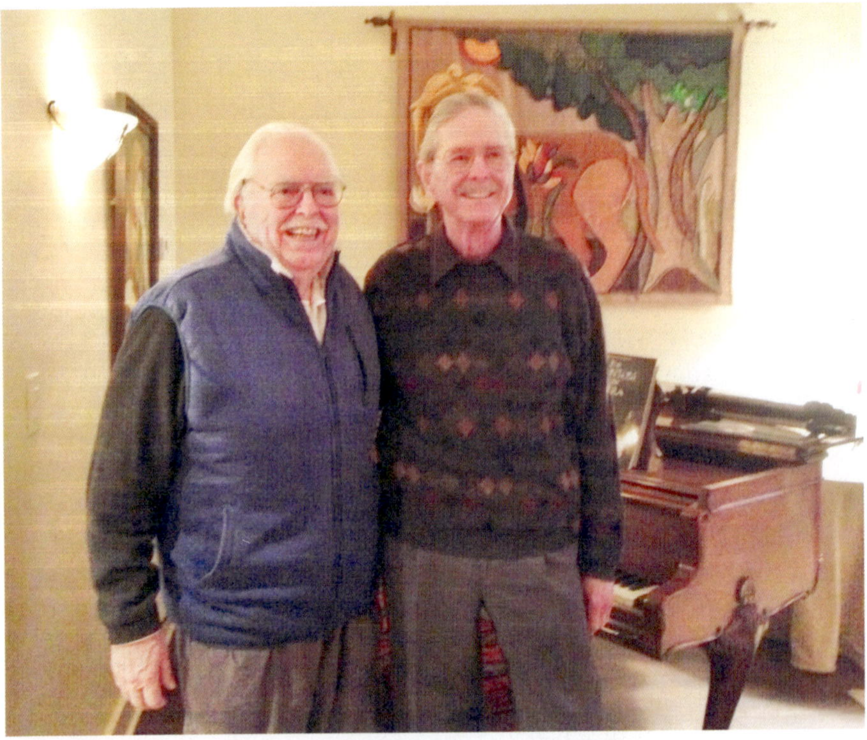

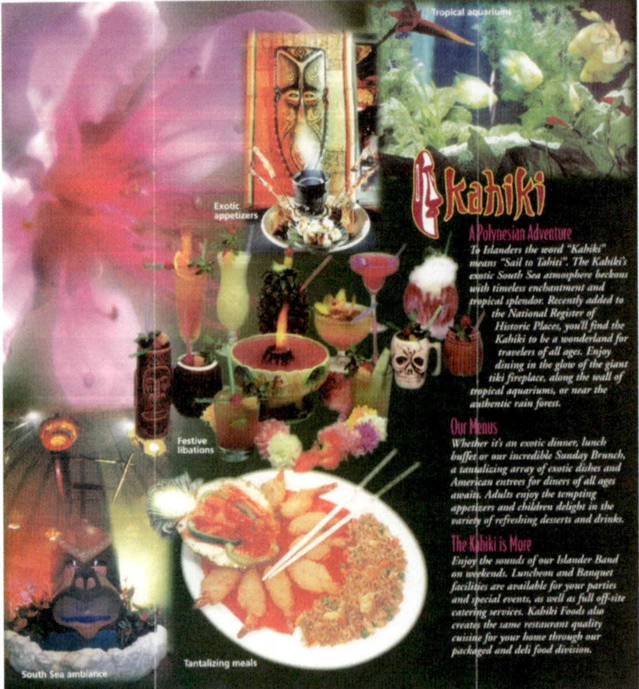

Above: The founders of the feast Bill Sapp (left) and Lee Henry in 2014. *Authors' collection.*

Left: A promotional brochure hinting at some of the delights to be found at the Kahiki. *Courtesy Candi Spencer.*

the wine bottle—the Kahiki restaurant. It was the wine—the food itself." Consequently, their mission became putting their wine in new bottles.

Late in 1997, the Kahiki won a place on the National Register of Historic Places. This was not a foregone conclusion since the building was only thirty-six years old and most structures are not considered until they have at least reached fifty. There was also some question about whether it was historically noteworthy at all. Then, in 1999, the International Restaurant & Hospitality Rating Bureau awarded the Kahiki Supper Club the Millennium Restaurant International Award of Excellence as One of America's Top 100 Restaurants of the twentieth century. For any restaurant, this would be a singular honor, but for a restaurant in Columbus, Ohio, it was almost an unimaginable achievement. However, instead of propelling the supper club to even greater heights, it served as its epitaph. Less than a year later, the Kahiki was no more.

By then, rumors had begun circulating that the Walgreens Company, the largest drugstore chain in the country, had its eye on this particular piece of property for one of its ubiquitous pharmacies, and these were confirmed in April 2000. At the end of June, Michael Tsao announced that he would sell the site to Walgreens. The decision was bittersweet; as much as he hated to part with the Kahiki, he was grateful that there was someone willing to buy it at all. "It was like the Field of Dreams—they built it and the people came," Tsao said, describing the restaurant's initial success when it opened in 1961. However, thirty-nine years later, "We saw the writing on the wall with Easton and Polaris [shopping malls] drawing people away. Everything has its life span."

Although in retrospect some people have questioned it, there is little reason to doubt he was being sincere when he said:

> *At this point, we look at, the Tiki culture has to be preserved. What we intend to do is take the current Kahiki and reproduce it as the same shape of the building, like a canoe, and then taking the interior, rebuild it using the same decorating packages, in fact, the same floor plan.*

The prospect of the Kahiki being bulldozed to build a Walgreens pharmacy led publisher Otto Von Stroheim of the *Tiki News* to write, "It would mean the devastation of the first or second most important tiki restaurant in the world!" Walgreens spokesman Michael Polzin said at the time, "Walgreens has a policy against destroying historic buildings...The company just doesn't think the Kahiki makes the cut. This building is unusual, but it's not very old." Of course, the National Register of Historic Places held the same opinion and elected to list it anyway because it was so unusual and historically significant.

With the turnover of the property to Walgreens, Tsao relocated his frozen food operation to a twenty-two-thousand-square-foot facility near Port Columbus International Airport. It had grown quickly to where it was producing ninety to one hundred varieties of frozen entrees, snacks and egg rolls each day for distribution to supermarkets, delis, cafeterias and warehouse stores such as Sam's Club and Costco. "It would have been so easy for my wife and I to just take the money and go to Hawaii and lay on the beach, but we didn't. We wanted to save the Kahiki brand and create jobs for a new immigrant base." His goal was to make it the preeminent provider of frozen foods in the country. Toward that end, he hired Alan Hoover, a marketing executive with International Paper Company and Sonoco Products Company, as vice-president of sales. The idea of rebuilding the restaurant would have to sit on a back burner until he got the frozen food division on a profitable footing.

Meanwhile, the Kahiki closed its doors to the public forever on August 25, 2000. Various artifacts from the restaurant were retained and put into storage. Some of them purportedly were donated to the Columbus Zoo; others resurfaced when the Tropical Bistro opened a couple years later. In 2004, Kahiki Frozen Foods was recognized for having the highest percentage gain of any publicly traded stock in Central Ohio, rising over 190 percent for the year. Then, on July 22, 2005, Michael Tsao passed away due to heart failure resulting from diabetes-related complications. Any hope of the Kahiki rising again died with him.

13
TROPICAL MEMORIES

It's often hilarious to me that I'm writing about Tonga or some tropical place and there's a blizzard outside and the cows are on their backs with their hooves in the air.
—Tim Cahill

Coincident with the proliferation of tiki culture was the appearance of such shows as *Hawaiian Eye* (1959–63), *Adventures in Paradise* (1959–62), *Surfside Six* (1960–62), *Gilligan's Island* (1964–67) and, later, *Hawaii Five-O* (1968–80) and *Magnum PI* (1980–88). All of these programs incorporated elements of tiki culture in their settings while *Gilligan's Island* is a practically visual textbook of all things tiki. Columbus Coated Fabrics, manufacturer of Wall-Tex, went so far as to once sell a "Kahiki" wall-covering pattern. And in part, this was what drew customers to the Kahiki.

Christine Hayes, daughter of the late Columbus newspaper columnist Ben Hayes, described one of her Kahiki experiences in the *Short North Gazette*:

> *When we went to the Kahiki in the afternoon: gray wintry day outside, coziest blue aquarium room inside. The one-year-old with us tramped all over the place, from fish-admiring to mock-thunderstorm-on-birds. There were few customers, so the young parents and the delighted grandmother (me) chose the best table and ordered fancy drinks. In lighting the grog, the waiter spilled the drink all over the table. Flames leaped up, but they did not burn the surface, or us. The orange-red glow on our faces contrasted sharply with the marine-blue of the aquariums. The one-year-old was impressed, we were elated.*

At the Kahiki, the key to making each visit a memorable experience was having the right staff. Wanda Stevens was Bill and Lee's secretary and the "Mother Superior" of the Kahiki. Bill readily concedes that she was "the glue that held everything together." Anytime anyone needed anything at all, they turned to Wanda. If a problem arose, she would listen to what Bill and Lee had to say and then tell them how it ought to be done. "She had the pulse of the Kahiki," he says. When she suggested that Linda should start learning the business because she "needed something to do," she was put to work blacking out the photo in the brochures. Once a Vietnamese lady who worked in the gift shop got sick with cancer. Wanda took care of her when she couldn't care for herself and continued to do so until she died.

Lee and his wife, Marilyn, plucked Craig Moore from the Cornell University School of Hotel Administration to be the manager of the restaurant and added Phil Chin, a mechanical engineer, to be the head chef. William D. "Bill" Harrison asserted that he basically bluffed his way past eighty others who were applying for the job of *maître d'* by claiming to have experience at Germany's famous 4 Seasons restaurant and then chatting with Bill Sapp in German. Marek "Chills" Verne had formerly been with Mario's International. He worked his way up from waiter to bartender and then *maître d'*. Johnny Gim worked in the kitchen, tended bar and later became an assistant manager. With 180 employees, there was plenty of opportunity for upward mobility.

The Outrigger Bar acquired its name from the full-size outrigger canoe that hung over it. One day, Bill told two of the bartenders, Tommy Joseph and Robert "Bob" Karst, "You guys be careful. There's money missing, and Lee's lying up in the canoe, watching." Apparently, they believed him and spent much of the evening looking over their shoulders.

Karst, a longtime employee of both the Kahiki and the Wine Cellar, had grown up in the restaurant business, and his wife, Mary, had worked at the Top. His family had owned and operated the Broad-Nel Restaurant.

Bill and Lee were upstairs in the office talking one evening when the phone rang. Bill picked it up and heard someone say, "Where's the pizza?"

"What're you talking about?" Bill asked.

"Where's the pizza?" the voice repeated.

"Who is this?"

"Tommy Joseph."

"Tommy, you've got the office upstairs."

"Ohhhhh," Tommy said and then hung up.

On another occasion, Tommy called Bill Harrison on the intercom at the bar. "Hey Sarge," he said, "We got carry-out." Harrison was nicknamed

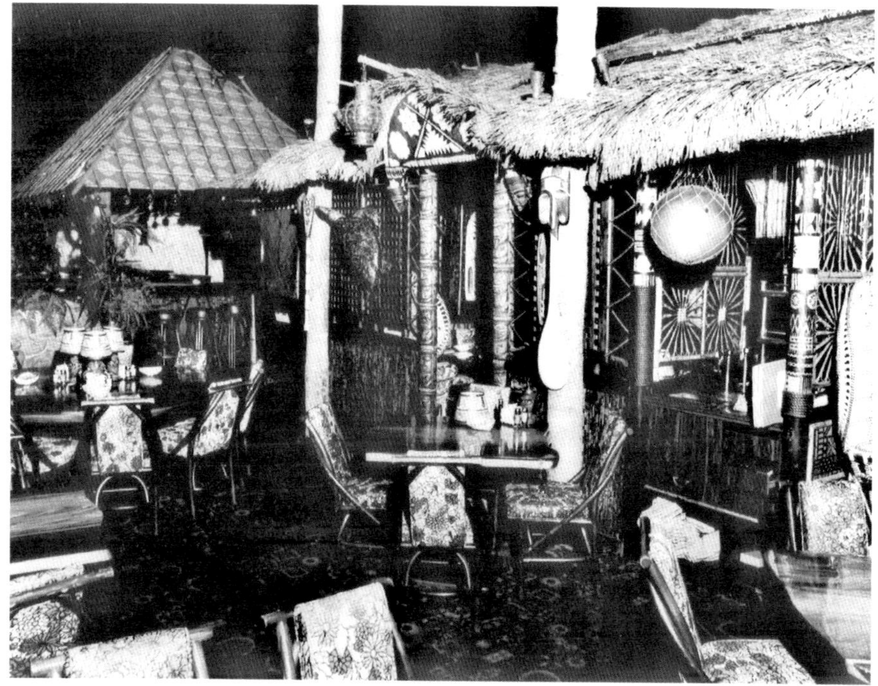

Customers dined in a variety of huts that formed a make-believe Polynesian village. *Courtesy Kojo Kaman.*

Sarge from his time in the army. Harrison replied, "We don't do carry-out." Tommy said, "You do now—she's passed out at the bar and needs [to be] carried out."

Hal Naguchi from Chicago was hired as general manager. He was, Harrison said, "a strong and gifted manager" who got things off on the right foot. "The cooks were all chow hands," Lee pointed out. "We couldn't get any at first, so we put ads in Chinese newspapers in San Francisco, Chicago, etc., and interviewed them over the phone." They bristled under Chin's direction.

As Harry Truman famously said, "If you can't stand the heat, get out of the kitchen." Well, the kitchen at the Kahiki got heated at times. Once a Chinese chef who will remain nameless got in an argument. Grabbing a cleaver, he took a swing at another employee and cut through a copper water line. Water sprayed out all over the place.

Another time, as Lee and Marilyn pulled into the parking lot at the Kahiki, they were met by manager Craig Moore, "wearing a white suit and a face to match. One of the dishwashers had stabbed another in the buttocks."

When the Kahiki first opened, large-scale aquariums—both fresh and salt water—were not common outside of zoos. Naturally, they required regular maintenance, and a company was hired to clean them. One day, a substitute worker showed up to clean the restaurant's wall of aquariums. He proceeded to put all of the fish, over one thousand, in the same tank—with the piranha. And the piranha proceeded to eat all of their exotic (and expensive) fish. Bill was not pleased.

Artificial rain forests weren't common either, inside or outside zoos. Bill Spencer moved his family from Memphis to Columbus to take a job. According to his daughter, Candi, the first time they went to the Kahiki, he was startled by the rain streaming down the windows so he ran outside to put the top up on their convertible. Of course, it wasn't truly raining; they were seated next to the artificial rain forest.

Many nights when her parents were socializing with their friends in the Outrigger Bar, Candi slept upstairs in the offices of the Kahiki rather than being left with a babysitter. Having been imprinted on her at such an early age, she admits to having been a frequent patron herself when she was older and has the menu collection to prove it.

The birds not only flit around inside the rain forest but were also on display elsewhere in the restaurant. Sam, a blue-and-gold macaw, "worked" at the restaurant from 1982 until it closed in 2000. He was a denizen of the Outrigger Bar, where he entertained patrons with his chatter. Jim Rush was the Kahiki's animal caretaker, tending to the fish and the birds. He continues to be the keeper of Sam, who lives with him and his wife.

Lee remembered that they bought items for the Kahiki from Tropic Trader and a half dozen other places in Florida. During one trip, they rented a car and drove to Joe's Stone Crab. After they had eaten their fill, they bought some extra crabs. They then went about tracking down an eccentric carver who was living with a harem of a half dozen women. While talking to him, they forgot about the stone crabs in the car. By the time they returned to the car, the smell of the rotting crabs was so bad that they couldn't get within fifty feet of it. The car had to be junked.

One of the secrets to the restaurant's success was Bill and Lee's insistence on buying quality ingredients. For instance, they purchased produce from China Farms in Chicago. A local guy kept begging them to buy Thai leaves from him. He was so insistent, they finally told him to send them a carload. Naturally, he couldn't deliver because he was growing them at home.

Various websites provide numerous testimonials to the good times that were had at the Kahiki. One anonymous contributor said, "In 1969, my high

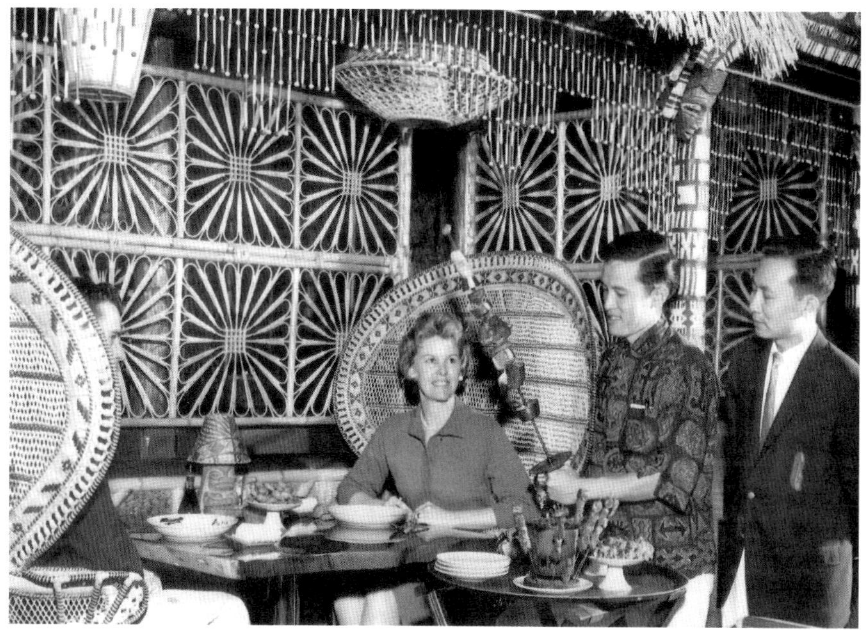

Always emphasizing showmanship, Johnny Gim serves Marcy Sapp her dinner on a sword. *Courtesy Sapp/Henry.*

school [in Chillicothe] put on a performance of 'South Pacific'...One of the faculty called the Kahiki and got permission for the cast to come during the off-hours, to shoot publicity photos. What a great experience. We had the whole place to ourselves...fantastic. I still remember my amazement at the indoor rain forest that towered overhead." Jon Foster, a former Columbus resident, exclaimed, "Man that place was so great. I remember being wowed as a kid when my mom took us there. I always got this big drink thing where they put dry ice in the punch glass and made it steam...it was like the volcano punch or something. And the food, to my very then untempered palate, was sensationally exotic."

"There's something about the Kahiki," *Columbus Dispatch* columnist Joe Blundo wrote, "that makes people want to get married." For example, Laure Beeckner of Westerville was leaving for Chicago to become a flight attendant. The night before, her boyfriend, Chris, took her there for a farewell dinner. Because of her new hairstyle, he had nicknamed her Poodle Head. When she opened a fortune cookie after she had finished her meal, she found a message inside: "Poodle Head, I love you!! Will you marry me?" With the entire Kahiki staff looking on, she said, "Yes."

Sue Wellmerling of Dublin said that her boyfriend, Jack, popped the question to her by hiding a jewelry box with a ring in it on the bread plate. "I hadn't even noticed the little tan box, since it was the same shape and color as my roll." Blundo wrote that Jack finally had to ask, "How's your bread?" to get her to spot the ring.

It was only by chance that Dan Bringardner happened to find the following fortune in his cookie: "You soon will be engaged in a new business venture." As he told Blundo, "Seizing the opportunity, I handed Barb [his future wife] the first half of the fortune. We celebrated our 20th anniversary last September." Although Lee and Bill always tried to accommodate customer requests, they drew the line at allowing couples to get married in front of the fireplace moai.

Many rehearsal dinners were held at the Kahiki. Larry Rummell told Blundo that when his daughter held hers there, "The wedding party, mostly Katie and Jeff's classmates from Miami U., ordered many Mystery Drinks. The drinks were so popular that the guests connected eight to ten straws end-on-end so that everyone at the far corners of the tables could sample them." When another restaurant cancelled her daughter's reservations at the last minute, Joan Miller of Worthington said of the Kahiki: "On very short notice they gave us a lovely room and served a scrumptious meal. My daughter sat in one of the peacock chairs, looking like a princess. The atmosphere was beautiful and what could have been a disaster turned into a thoroughly pleasant and memorable evening."

Then there were the proms. Jim Smith and Joe Francisco and their dates went to the Kahiki after the Bishop Watterson High School prom in 1962. "When the check came," he told Blundo, "we were going to be short if we put much of a tip down. To impress the girls, Joe laid down a $10 bill for the tip. As he and the girls got up and moved away from the table I picked the tip back up to pay the bill."

Linda Rodichok's memory of the Kahiki dated back to a night in 1961 when a "gorgeous male" asked her and a friend for directions to the newly opened supper club. Captivated by the young man, they decided to follow him there and even went inside when he did. "Having only $1.80 between them," Blundo reported, "they ordered the cheapest thing on the menu, which turned out to be ice cream molds. They never did find the handsome stranger."

To drama teacher Susie Gehrisch, "It was like eating in a dream." Someone calling himself Hodge wrote on an Internet chat board, "It was so over-the-top, it was basically a *Mad Men* set: aquarium walls, an Easter-Island-style fireplace, palm trees, and a freakin' rainforest inside with storm

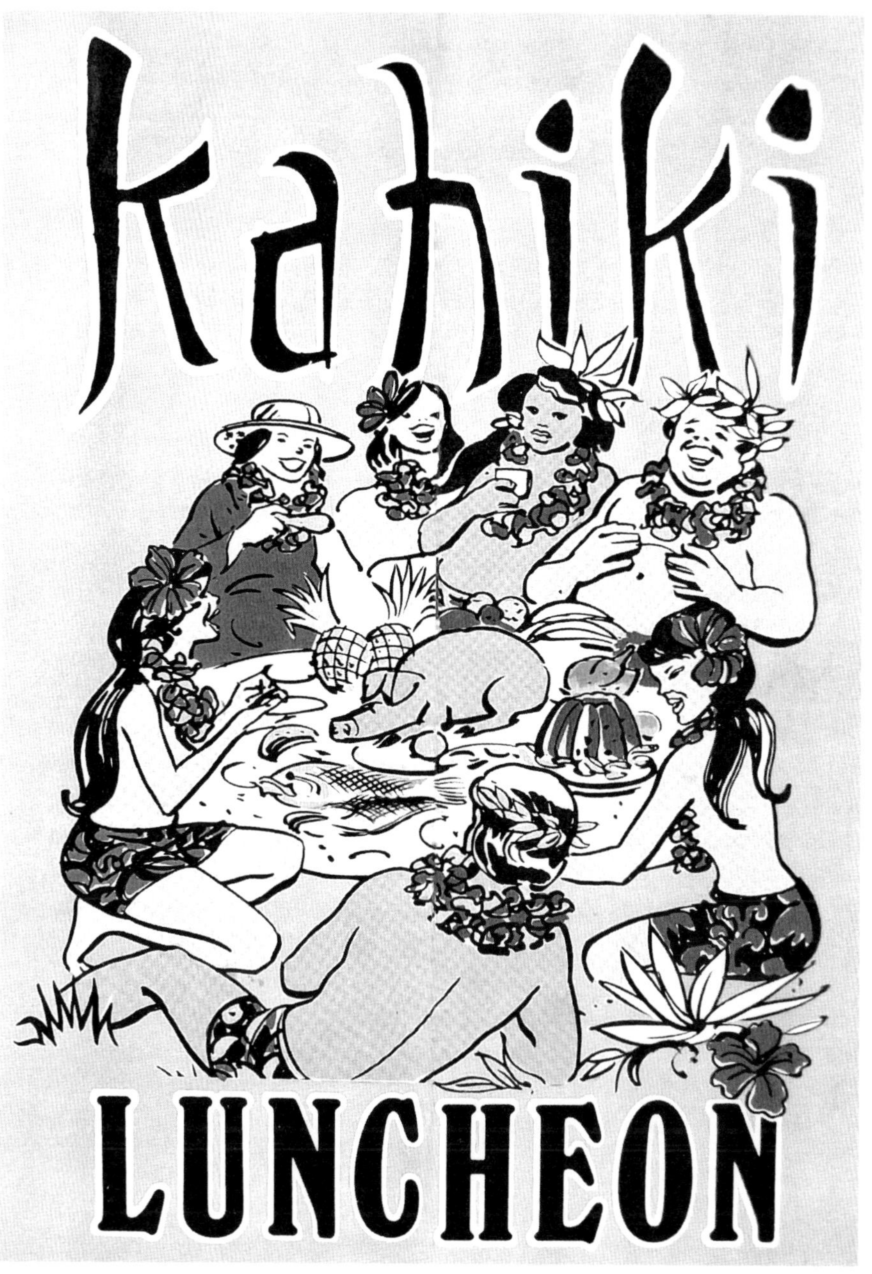

The Kahiki was a popular spot for lunch, providing customers with a break from the workaday world. *Courtesy Candi Spencer.*

effects." Perhaps Elizabeth Gibson said it best: "No restaurant with a fire-breathing stone head has ever captured the hearts of Columbus quite like the Kahiki."

Michael Tsao's son, Jeff, was three years old when they moved to Ohio. He grew up in the family business, first at the restaurant and then the frozen food division, rising to the position of director of research and development in the latter.

"I started as a dishwasher when I was thirteen," Jeff said. "I had no idea what I was doing, but everybody knew I was the boss's son. I remember I was spraying down a plate and the food and water went all over [a co-worker]. I remember him giving me a glare like, 'If you weren't the boss's son…' Now, of course, we're friends."

Jeff candidly admits that he had "a different experience. I could walk by the ice cream bin and have as much as I wanted, and I wasn't allowed to drink. Well, there was the whole parent guilt thing, at least, but I snuck a little sip every now and then like the whole staff did."

There are many who will never forgive the Tsaos for closing the restaurant and then for not building another one. Jeff admits, "The last days were bittersweet at the Kahiki. It was great, but I think my father's business is a more lasting legacy." In his opinion, there were three factors that prevented his father from reopening the Kahiki: 1) the frozen food plant got too busy, 2) the political support was less than he needed and 3) he died before he really had the chance. What he left unmentioned was that Kahiki Frozen Foods had not turned a profit when his father died and would not do so for several more years. As much as Michael Tsao might have wanted to build a new restaurant, he couldn't have done it alone.

According to Lee, the Kahiki served over two thousand dinners on one day. "It wouldn't be possible to duplicate the drinks today because too many ingredients were from Mexico and South America. Lot of rum goes down like soda pop. Sandro made the Navy Grog mix twice a year. Only one or two bartenders knew how to make it." He went on to observe, "I don't know how restaurants survive today. If we didn't have them lined up on Tuesday, we were worried."

14
TROUBLE IN TAHITI[27]

The most difficult crime to track is the one which is purposeless.
—Arthur Conan Doyle

For most people, the Kahiki was an oasis away from the problems of the outside world. Even now, it conjures up many pleasant memories: high school proms, birthday parties, weddings, graduations and other celebrations. However, there are some who cannot think of it without recalling certain tragic events that occurred there—the dark side of paradise.

As can be expected wherever large sums of cash are exchanged, the Kahiki was robbed on several occasions. No less than four times between 1963 and 1969, thieves struck the supper club. The earliest incident occurred in April 1963. Some rather sloppy burglars broke out a side window after business hours. After ransacking an office on the second floor, they managed to get the safe open. In their haste, they left a large amount of money scattered on the floor of the accounting room. Perhaps, this was the incident that Mike Ballen was referencing when he posted the following on a tikichat board:

> *My brother Gary and I were walking to school one morning when we noticed some loose change in the street in front of our house…a whole lot of it. We picked it up as fast as we could, and when we counted it, it added up to $86. What a score. Later that night, we found out that the Kahiki was robbed and the robbers threw some of the money (bags of change) as they sped down Napoleon. Our father, after a lot of arguing, convinced us to turn the money into the Kahiki, which we did.*

The next robbery was a little more serious. At about 10:45 p.m. on October 3, 1965, Bill Sapp, then thirty-seven, was taken hostage by two thugs he caught going through a filing cabinet safe after closing. He described them as clean-cut white men in their twenties.

> *I'd been playing in a golf tournament in Dayton, and I came back. There was a back stairs on the Kahiki that leads to the offices. So I came up the stairs, walked in the back door and walked into my office, and there's two guys in there. I thought they were working on the fish tank over my safe in the office. Then all of a sudden, I'm looking at a gun. They said, "We need you to open the safe." I said, "Hell, I can't open the safe; I don't even know the combination." They said, "Well, who does." I said, "The only one I know that does is the secretary, and she's not here." So he says, "You get her on the phone and get that combination or something's going to happen to you like the guy last night." There was a robbery the night before and they shot the guy. I didn't know that at the time, so it didn't bother me. Anyway, I called the secretary up; and she gave me the combination, and I opened the safe for them. There was a couple thousand dollars in it. So when they left they wired me up, and as an afterthought, they took the money I had on me, which pissed me off. I had won a money clip in that tournament over there. I said, "Hey, leave me that money clip. I just won it in a golf tournament." He said, "OK" and gave it back to me.*

Having been tied up with electrical cords ripped from office appliances, Bill managed to free his legs after about thirty minutes. He hopped downstairs, out the door and to the Ranch Drive-In restaurant next door, where he was able to call the police.

According to Lee Henry, his Mynah bird saved his friend's life. Both of them had offices, and each had a Mynah bird. Lee's bird would often whistle and say, "Hi, baby." When the two crooks were arguing over whether to kill Sapp, the bird whistled and said, "Hi, baby" from the adjoining office, frightening them away.

Either late Sunday or early Monday, February 16–17, 1969, someone broke into a side door with a screwdriver. They used a cutting torch to open the safe and collect the weekend receipts. Reports indicated that the restaurant's losses were "very small." Nine months later, on Monday, November 10, 1969, a single gunman got away with $10,000. He came in through the kitchen door, dressed in a nice gray suit with black gloves and carrying a black briefcase. He went upstairs and took the money from two

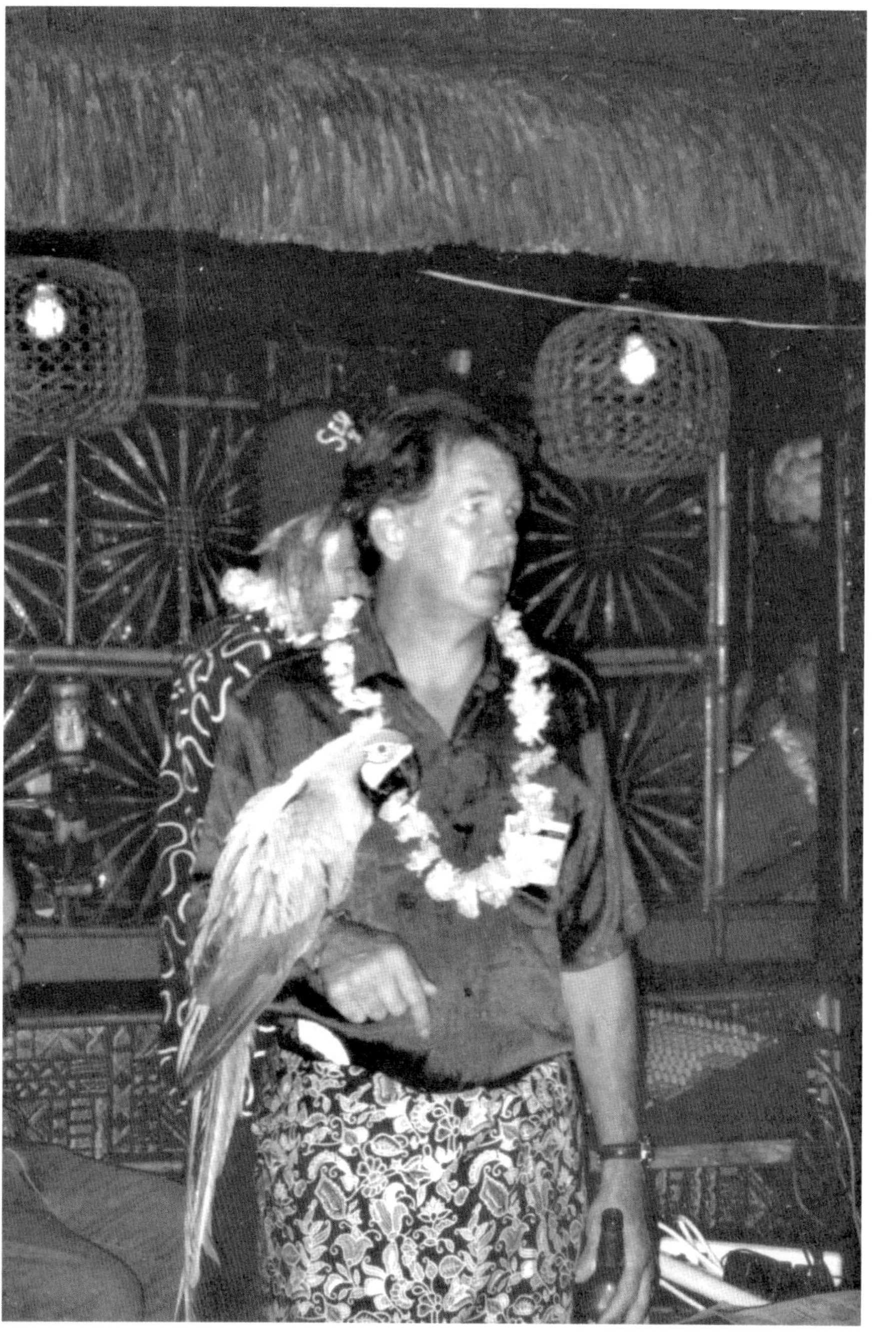

A horticulturalist by trade, Tilly was the birdman of the Kahiki. *Courtesy Sapp/Henry.*

women working in an office. Although the restaurant was open, no one else knew that the robbery was taking place until the assailant had left. Due to his manner of dress, the "bandit" (as the *Columbus Dispatch* called him) was able to blend in with the regular crowd of businessmen who dined in the restaurant and slip away unnoticed.

A former employee, Todd A. Pahel, age nineteen, was arrested in November 1978, for breaking into the restaurant. Twenty-five years later, Pahel made the news again when he and a friend decided "it would be funny" to shoot a BB gun at the house of an acquaintance. In the early morning darkness, the teenage resident of the house returned fire with a shotgun, and both men were wounded. Pahel subsequently died; the shooting was ruled self-defense.

The employees themselves were sometimes the targets of crimes. The restaurant had been open little more than six months when, on September 11, 1961, twenty-two-year-old Alice Taylor, a hostess at the Kahiki, was leaving work with her sisters Andriana, age nineteen, and Wilma Lambropoulos, eleven, and her two-year-old son, Billy, when her estranged husband, Allen Taylor Jr., rode a motor scooter up to the car. He fired three shots into the driver's side window. Both Alice and Andriana were hit with flying glass. They were taken to Saint Anthony Hospital and later released. Alice had filed for divorce from Allen on May 15 of that year. The same day, Allen set fire to his mother-in-law's house at 1448 Deshler Avenue. He was indicted by a grand jury for arson in August and was released on a $1,000 bond for setting the fire and a $50 bond for assault and battery when he shot the car his wife was driving.

Another "employee" crime victim was Sam, the Macaw. He was known for his big and sometimes saucy mouth (he knew about ten different phrases, not all acceptable in polite company). In the early 1990s, Sam was kidnapped by a disgruntled employee. He was missing for several days before being found in a Short North pet store. Before returning to the bar, he was implanted with a pet-tracking chip so that he could never be stolen again. After the closing of the restaurant, Sam retired to the Powell home of friend and keeper Jim Rush. Jim says Sam misses the patrons. In domestic life, he rarely has the opportunity to say another one of his favorite lines, "What, no tip?"

The most tragic loss suffered by the extended "Kahiki family" was the death of fifty-five-year-old Yung Mo Yang. A beloved employee of seventeen years, "Uncle" Yung was shot to death behind the restaurant on Monday, May 28, 1990. The headwaiter, he was alone when he closed the restaurant and set the alarm at 2:00 a.m. Police were called to the scene at 8:00 a.m. after concerned family members went looking for him when he failed to return home. Yung was shot two times in the head in an apparent robbery. A former member of the South Korean Marine Corps, Uncle Yang loved his job. He began as a bus boy, after getting help from his sister, Bong Im, who was a waitress at the time, and rose through the ranks. He left behind a wife and four children.

Two days after his death, someone tried to return his wallet to the restaurant. After asking to see the manager and learning he was not immediately available, the man quickly left, saying he would come back another day. Later, the wallet was mailed to Uncle Yang's family with a signed letter from the man who found it. He claimed he had stumbled upon it in the grass near an apartment complex on Hamilton and Refugee Roads. The wallet contained Yung's driver's license, social security card and family pictures but no money. A different man also tried to return it. Neither one was believed to be a suspect. A $10,000 reward was offered, but no one has ever been arrested for his death. It remains a "cold case" in the Columbus Police Department files.

The parking lot was a particularly dangerous spot for some Kahiki patrons, even when they were themselves law enforcement. John Daily, a used car dealer from Dayton, and his friend Detective Kenneth P. Jones of the Dayton Police Department were held at gunpoint at 1:12 a.m. the day after Independence Day in 1966. They had just left the restaurant and were sitting in John's car, a new model Cadillac, when the six-foot-tall, thirty-something assailant came up to the driver's side window and pointed a gun at them. In what must have been a fantastic night for the gunman, he got away with $2,140 in cash ($2,100 from John and $40 from Kenneth) and more than $42,000 in jewelry composed of John's diamond set in white gold ring and diamond tie tack. Luckily for Daily, both items were ensured with Lloyds of London. He later told the *Columbus Dispatch*, "I always carry a couple of thousand on me." Detective Jones had come to Columbus unarmed.

In another parking lot incident, Joyce E. Finke was killed in 1998 when she was hit by a car while riding her bicycle out of the Kahiki parking lot. While the driver of the car was known, no charges were filed.

Many Mystery Girls came and went before the Kahiki closed in August 2000, but a real mystery girl made her first and last appearance a year earlier on November 28, 1999. A white woman, believed to be about twenty years old with short brown-red hair and blue eyes, was found dead in the parking lot. Standing at five feet, seven inches and weighing approximately 140 pounds, her ears were pierced one time on the left ear and twice on the right. She also had small scars on the left side of her face and nose. This

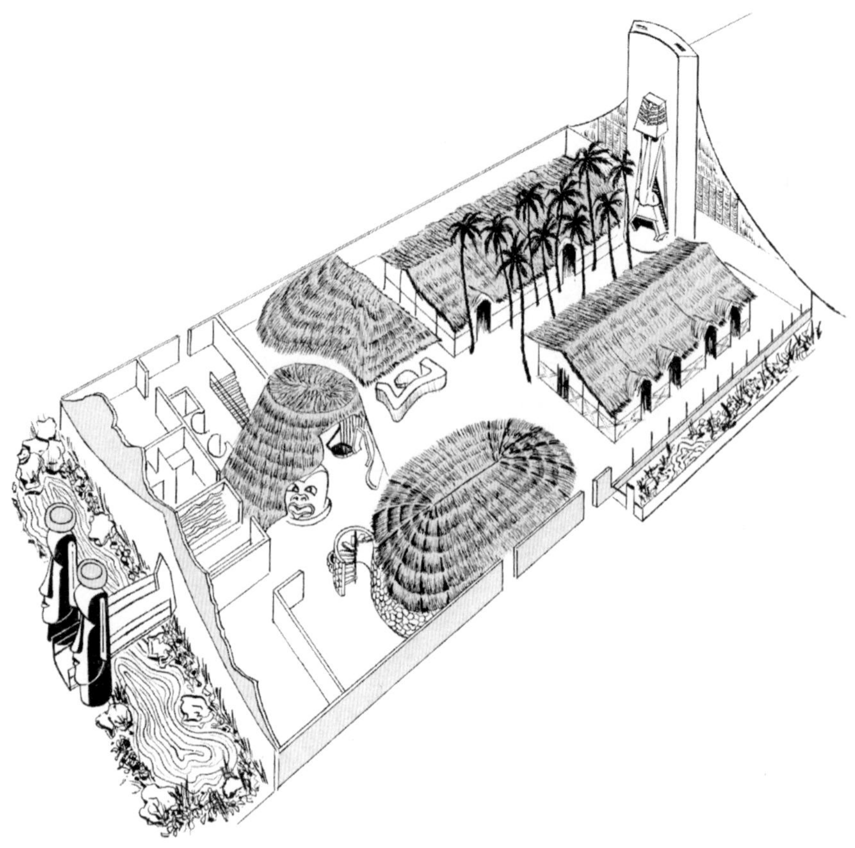

A cutaway illustration of the main dining floor showing the layout of the "village." *Courtesy Sapp/Henry.*

mystery girl wore overalls, a blue coat and a straw hat. Her identity remains a mystery, and she is known only as Case 185 in the Ohio attorney general's unidentified remains directory.

15

ALL IN THE OHANA

Ohana means family. Family means nobody gets left behind or forgotten.
—*Stitch,* Lilo & Stitch

In the spring of 1975, the Kahiki Supper Club became the epicenter of one of the ugliest affairs to ever occur between the Columbus Division of Police and the local minority community. The incident involved three African Americans and a handful of police officers who had been summoned to the restaurant because of a disputed bill. In the end, the U.S. Department of Justice was called in to investigate allegations of civil rights abuses. Ironically, the Justice Department was denied access to the police division's internal records by U.S. district judge Robert M. Duncan.[28]

The Kahiki incident and its aftermath inflamed racial tensions in the city. Eleven people, including eight police officers, were injured, and two officers were fired (although they later were reinstated with all but thirty days' back pay). City councilman Jerry Hammond later commented, "It was an intense situation, because the African-American community was justifiably angry." Hammond, who is black, found himself "squeezed" between city officials who wanted to cover it up and black activists who wanted answers. In many other cities, it might have culminated in race riots. Fortunately, cooler heads prevailed, and the whole episode was allowed to play out in the criminal court system. But whether justice was served in the end is still being debated.

On the evening of Friday, May 30, 1975, twenty-three-year-old Samuel Bryant was dining with his common-law wife, Jo Anne Johnson, twenty-one; her brother Jerome Johnson, twenty-three, a graduate student at Ohio State

University; and, apparently, Jerome's girlfriend. When presented with a bill for $98.96, Samuel, a Vietnam War veteran, got into a dispute with the waiter. He insisted they could not possibly owe that much and that they were being charged for items they didn't order. (The facts are unclear, but it is possible that a gratuity had been added.) The group, all African Americans, were said to have left without paying. According to Diana Tanaka, a gift shop employee, they had reached their car in the parking lot when they were invited up to the office of general manager "Chills" Verne to settle the matter.

Once in Verne's office, they were joined by assistant manager Johnny Gim. Columbus police officer Ronald Bentley and auxiliary officer Rocco Eramo arrived a few minutes later, having been summoned at Verne's request. According to Bentley, he suggested that Jerome pay the bill and later seek legal recourse in civil court. So Jerome paid up, and the unhappy customers started to depart. At this point, the accounts of what happened start to diverge. Officer Bentley testified that Jo Anne, who was holding her nine-month-old baby in her arms, struck him on her way out. Other witnesses say that the one-hundred-pound woman elbowed him.

It was JoAnne's contention that she accidentally bumped the officer as she passed by him. Then, as she was being placed under arrest, she dropped the baby, who, luckily, was caught by Samuel. (Apparently, he then handed the child over to Jerome's girlfriend.) JoAnne was then taken back to the office. At some point, Officer Bentley called for back up. The message apparently went out over the radio as "officer-in-trouble." After no more than ten minutes, up to thirty police officers arrived at the scene, including members of the Special Weapons and Tactics Team. Among them were Officer Harlan G. Hill, Sergeant Harold E. Moore, policeman Ira P. Benedict, policeman John Hunt, Robert W. Stout and policeman Rick A. Newpoff—all of them white men. What occurred next is described in court records as a "mêlée or free-for-all."

Officer Hill admitted that he struck Jo Anne with his flashlight after she allegedly attacked his face and bit his leg. She also fell headfirst into the fountain in the foyer, either in an attempt to escape (as the officers claimed) or as the result of police brutality (as she claimed). Jo Anne was subsequently carried out the front door and placed on the floor of the police van. Officer Hunt claimed that during the trip to jail, Jo Anne, while in handcuffs, reached up and unsnapped his holster in an attempt to grab his service revolver. Officer Newpoff testified that she also bit him. Both officers retaliated by punching her. Officer Newpoff got out of the wagon at Champion Avenue and Broad Street and transferred to a cruiser so he could be taken to Grant

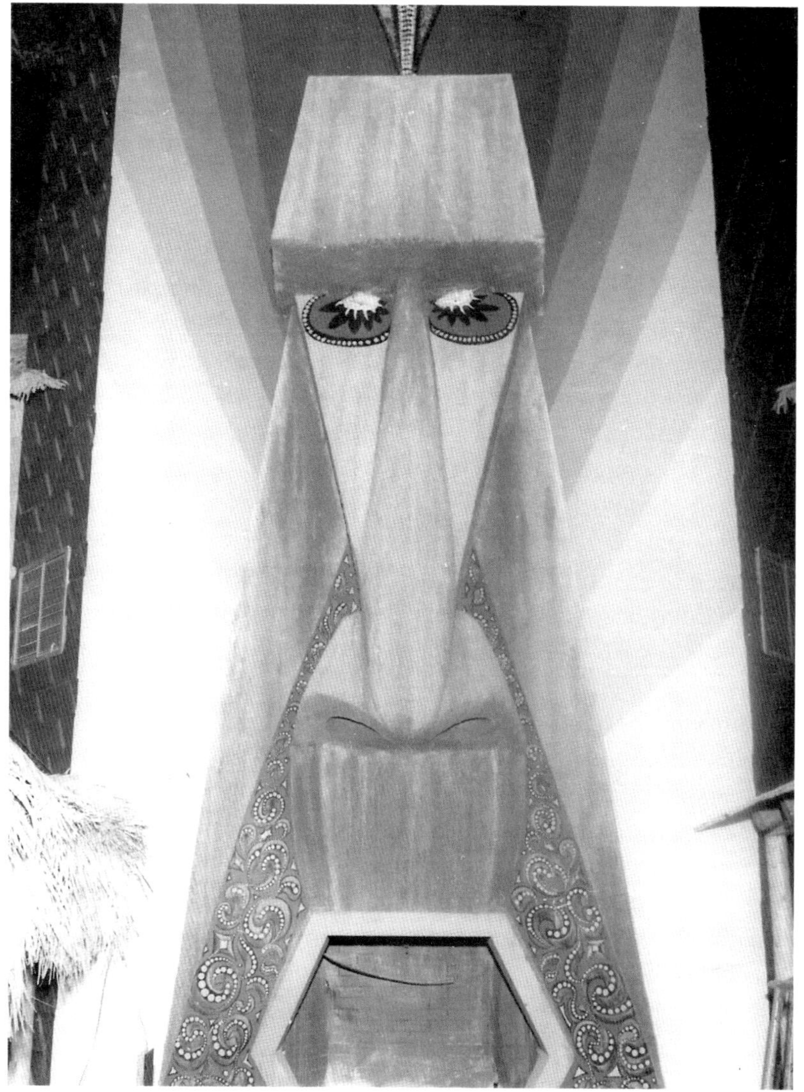

A photo of the fireplace moai, which appears to have been used in designing the menu. *Authors' collection.*

Hospital. Jerome and Samuel were also removed from the wagon, while Officer Hunt remained with Jo Anne, joined by Officer Stout. It is believed that Officer Stout hit her several times with his baton. They all then drove straight to Grant Hospital. Jo Anne received seventeen stitches and was taken to the Women's Correctional Institute. Samuel also received stitches.

As Stout later recalled, "When we opened up the back of that van, [Officer Rick] Newpoff was being bitten by this woman, through to the bone. Some other officers restrained the two males, and I went to Newpoff's assistance." He denied striking her with a club but did admit to using "the force that was necessary to get her off Newpoff."

General manager for WVKO radio, Les Brown was doing a report on the "Project '75" voter registration drive when Tom Catron, a white man, called in to relate what he was seeing. At the time, WVKO reached 80 percent of the black audience in Columbus. Catron was listening to his police scanner in his home at 278 Grubb Street when he heard the distress call go out. He got in his car and followed the police to Grant Hospital. There, he witnessed Jo Anne being beaten. He would later describe his disgust at the officers' lack of respect for her modesty. He subsequently filed police brutality charges.

Another witness at the hospital was Frederick Gouch. There to visit a friend, he saw Jo Anne, Jerome and Samuel being brought in. He asserted that he saw an officer push one of the men against the wall. He also claimed that Jo Anne was dragged in on her face while the officers were uttering racial slurs.

In January 1976, the "Kahiki Three" were found guilty of a total of nine charges relating to the incident and not guilty of four others. Jo Anne was convicted of five charges of assault and one of resisting arrest. Jerome was found guilty of resisting arrest but not guilty of obstructing official business and two charges of assault. Samuel was guilty of one count each of assault and resisting arrest but not of obstructing official business. They were originally given twenty-five charges, but twelve were dropped by the prosecution before trial. In total, Jo Anne was sentenced to six months in jail and a $1,500 fine. Jerome and Samuel both received sixty days and a $500 fine, although the judge commended Samuel on his attempts to peacefully pay the bill. Samuel made the statement "I don't feel that I'm guilty, but I assume every man or woman who comes into court feels that way. I don't feel that I was found justly guilty, but whatever your honor would choose to enforce, so be it." They lost all appeals.

Before going to trial, all three defendants met with then mayor Tom Moody, who promised them, African American leaders, the Committee Against Racism (CAR) and community members that he would personally follow up on their allegations. He was also contacted by the National Organization for Women (NOW) over concerns that Jo Anne was beaten while serving time in the Women's Workhouse.

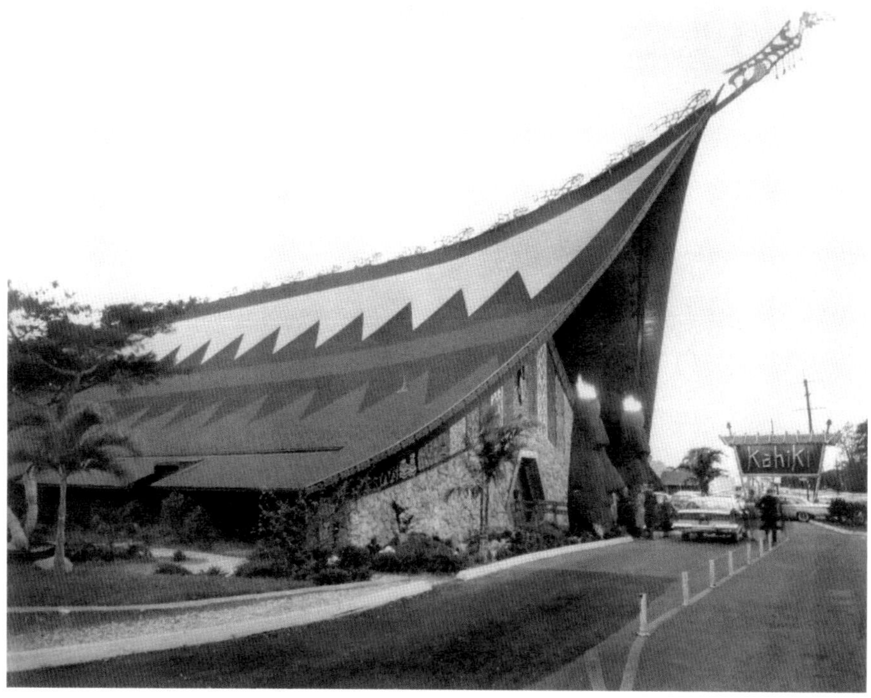

A photo of the Kahiki showing the "good luck" pelican figure extending out from the roof. *Courtesy Sapp/Henry.*

In the subsequent investigation by Chief Earl Burden, 165 interviews were conducted with 139 witnesses. Twenty-seven officers were ordered to take lie-detector tests. Two of them—Robert Stout and Robert Morgan—were suspended without pay on June 11, 1975, for their roles in the incident. Later, city safety director Bernard Chupka fired them for using excessive force. Morgan, who had been the turnkey[29] at the city jail, was specifically charged with striking Bryant during the booking process. Stout became involved when he was summoned to East Broad Street and Champion Avenue after a squabble broke out in the police paddy wagon that was en route to Grant Hospital with the three prisoners.

In July, following an investigation by the Columbus Police Internal Affairs Division, Officers Stout and Robert A. Morgan were fired. Curiously, Frederick Gouch had refused to give a statement. When the official 716-page report was released, Officers Stout and Morgan were the only ones listed by name. Morgan had not previously been mentioned in any of the news accounts.

Morgan might have first met Samuel Bryant during the booking process and was charged with misconduct for hitting him with his nightstick. He was condemned by the testimony of fellow officers Michael Thomas and Ralph Davis. A video of the room where the abuse was alleged to have taken place did not provide confirmation, but the recording was of poor quality and might have malfunctioned during taping. Stout was charged with violence against both Samuel and Jo Anne, as well as failure to report use of force and lying to investigating officers.

Neither the People's Coalition for Justice nor the Fraternal Order of Police was happy with the report. The former felt it was too easy and the latter too hard on the officers involved. Diana L. Morgan felt that her husband was being treated as a scapegoat. A group marched on city hall in support of the police.

By September, both officers had been reinstated by the Civil Service Commission, a group of two white men and one black man, after having their dismissals commuted to thirty-day suspensions. Both votes were 2–1 with David Barker, the only African American, dissenting. The suspensions were served retroactively, and both men received backpay covering the end of their suspensions to their official returns. The officers were subsequently given assignments that kept them away from the public, with Stout on the dispatch radio and Morgan in the police garage.

The reinstatement of the officers was protested by a number of mixed-race groups, including CAR and "Yes We Can," a proto-PAC founded by Les Brown to create political literacy in the African American community.

Following the Kahiki incident, there was a boycott of the *Columbus Dispatch* that led to the loss of two thousand subscribers, according to Ohio State's newspaper, the *Lantern*. Reverend Cameron W. Jackson of the First African Episcopal Church acted as de facto spokesperson for the boycott. He and his followers targeted the *Dispatch* because they felt it would cause the most economic stress in Columbus.

U.S. district judge Robert Duncan, who would later oversee the desegregation of Columbus public schools, issued a court order forcing the Columbus police to maintain a percentage of African American officers equal to the black population of Columbus (at the time 18.5 percent). Until they reached that point, 45 percent of police academy recruits had to be black. One of the 1976 recruits was George Garrett from Sandusky. He applied to the force after hearing a recruitment ad on Les Brown's WVKO. To adhere to regulations, he needed to shave his full beard and cut his Afro.

Les Brown was fired from his job at the radio station after a 1975 free-style editorial regarding the Kahiki incident and police brutality, during which he locked himself in the studio. He went on to become state representative for Columbus and a motivational speaker. He was also briefly married to Grammy Award–winning singer Gladys Knight.

In 1990, Officer Morgan retired from the Police Division. Over the next decade, his health declined precipitously. Ten years afterward, he told a reporter, "It was a long time ago; let sleeping dogs lie." Officer Robert Stout was dismissed from the Columbus Police Department for the second and final time in 1993, after being found guilty of six departmental charges. He retired while appealing the dismissal. Between 1974 and 1989, he had been investigated fourteen times for excessive use of force. In twelve of the incidents, his actions were ruled justified. In 1969, Stout was shot by a suspect fleeing a burglary; he returned fire and killed the man. Four years later, he was shot again. The same year, the Exchange Club named him Officer of the Year. But that is not how he will be remembered, and in the end, he would prefer not to be remembered at all.

16

NATIONAL TREASURE

I don't like to do firsts and biggests and bests and lasts, but I can say with certainty that this is the only Tiki listed.
—Beth Savage, architectural historian

By 1997, preservationists realized that they could not count on the Kahiki Supper Club, let alone the magnificent building, to be around forever. They had undoubtedly begun to notice that the neighborhood was changing (had, in fact, changed) and that the structure was beginning to show its age. In the hope that they could somehow forestall its possible demolition, they pushed to have it listed among the seventy thousand other sites on the National Register of Historic Places. While experience has shown that a listing on the register does not guarantee that a building will be preserved, it can help garner publicity, mobilize public sentiment and support and, less frequently, attract investors.

Placing the Kahiki on the list was in large measure due to the dogged determination of Nathalie Wright, the National Register coordinator at the Ohio Historic Preservation Office. And not everyone agreed it belonged there. Wayne Curtis in the *Atlantic Monthly* posed the question, "How do we distinguish the historic from the sentimental?"

> *Built in 1961, the Kahiki wasn't the first Tiki restaurant in the nation (that honor goes to Don The Beachcomber's, in Hollywood, which opened in 1934), but it may have been the most elaborate. Last June, The* New York Times *dubbed the Kahiki "the grandest and best-preserved of a nearly*

> *extinct form of culinary recreation." Otto Von Stroheim, the publisher of* Tiki News, *a newsletter devoted to Polynesian pop, once called the Kahiki "the first or second most important Tiki restaurant in the world."*

The application for the listing noted that "as Ohio's only Polynesian restaurant and a significant example of the once popular national restaurant trend and unique building type, the Kahiki is being nominated under criteria A and C, consideration G at the state level of significance." It emphasized the "rarity and fragility" of the property.

Criterion A requires that the structure is "associated with events that have made a significant contribution to the broad patterns of our history." In brief, the application makes the case for the Kahiki being "an important representative of 1950s and early '60s entertainment. It is part of a broader pattern of national restaurant and entertainment trends from that era. The Polynesian restaurant motif was the beginning of today's theme restaurant fad."

To support the argument, a review of U.S.-Polynesian relations was presented, highlighting its treatment in popular culture.

> *Polynesian restaurants...sought to transport the dining guests away from reality to a distant tropical island free of worries. An atmosphere of enchantment was created. The food was exotic in comparison to other restaurants. It arrived on fire or billowing with smoke, created by dry ice. Entertainment was provided by a live band or a floor show featuring hula and sword dancers. In essence Polynesian restaurants were more than eating establishments; they were places of entertainment where customers could spend a few leisurely hours.*

Under Criterion C, the structure is required to "embody the distinctive characteristics of a type, period, or method of construction, or that represent the work of a master, or that possess high artistic values, or that represent a significant and distinguishable entity whose components may lack individual distinction."

It was also argued that the Kahiki was "an excellent and remarkably intact example of the Polynesian restaurant building type." The structure represented an amalgamation of architectural traditions drawn from various Polynesian, Micronesian and Melanesian cultures. Not only was the exterior modeled after "young men's houses of the Yap Islands and the men's ceremonial houses of New Guinea," but also the interior

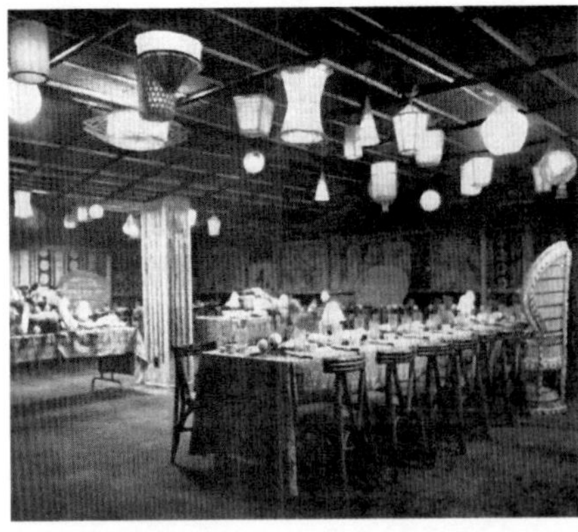
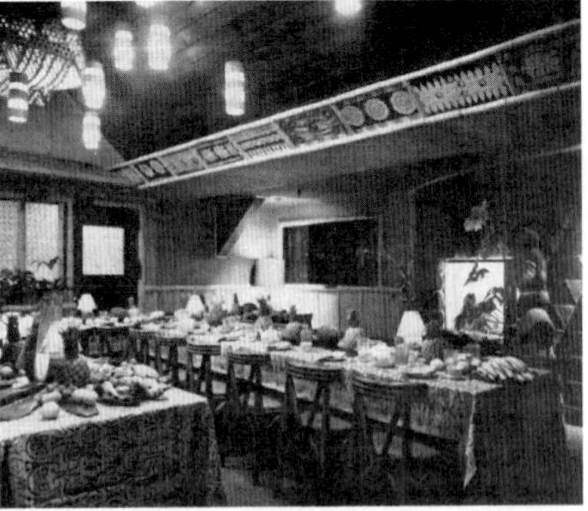

Continuing the Polynesian theme, the basement party rooms were also popular spots for events of all kinds. *Courtesy Sapp/Henry.*

included a number of dining huts that were based on the grass huts seen in Hawaiian villages.

> *A certain level of decorative elements had to be present in order to carry the diner's imagination to the South Seas. Tiki statues, shells, glass fishing weights, fountains, and aquariums were always used for creating atmosphere. The Kahiki designers took these pre-requisites seriously, employing an abundance of the decorative items. Combining them with other design features the Kahiki truly does transport dining guests to a magical island paradise.*

Author Michael J. Rosen, longtime literary director of the Thurber House in Columbus, gave the following response to the suggestion that the Kahiki was "kitschy":

> *You do know that what your suggestion of the place as kitschy (admittedly!) has to take into account that it was an authentic Papau New Guinea long house, created with incredible authenticity, unique to the time. Okay, the Polynesian valet parking was a little eccentric. And maybe the dry ice in the various "tropical" drinks. Okay, and maybe the blue-light entrance with waterfalls. Okay, maybe the birds in the "rain forest" and the series of aquaria...the whole enterprise. But I know the place from childhood birthdays to the moment of its closing.*

Finally, Consideration G calls for "a property achieving significance within the past 50 years if it is of exceptional importance." The application stated that

> *it is a significant representation of a form of entertainment and building type that was once popular at mid-century. It provides physical evidence of a larger societal enchantment with Hawaiian culture (often a perceived culture) and a reflection of Cold War escapism. Thirty to forty years have passed since the popularity of these restaurants were at their peak, thus allowing sufficient time to pass to examine their place in American culture.*

In conclusion, it was argued that

> *Polynesian palaces were America's first theme restaurants. In as much as these seem to be the future of the food-service business in this country, Polynesian restaurants may prove to be almost as important to our national heritage as the first automobile assembly line.*

Although Nathalie Wright and the others involved succeeded in having the Kahiki added to list, in the end it did nothing to change or even delay the restaurant's fate. Ironically, the same year the Kahiki was going up, the Alfred Kelley Mansion was coming down. An outstanding example of Greek Revival architecture with four porticos supported by massive stone columns, this was once the home of Alfred Kelley, "Father of the Ohio-Erie Canal," and one of Columbus's most prominent citizens. Built in 1838, the mansion stood at 282 East Broad Street, once the very outskirts of town. Four years later, Kelley "singlehandedly propped up the state's credit, pledging his personal property, including the mansion, to back a note to pay the overdue interest" owed the U.S. government on bonds issued to build the canal system. By 1961, however, Kelley's home was a sad shadow of its former self, having been purchased in 1907 by the Catholic Diocese of Columbus, which used it as a school. A year earlier, the church had sold the building to a developer who had big plans for the site.

To appease those who raise a hue and cry whenever historic structures are sacrificed to the gods of progress, it was agreed to dismantle the façade of the house, number every stone and store them somewhere so that it could be reconstructed somehow, sometime, somewhere. For a time, they were deposited at Wolfe Park and later moved to the Ohio State Fairgrounds. But by then, most of markings had weathered off the stones. Finally, they

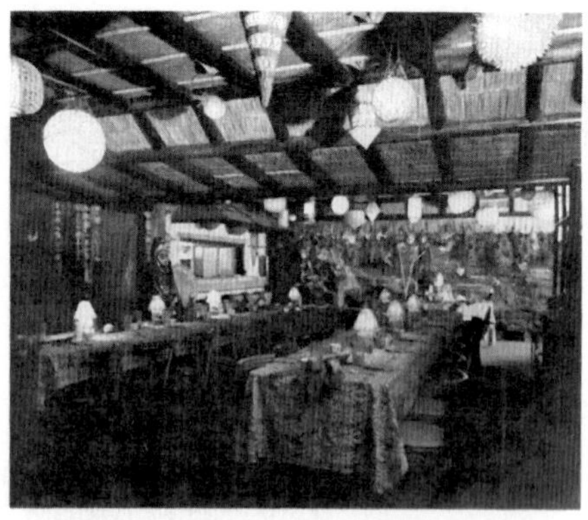

the OAHU ROOM

The beautiful Oahu Room has been called the most intriguing party room in the country. Even this could be a modest claim, for the Oahu Room is truly a magnificent setting to hold an informal gathering or banquet up to about 45 guests. Central theme of the Oahu is the trio of shimmering waterfalls, cascading majestically out of volcanic rock. Tropical island foliage is everywhere, heightening the island adventure. The multi-colored low key lighting effects are carried out through the use of various native lanterns and illuminated blowfish. The private bar serves all the famous Kahiki drinks, and a display of the various containers is featured. Why not plan your next party for the Oahu Room? Make reservations now! Get away from the ordinary and have the time of your life in a tropical paradise!

This ad for the Oahu party room suggests it is "the most intriguing in the country." *Courtesy Sapp/Henry.*

were given over into the custody of the Western Reserve Historical Society in Cleveland.

The old homestead was replaced in 1963 by the Christopher Inn, a hotel and restaurant famous for its circular design, not unlike the Capitol Records Tower in Hollywood. The fifteen-story building with 137 pie-shaped rooms was demolished in 1988. Some preservationists weren't happy about that, either.

At the end of his article, Curtis didn't reach a conclusion, but posed more questions:

> *But what to save? Early strip malls? Subdivisions filled with tract homes? Drive-in theaters? White Castle hamburger stands? (One paper presented in Philadelphia was titled "The Ubiquitous Parking Garage: Worthy of Preservation?") After all, these are icons of the twentieth century, much as canals and carriage houses and Richardsonian Romanesque train depots are icons of the nineteenth. Isn't it important to preserve the best*

> *architectural examples of our era for our grandchildren? How do we decide which are the best?*

In Columbus, there are many who would probably say that it is time we started saving something. Stu Koblentz, who helped to classify the Kahiki as one of the top ten endangered historic buildings in Ohio when he served on the Ohio Preservation Alliance, says, "I think a lot of people are still bitter about it. We all miss it."

17
BON VOYAGE

The true paradises are the paradises that we have lost.
—Marcel Proust

For much of its history, Whitehall was a blue-collar community of safe, clean and respectable neighborhoods. It was a good place to live and a good place to work. No doubt this was what prompted developer Don M. Casto Sr. to open Town & Country Shopping Center in 1949. A strip mall–style development dubbed the "Miracle Mile," it was a novelty at the time. During the next two decades, Main Street was known as "the strip" and was home to modern motels, nightclubs and restaurants, not the least of which was the Kahiki. By the 1980s and 1990s, however, many of these businesses had closed. The motels had gone to seed and were used only by drug and prostitution rings. As Nathan Miner, a visitor from Baltimore, blogged shortly before the Kahiki closed:

> *It was worth the drive, but I should warn anyone visiting for the first time that the Kahiki is located in a dirty, ugly, depressing, "down-trodden" part of town that had its "hey day" long, long ago and is now slipping into poverty, vacant lots, etc. I can understand why the Kahiki is glad to get out—and I have absolutely nothing but compassion for the decision to close and move elsewhere!! I know the Kahiki owners were celebrating that someone actually wanted to open a business on the property.*

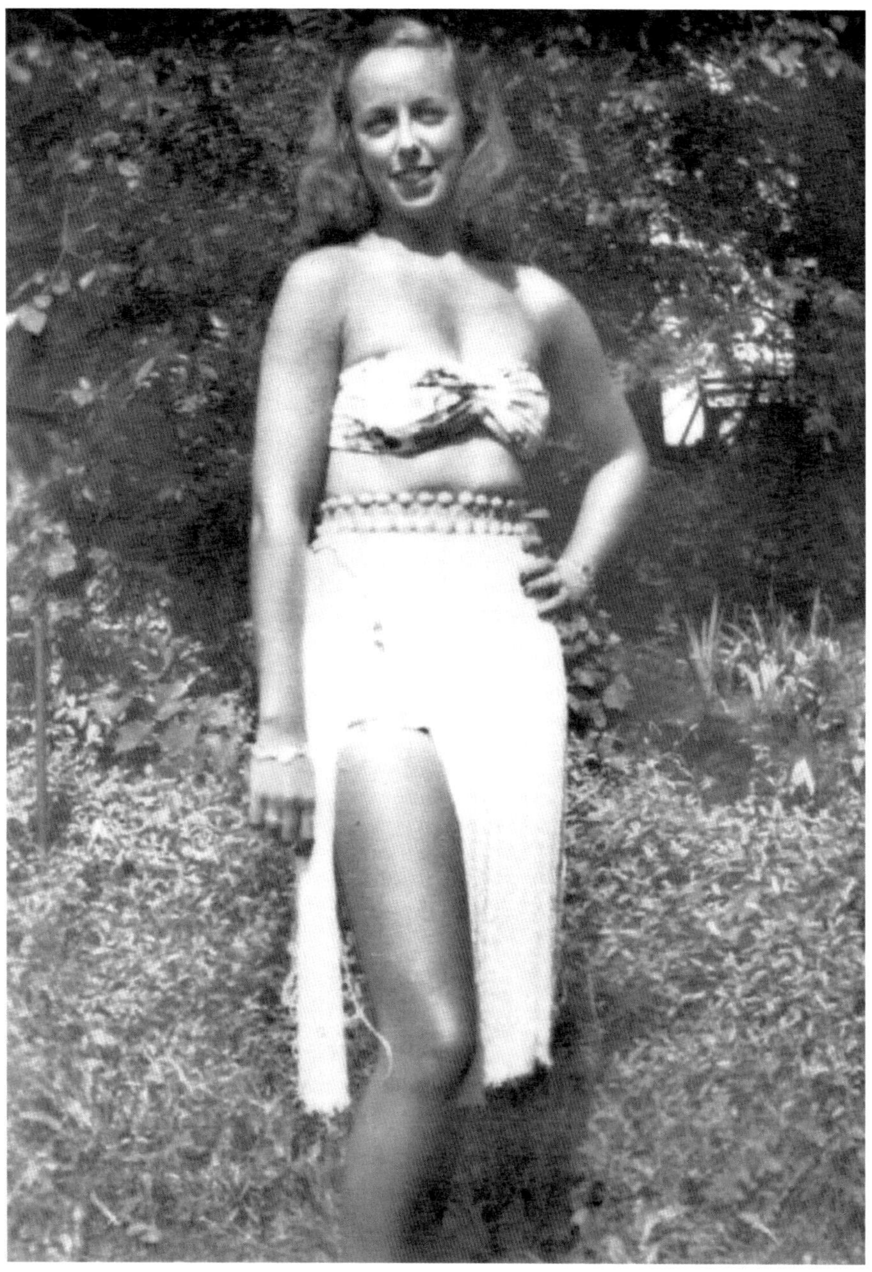

An early photo of a young woman posing in one of the Kahiki costumes. *Courtesy Sapp/Henry.*

Kristen Schmidt reported in *Columbus Monthly*: "Outdated housing, a transient population, language and cultural barriers and a high crime rate are phenomena that chase each other in cities like Whitehall."

In a study of restaurant failures, H.G. Parsa et al. made the following observation:

> *For example, Kahiki Restaurant located in Columbus, Ohio was ranked as one of the Top 100 restaurants in the US. It was visited by several Hollywood and national celebrities as a destination restaurant. Over* [the] *next three decades, this particular location continued to become less attractive as the affluent of the neighborhood moved, leaving empty spaces, vacant houses, and "brown fields." Eventually Kahiki was closed for good as the location became impossible to operate profitably. In this case, the geographic factors of the location did not change much, but the demographics changed; resulting* [in] *restaurant failure.*

As hard as it is for Kahiki-ophiles to accept, there were sound business reasons for closing the supper club. The restaurant simply was no longer a viable proposition. Sales had plateaued at $2.5 million. The building itself was in need of extensive renovations (there had always been problems with the rain forest plumbing, backed-up drains, rotting timbers, etc.). And as much as he would have liked to, Michael Tsao couldn't afford it.

In the restaurant game, location is everything, and the Kahiki's location at 3583 East Broad Street was militating against its continued survival. In the nearly forty years since it opened as a destination dining attraction, the area between Bexley and Whitehall had undergone many changes, few of them for the better. Although the term "changing demographics" was bandied about, what was really meant was the steady decline of the neighborhood. Bad things were happening there, the type of things that discourage customers. The location was no longer attractive to diners.

A second and possibly equal factor was the cost of renovating and maintaining the property. Although the building had been awarded historic preservation status just two years earlier, that didn't fix anything. You don't throw good money after bad. "We're looking at the physical maintenance of this facility catching up with us in the next 10 years," Tsao said. "It'll best serve us and the community if we move."

Although Michael Tsao downplayed Walgreens' influence on the decision to close the restaurant, he couldn't deny that money talks. The drugstore "just moved our process along faster."

"Tsao, dressed in a flowered shirt and a pink lei, said he wants to re-create the restaurant at a downtown location within two years, perhaps along the riverfront," a reporter for the *Jackson Florida Times Union* wrote. "He said Walgreens is not responsible for the closing and is getting undue criticism."

Preservationists, naturally, were upset by the prospect of losing the Kahiki. However, Tsao attempted to soothe ruffled feathers by insisting that the restaurant would not die. He noted that although the company (of which he was president) wanted him to consider relocating it to a destination city such as Orlando or Chicago, he felt that "this restaurant belongs in Columbus"—specifically, on the downtown riverfront. "We have a nice riverfront downtown, but there's not enough activity to support anything—not even the [replica of the] Santa Maria."

Tsao had his eye on several sites on the west bank of the Scioto River in the vicinity of the Veterans' Memorial and the Columbus Health Department. "We can be the catalyst for commercial development of the riverfront." Meanwhile, he planned to store artifacts and architectural details from the original Kahiki in the hope that they could be incorporated into any new building. He went so far as to discuss his idea with Mark Barbash, the city's director of trade and development. "What the city chooses to promote downtown needs to make sense in terms of the overall plan," Barbash said. "We're not going to piecemeal this. With that said, Michael's a good business person with a lot of good ideas. I just haven't seen his more recent plans."

Other movers and shakers gave their conditional support. Developer Ron Pizzuti, who was in the process of building the Miranova condominium complex, suggested, "Maybe that restaurant could be floated in the middle of the river or perhaps at Confluence Park." Keith Myers, a partner in Myers-Schmalenberger Landscape Architects, emphasized that "the architecture and design would be important. Any structure like that on the river has the potential to be very visible. It would be difficult to get something that would fit in with the cultural institutions developing over there" on the west bank. Richard Nolan, general manager of the Veterans' Memorial, said, "I think what Michael wants to do is exciting and he wants to find the right place for it."

On August 26, 2000, the Kahiki officially passed away at the age of thirty-nine. But instead of holding a wake over the deceased, those who were in attendance partied like it was 1999. Otto Von Stroheim, publisher of *Tiki News*, was among those covering the festivities. "Guests traveled from all over the U.S. and abroad," he wrote. "Some of the cities represented were Atlanta, Chicago, London, Los Angeles, Madison, Melbourne, Minneapolis,

New York, Pittsburgh and San Francisco." Artists, musicians, journalists, filmmakers, celebrities big and small, longtime customers and the merely curious converged on this the center of the tiki universe to rub elbows and shake hands with Bill Sapp, Sandro Conti, Herman Leitwein and others who had a hand in creating the legendary Polynesian palace.

When Otto Von Stroheim asked Michael Tsao directly whether he thought the Kahiki would really reopen, he answered, "I have almost 100 people that rely on me for their livelihood…I want to make sure that Kahiki lasts another 40 years. That is why we are moving." Even had he lived, however, it is unlikely it would have been resurrected.

18
AFTERLIFE

To begin with, the "goals" of all Polynesian peoples seem to have been limited to those of the Ao, the mortal everyday world—i.e., generally speaking, individuals did not act in ways aimed at securing a desirable existence in the afterlife, in the Po.
—Douglas L. Oliver

Although the Kahiki is no more, there are many people who do not want it or the memory of it to pass away. They have endeavored, some more successfully than others, to provide it with an afterlife. A surprising number of them had never experienced the restaurant—or even stepped foot in Columbus—but recognized that it was a very special place and keenly feel the loss. Their desire to pay tribute to the Kahiki Supper Club has expressed itself in a variety of ways.

Scott Kramer and Steve Zurnoff opened Pittsburgh's Tiki Lounge at 2003 East Carson Street in the autumn of 2002. According to tikiophile James Teitelbaum in *Tiki Road Trip*, it was

> *inspired by Columbus's universally missed Kahiki (right down to the shell sinks in the washrooms). One enters the two-story building through a mammoth tiki, to find a bar across from some booths. The rear of the room contains a dance floor, and the basement level is a non-smoking bar. The TiPSY Factor here is high; two waterfalls and plenty of tikis exist among the dense foliage, and two glass cases house a pair of cannibals (fake).*

Until it closed forever in August 2008, Marion's Continental, a retro-chic bar and restaurant at 354 Bowery between East Fourth and Great Jones Streets in New York, hosted an annual tribute to the Kahiki. For several weeks each year, Marion's broke out the flower leis and decked the halls with paper palm trees, some thatching and flowers to create a "tasteful Tiki" décor. The kitchen served up pu-pu platters galore, along with other Asian Pacific dishes, and the bartenders deviated from their usual cocktail-heavy fare to mix up a variety of exotic drinks. For entertainment, the World Famous Pontani Sisters tapped up a storm with their "glamorous Las Vegas style showgirl dance numbers with a downtown twist."

A 2005 press release stated that Marion's salute to the Kahiki originated from an incident that occurred when Marion Nagy, a New York socialite, and her husband, Harry, were flying to Los Angeles to attend to the wedding of Harry's brother at baseball star Sandy Koufax's house. When their plane was unexpectedly diverted to Columbus, they called some friends who took them to the newly opened Kahiki Supper Club. With its over-the-top décor, Mystery Girl, volcanic drinks and Polynesian dishes, the Nagys "had a hoot of a time."

Ty Wenzel, longtime bartender at Marion's, described the scene during the Kahiki celebration:

> *The usual fifties shabby-chic is still apparent under the explosion of Tiki-ware. The largest tables…are under gigantic thatch roofs dressed up with stuffed plastic parrots hanging from the center on their perches. One of them is dangling lopsided, prepared to nosedive into someone's frozen daiquiri. The other side of the room, where the two-top orange booths…are lined up against the wall, it is also covered by an elongated version of the straw roof, edged with a chintzy multicolored gigantic lantern light set.*
>
> *Scattered all over the room, including the bar, are paper and plastic palm trees, plastic totem poles, head-bobbin' hula girls, plastic fish tied in nets, gardenias, leis, grass skirts, coconut bras, and other silly island accessories. It looks garish and cheap in the sunshine coming in through the front windows, but it takes on a kitschy island charm at night. And believe me when I say New Yorkers love nothing more than a Tiki theme.*

Although the staff dressed in Hawaiian shirts, grass skirts and sarongs, Marion's remained pretty much rooted in its usual "Rat Pack" ambiance. As one customer wrote, "It basically looked like they were throwing a tropical themed birthday party for someone. It was that lame."

While the preservationists had failed in their attempt to prevent the Kahiki from being demolished, others were determined to keep it alive by saving some of the artifacts and recording its history. Initially, these efforts were undertaken by disparate individuals acting on their own. However, in 2005, Matt "Kuku Ahu" Thatcher, Jim "Chisel Slinger" Robinson and Joel "Cowtown Kahuna" Gunn formalized their efforts with the founding of the Ohio-based Fraternal Order of Moai. With a mission of serving as the "premier fraternal organization and social network for all men and women interested in tiki culture and the Polynesian pop era," the Moai espouses the following core values: good words, fellowship, spirit, presence, preservation and celebration.

In 1994, Steven Schussler opened the first in an international chain of Rainforest Cafés at the Mall of America in Blooming, Minnesota. The theme is a tropical rain forest with plants, waterfalls, aquariums and animatronic figures, from elephants to gorillas and even a talking tree. The optical fiber ceilings are designed to suggest a starry night. And occasionally a "thunderstorm" rolls through, just as it did at the Kahiki. As befitting an operation that includes branches at Downtown Disney in Anaheim, California; Disney's Animal Kingdom, Lake Buena Vista, Florida; and Downtown Disney, also at Lake Buena Vista, the staff are all "cast members," with waiters acting as Safari Guides, hosts and hostesses as Tour Guides, bartenders as Navigators, etc. The menu plays it safe, offering burgers, salads, nachos, pizza, pasta and similar entrées. Everyone yells "Volcano!" when someone orders a volcano sundae.

Early in 2006, Theang Ngo, age thirty-four, and Soeng Thong, thirty-nine, opened the Tropical Bistro at Mill Run next to Lowe's. "We want to give the people the spirit of the Kahiki," Ngo said. He had been a general manager when the celebrated Polynesian supper club closed, while Thong was a headwaiter. Joining them at the new pan-Asian venture was Mickey Cheung, former executive chef at the Kahiki. Obviously, this venture was a little closer to the heart than Marion's Continental.

Located at 3641 Fishinger Road in Hilliard, a Columbus suburb, the restaurant featured some tables, lanterns, masks, wooden tikis and turtle shells from the original Kahiki. However, the overall décor largely reflected its previous life as Mark Pi's China Gate.[30] The tables were a gift from Alice Tsao, widow of Kahiki owner Michael Tsao. Other items were provided by Kahiki Foods, Inc. Although the food ("From the East," "From the West" and "From the Island") and drink recipes ("Zombie," "Smoking Eruption," "Headhunter," "Suffering Bastard" and, of course, "Mai Tai") remained the

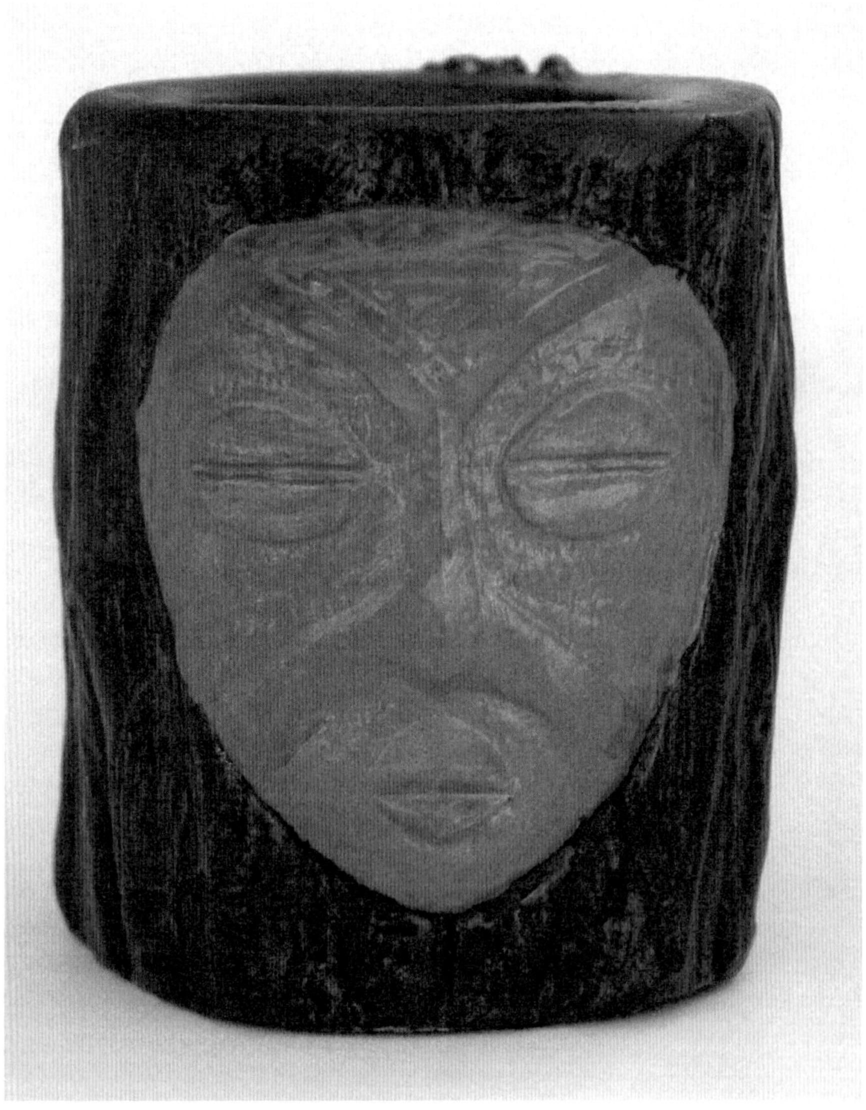

The face on the original Zombie drink sleeve was also incorporated into the main doors. *Courtesy Joe Schuster.*

same (with the addition of a sushi bar), the Tropical Bistro, as one article put it, was "Kahiki Lite."

Diners still raved about such dishes as the "Tahitian Mermaid" (steak stuffed with crab and cream cheese) or the "Malagasy New York Strip

Steak" (with a green peppercorn sauce), but by 2008, the Tropical Bistro had closed—good food and good drinks couldn't trump a bad location. The Tropical Bistro was saddled with a dying strip mall and suffered from the lack of a distinctive building that had only a couple stone moai out front.

If anyone in Columbus knows how to work a restaurant concept, it's Elisabeth "Liz" Lessner. In 2011, Lessner, co-founder of the Columbus Food League, announced plans to add a sixth restaurant to her rapidly growing portfolio. The Grass Skirt opened the following year at 105 North Grant Avenue, a small brick building whose former tenant was the Mad Lab Theater and Gallery. She noted that she and her partners "all grew up loving the Kahiki," so they wanted to bring back the kitsch of the tiki bar. "We try to find niches," she said. "Our restaurant group goes for a fun vibe." Joining her were the other members of the league: Carmen Owens, Amy Brennick, Tim Lessner and Harold Rue. Although the Grass Skirt, by design, is even more "Kahiki Lite" than the Tropical Bistro was, it has demonstrated that the city still has a soft spot in its heart for tiki bars.

Then there is Kahiki Foods. In December 2002, Michael Tsao bought a new building in Gahanna for $2.2 million, which included an additional fourteen acres for expansion. He also secured a $4.2 million industrial bond from the state that would allow him to refurbish and equip the building, bringing the total cost of the project to nearly $7 million. Two years later, the 119,000-square-foot, state-of-the-art Gahanna plant was ready for occupation and none too soon.

The executive, administrative and sales offices were first to move in. Manufacturing was scheduled to follow, beginning in mid-October. However, the move was not completed until May 2005. Ten weeks later, Tsao died unexpectedly. He had lived long enough to see his dream of a larger factory, but not to enjoy its fruits. Although his family was in mourning, they were also understandably anxious about the company's future. The visionary was dead, and Kahiki Foods was deeply in debt. Nevertheless, they were determined to continue his legacy.

In May 2007, ABARTA, Inc., a Pittsburgh holding company, purchased Kahiki Foods for $11.7 million. A family-owned business, ABARTA is involved in newspaper publishing and oil and gas exploration and is also one of the nation's largest bottlers of Coca-Cola soft drinks. The company decided not to move the Kahiki factory from Gahanna. The transition was so quiet that few Kahiki enthusiasts seemed to realize that the tiki torch had been passed to an out-of-town concern.

Then, in 2010, Hills Market, a gourmet foods store in north Columbus held a special Kahiki tribute day in conjunction with Kahiki Foods. There were food samples, cooking demonstrations and a three-course dinner. The market also served three rum drinks using the original recipes: Tonga Tale, Suffering Bastard and the Mystery Drink.

Three years after that, the Columbus Historical Society started its Historical Dinner Club series. The initial offering was a tribute to the Kahiki, held at Alana's Food and Wine. The special event was limited to forty diners, who were treated to a Kahiki-like meal by owner/chef Alana Shock. At $125 each, the tickets were snatched up immediately by locals as well as one couple who traveled from Maryland just to revisit the Kahiki experience.

Ten years after Walgreens rose up out of the dust of the Kahiki, Alan Hoover, president of the Gahanna-based frozen food company of the same name, was leaving his office one evening when "a couple was walking up the front walkway. I asked if I could help them, and they said, 'Yes, we'd like to have dinner tonight.'" He didn't say whether he tried to steer them toward the frozen food case.

APPENDIX A

KAHIKI DISHES

"Polynesian cuisine" sprang largely from the imaginations of Victor Bergeron and Ernest Gantt, including such popular entrees as crab Rangoon and rumaki. Inspired by what he saw at Don The Beachcomber, Bergeron (to quote Nathalie Wright),

> *traveled to Cuba, Florida, and Polynesia looking for new drink and food ideas, as well as additional artifacts for Trader Vic's. In the end he settled on Chinese food with pineapple, coconut and bananas added to give a "Polynesian" flare. His opinion was that Americans would not like real Polynesian food, therefore, he compromised with food that would be considered exotic, but not too foreign.*

As restaurant historian Jan Whitaker has pointed out, so-called Polynesian cuisine had little to do with what real Polynesians ate.

> *The Kahiki's reference point was Tahiti. So, what were Tahitians eating in 1961 when the Kahiki opened? According to a geographer, the traditional Tahitian diet consisted of baked fish, breadfruit, and taro, but natives then preferred French baguettes with Australian butter, rice from Madagascar, canned beef from New Zealand, and Canadian canned salmon, all "washed down with generous drinks of Algerian red wine."*

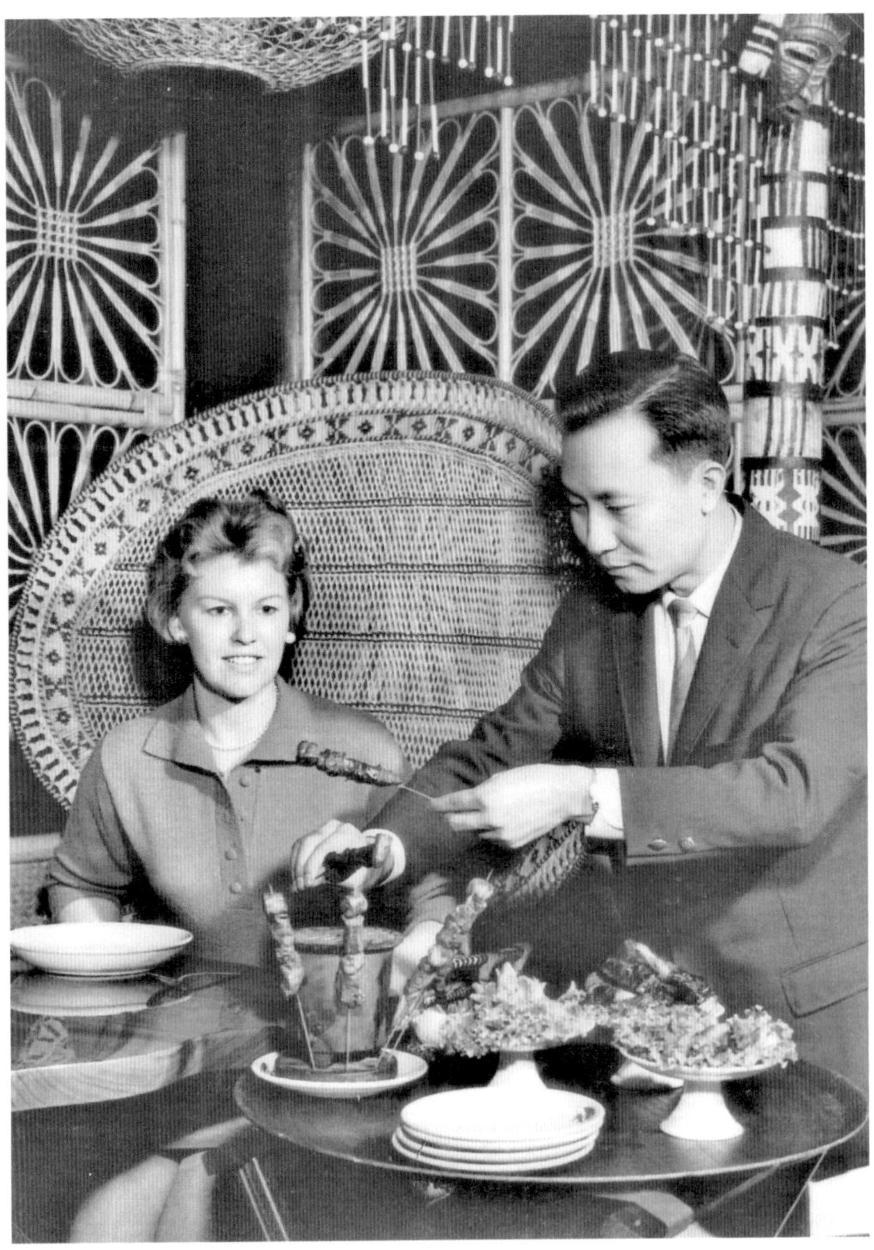

A former print model, Marcy Sapp appeared in many of the staged photographs used for advertising. *Courtesy Sapp/Henry.*

Whittaker doubted "that Tahitians ate much in the way of Oriental Beef or Tahitian Flambé (flaming ice cream with rum). Not to mention Tossed Green Salads, Eggs Benedict, or Reuben Sandwiches." A true Polynesian would undoubtedly find the offerings on the Kahiki's menu every bit as exotic as the typical patron did. But people didn't go to the Kahiki primarily for its food, although some undoubtedly did. As an unenthusiastic reviewer wrote in 1975, "If decor is your reason for dining out, the Kahiki in Columbus is the place for you."

Philip C.W. Chin, a graduate of Texas A&M, was the executive chef and general manager of the Kahiki for a time. He oversaw a kitchen that included everything from a radar range to ancient Chinese kettles. Where possible, an emphasis was placed on showmanship. For example, the *maître d'* would prepare a tableside Caesar salad.

Joe Blundo is the oft-quoted (but seldom credited) pundit who wrote, "Some entrees are served in whole pineapples, others are delivered on fire. The Kahiki is one of the few restaurants in Columbus in which food can injure you." He was thinking of William E. Thompson of Columbus, who recalled, "My wife ordered a flaming dessert. When the waiter ignited the dessert, the flames were about 2 feet high and quickly advanced across the table and engulfed the bread basket." It required several waiters to extinguish the blaze.

Similarly, "Christine Rodabaugh of Lima, Ohio, once mistakenly dipped a meatball on a stick into an accelerant fueling a tableside fire. She thought it was the sauce pot." Blundo wrote, "I quickly noticed it was flaming as fiercely as a marshmallow left too long in a campfire, totally engulfed in leaping flames…My entire family was falling off the sides of their chairs laughing uncontrollably. Now, where else can you get that kind of entertainment?"

Judy Frye of Tucson, Arizona, and Judy Ottney of Dublin, Ohio, have both admitted to mistaking the hot hand towels, served in a wicker basket, for egg rolls. *Maître d'* Bill Harrison described one incident in which a young lady told him they were the worst egg rolls she had ever had. He could hardly keep a straight face as he saw that she had covered the towels with mustard and sweet and sour sauce. So he said, "I'm sorry. Please excuse me. I'll have them bring you fresh egg rolls right over." Then on the way out she told him, "Thank you very much. The second was delicious." He then thanked her for giving them a second chance.

If there is a Kahiki recipe book in existence, we have not seen it. If there were, we could sell a few copies. However, we have tracked down several authentic—or allegedly so—recipes from various sources.

KAHIKI BEEF KATIKI

This recipe was published in a restaurant journal in 1963 and attributed to the Kahiki.

1½ pounds lean beef, cut against the grain and sliced
1 medium yellow onion, chopped
1 clove garlic, chopped
1 pound precooked green pepper, chopped
1½ pounds tomatoes, chopped
1 stalk celery, chopped
1 cup tomato ketchup
1 tablespoon soy sauce
1 teaspoon salt
1 tablespoon sugar
½ teaspoon seasoning powder
2 tablespoons cornstarch, dissolved in ½ cup water

Sauté meat, onion and garlic in skillet on medium-high heat. Add green pepper, chopped tomatoes, celery, ketchup, soy sauce, salt, sugar, seasoning and cornstarch mixture. Bring to a boil. Then turn down heat and simmer until the water has been absorbed and the mixture thickened. Makes 4 servings.

TAHITIAN MERMAID

Mickey Cheung, former chef at the Kahiki, provided the Ohio Department of Agriculture with this recipe for the *1998 Ohio's Heartland Cuisine* cookbook. The 1/16 tablespoon lemon juice is an odd measurement, but that's what the recipe says.

2 6-ounce beef filets
½ teaspoon Worcestershire sauce
½ teaspoon seasoning salt
¼ teaspoon pepper

FILLING:
3½ ounces crabmeat
3½ ounces cream cheese

½ cup coarse bread crumbs
¼ teaspoon hot sauce, such as Tabasco
¼ teaspoon Worcestershire sauce
¼ teaspoon salt
⅛ teaspoon pepper
⅛ teaspoon garlic powder
1/16 tablespoon lemon juice
1 tablespoon chopped onion

In a medium bowl, combine the filling ingredients. Set aside. Butterfly the filets of beef (they will look like an open shell.) Season with the Worcestershire sauce, seasoning salt and pepper. In a skillet, sear the inner part of the steaks over high heat for 30 seconds. Remove from heat, and stuff half the filling into each steak. Then slightly close each and return to the skillet. Cook each side of the steaks on high heat for 1 minute. Serves 2.

Chicken Pineapple Kahiki

The next three recipes were published in *A Taste of Columbus* by Beth Chilcoat and Cindy Kusmer (Corban Productions, 1978). The entire series is a tremendous resource for food historians.

1 ripe pineapple
2 meaty chicken breasts, cut into ½-inch pieces
butter
1 tablespoon white wine
1 cup water
1 green pepper, diced
½ cup sugar
½ cup vinegar
½ cup water
½ cup ketchup
pinch ginger powder
pinch garlic powder
cornstarch

Wash pineapple; cut lengthwise into two halves. Using a grapefruit knife, cut meat from the shell leaving about a ½ inch of pineapple. Working around the core, dice pineapple meat into ½-inch cubes; discard core. Set aside pineapple meat.

Brown chicken in butter and wine. Then add 1 cup water, the prepared diced pineapple and green pepper. Bring to a simmer. Mix together sugar, vinegar, ½ cup water, ketchup, ginger powder and garlic power to make sweet and sour sauce. Add sauce to chicken/pineapple mixture. Cover with pineapple shells for five minutes. Remove shells and thicken with cornstarch. Put chicken mixture into shells and serve. Serves 2.

Kahiki Egg Drop Soup

½ cup fresh or frozen peas
1 teaspoon chicken base (homemade or from gourmet grocery)
½ teaspoon sugar
1½ cups water
2 stalks green onion, finely chopped
2 eggs, well beaten

Combine all ingredients except the eggs in a saucepan over medium heat and bring to rapid boil. Boil for 2 minutes. Remove from heat. Add well-beaten eggs, combining thoroughly. Serves 2.

Kahiki Ham Fried Rice

1 tablespoon cooking oil
½ yellow onion, chopped
½ pound cooked ham, diced
2½ cups cooked rice
2 tablespoons soy sauce
pinch salt
1 teaspoon sugar
2 eggs, scrambled
2 green onions, chopped

Heat oil in a large skillet over medium-high heat. Brown onion and ham until onions are tender. Add rice, soy sauce, salt and sugar and combine. Add scrambled eggs. Mix well. Top with green onions. Serves 4.

Chinese Chicken Sauté with Star Anise

This recipe is attributed to Chef Ping Lee of the Kahiki.

1 whole (fryer) chicken
2 tablespoons soy sauce
1 to 1½ teaspoons brandy or sherry
3 slices of ginger, mashed and then chopped
2 whole star anise, processed in spice mills or chopped
pinch sugar

1 ounce dried black mushrooms, soaked for 30 minutes
(or fresh sliced mushrooms)
2 or 3 green onions, cut in 1-inch strips
¾ cup chicken stock or water
cornstarch and water slurry (1 tablespoon cornstarch to 1 tablespoon water)

Bone the chicken and cook in halves, or prepare the recipe with halved bone-in chicken. (A bone-in chicken retains more juices, but a boned chicken is quicker to prepare.)

Make a marinade by mixing the soy sauce and brandy or sherry with the ginger, star anise and sugar. Thoroughly rub the outside of the chicken with the marinade.

Brown the chicken halves in a wok or heavy skillet and add mushrooms, green onions and chicken stock or water. In a small bowl, combine cornstarch and water; then add to skillet. Cover and simmer slowly for 15 minutes or until the chicken tests done (juices flowing from the chicken when stuck with a fork near the bone should be clear rather than pink). More stock or water should be added if needed.

Kahiki Caesar Salad

Having "bluffed" his way into the job of *maître d'*, Bill Harrison learned that he would be expected to prepare a tableside Caesar salad. So he borrowed a book from the library by the famous French chef Auguste Escoffier. It said to start with a coddled egg. "I'm a poor boy from Youngstown," Bill laughed, "and I didn't know a coddled egg from a bacon sandwich." But he looked it up. Unfortunately, his first customer was Ed Docherty, who was with his wife, Mary, the daughter of the owner of the rival Jai Lai Restaurant.

"The lettuce went up in the air," Bill recalled, "…and nearly all went into his lap. He had a beautiful sense of humor and said, 'Well, I would have preferred it on the plate' and then added, 'So far the show is nice.' It was ridiculous. I was sweating and I was dying, and the bus boy brought me another and I remix[ed] and he said it was very good and he tipped me ten bucks on the way out."

Note: This recipe is included for historical purposes. Many people are allergic to MSG, and salmonella bacteria may be present in raw eggs unless they are pasteurized.

1 medium clove garlic
2 or 3 anchovy filets
pinch salt
½ teaspoon Worcestershire sauce
pinch monosodium glutamate (MSG)
juice of ½ lemon or 1 tablespoon tarragon vinegar
2 to 3 ounces olive oil
1 raw egg
2 tablespoons grated Parmesan cheese
1 quart mixed Romaine and Iceberg lettuce, refrigerated
⅓ cup seasoned garlic croutons
freshly ground pepper

Drop peeled clove of garlic into a salad bowl. Use the back part of a spoon to mash the garlic down into a pulp. Add the anchovy filets with a sprinkle of salt and mash the garlic and anchovies together. Combine Worcestershire sauce, MSG, lemon juice, olive oil, raw egg and cheese. Mix ingredients together until almost creamy.

Add salad greens to the dressing and toss over and over in dressing until every leaf is coated, using a wooden fork and spoon.

Add garlic croutons and toss only a few seconds more. Serve immediately with a generous amount of freshly ground pepper.

APPENDIX B
KAHIKI DRINKS

Restaurant historian Jan Whitaker claims that what really made Polynesian restaurants attractive to investors was the high profit margin on rum drinks: "Their marketing relied on bar decoration, bartender apparel, drink names, elaborate serving vessels, and imaginative presentation." Kahiki co-founder Bill Sapp agrees. "It was all shortly after the war, and everyone was coming home and happy. And the economy was starting to boom again. They said our drinks tasted like fruit juice, and they certainly were strong. Our colorful drinks were good for the happiness." And happiness was good for business.

All such tropical beverages were American inventions and in no way representative of what Polynesian natives actually drank (besides Algerian red wine). A roll call of the drinks would include Mystery Blossom, Smoking Eruption, Kahiki Coffee Grog, Piña Passion, Idol's Cast, Barrelito, Zombie, Fog Cutter, Port Light, Native Nectar, Satan's Sin, Maiden's Prayer, Tonga Tale, Mai-Tai, Widow's Wail, Kahiki Pearl, Navy Grog, Bahía, Polynesian Spell, Pago Passage, Jungle Fever, Suffering Bastard, Mystery Drink, Hot Buttered Rum, Derby Daiquiri, Backscratcher, Kahiki Swizzle, Headhunter, Instant Urge, Malayan Mist, Penang, Coconut Kiss, Potent Potion, Misty Isle and Starboard Light.

The most famous beverage offered at the Kahiki was the Mystery Drink, which was served communal style in a large bowl. Trader Vic's had introduced the Kava Bowl during the 1940s. Don The Beachcomber's introduced the Volcano, which had "a central cone filled with overproof rum." Of course,

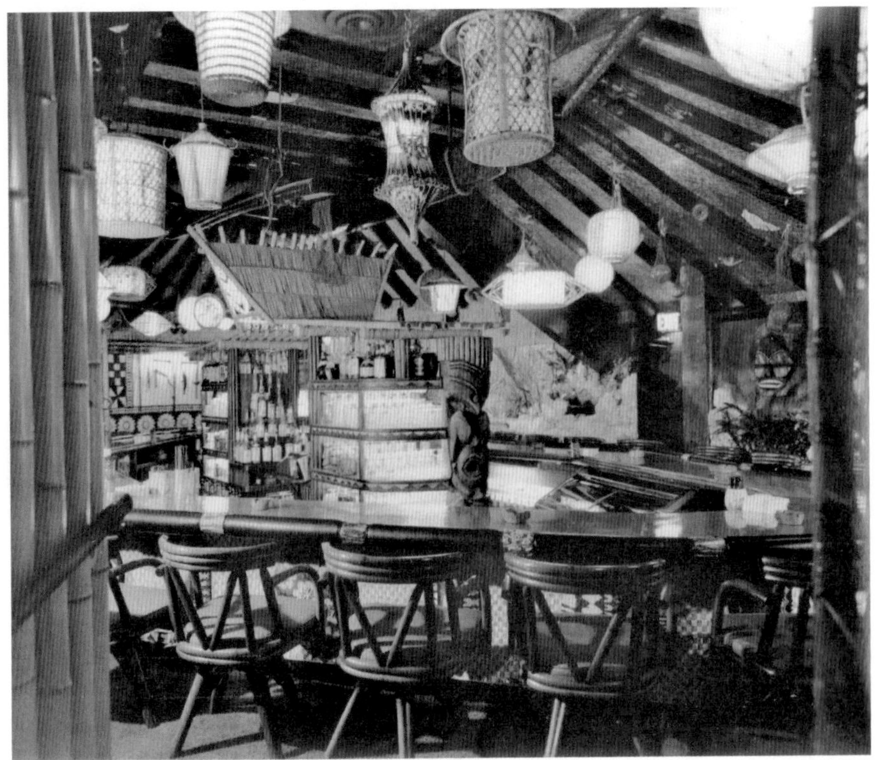

A view of the Outrigger Bar in the Kahiki. *Courtesy Sapp/Henry.*

there was a certain amount of ceremony accompanying the arrival of the drink at the customers' table.

Because the tiki bars would freely steal one another's prize drink recipes, Don The Beachcomber's resorted to replacing the labels on its liquor bottles with a series of letters and numbers. The bartenders were directed to mix drinks according to coded recipes that referenced the bottles by number and letter. In this way, the chain hoped to reduce the chance of their bartenders' taking their drink recipes with them when they were hired away by the competition. As a 1948 *Saturday Evening Post* reported, "Infinite pains are taken to see to it that the service bar help cannot memorize Don's various occult ingredients and proportions."

Skip Davis, who bartended at the Kahiki for twenty-one years, has a lot of stories from the Kahiki that can't be told in polite company. However, this one is worth repeating because of its contribution to local football lore. "There was a young man from my wife's hometown who was Brutus Buckeye one year," Davis wrote, referring to the Ohio State University mascot. "Long story short, the head on the costume didn't get turned back in right away. Well, we just kind of filled it up with some kind of concoction and drank out of it. Here was Brutus's [fiberglass] head upside down on the bar and we're all sipping out of it." He was also known to drink champagne from his tennis shoe on occasion.

Davis was one half of the popular bartending duo of Skip and Jim (Davis and Carasco). The latter had worked at the Kahiki for eighteen and a half years. During Skip and Jim's years of service, the recipe book fell by the wayside, but it didn't matter because they had memorized all forty of the drinks on the menu long ago. "Some of the drinks are easy: the only difference between a Zombie and a Barrelito is [a half ounce of] Navy Grog mix," Carasco noted. However, as he explained to Otto Von Stroheim of *Tiki News*, the Navy Grog mix is another story altogether.

> *The Kahiki Navy Grog mix is so complex and made so infrequently (once every 5 years) that the recipe was seldomly seen let alone memorized. Jim made it once when he was first hired at age 20, then again at 25. I noticed* [the recipe] *hanging on a wire one day in the kitchen and I thought "That's gonna fall off and get lost." Jim divulged* [it] *to me as I navigated my Navy Grog. So I copied it down and kept it at home. Months later when it came time to make the recipe the other bartender said, "It's gone!" and I said, "No it isn't I have it at home."*

Although he did not come away with the recipe for Navy Grog, Von Stroheim wrote:

> *Legend has it that making the mix requires a large pot and hours of patience. After pouring in the right amounts of sherry, three kinds of bitters ("Last time I had to purchase them at the pharmacy because the liquor stores don't carry them anymore" explained Jim), curaçao, rock candy syrup, orgeat syrup, cinnamon, etc., a stirrer is made from a stick and about a pound of cloves wrapped in cheesecloth. This is used to stir the mixture as it is slowly brought to a boil. The recipe fills 50–100 bottles!*

From the Kahiki's start, Señor Sandro Conti was the bar manager and devised many of the drinks served at the restaurant. Bill Sapp's first meeting with Sandro at the Top Steakhouse had been a memorable one.

> *It was on a Sunday evening. I had been tending bar, and at that time, according to law, you could only sell whiskey until midnight on Sunday. Another bar owner from Pataskala and I were the only ones sitting at the bar and this long-haired, blue-eyed guy came in the door. I was tired from playing golf all day, so I said in Spanish under my breath, "If you want a drink, go make your own." And he walked right back to the bar and said, "Sí, cómo no?"* ["Sure, why not?"] *and mixed himself a drink. It turns out he's Italian and lived until he was eleven years old in Italy. His family moved through a political appointment-type thing to Nicaragua. He grew up in Nicaragua and was fluent in both Italian and Spanish and then came to the U.S. in either 1958 or 1959. When he came into the Top that night, he could say "Hello," and that was the extent of his English. We talked* [in] *Spanish all the time, and that's how we became very good friends.*

The two men quickly became friends, which led to Sandro's becoming the chief mixologist at the Kahiki.

Conti came to know rums while living in South America. His drinks included Sandro's Sin, Malayan Mist, Blue Hurricane, Instant Urge, Headhunter, Jungle Fever, Potent Passion and Smokey Eruption. The Kahiki's bars would consume one thousand pineapples and about two thousand bottles of rum a month. They once sold over eighteen thousand Polynesian drinks during the months of May alone. And each drink came in its own distinct mug or glass.

Promoter Bruce Nutt said he consulted with a couple bartenders at the Kahiki when he opened Crazy Mama's, just south of the Ohio State campus in 1979. They helped him devise the drinks and the menu at "America's First Rock 'n' Roll Disco."

A book of drink recipes from the Kahiki would probably be in even higher demand than a book of food recipes. Sadly, if there is one, it is probably under lock and key in somebody's basement tiki bar. However, here are a few that have surfaced.

PORT LIGHT

This drink recipe is one of Sandro Conti's best known. It is unusual in that it is a whiskey- (not rum-) based drink. The name might refer to the fact that it has a red tint like the port light on a boat.

1 (or 1½, according to some sources) ounce bourbon
1 ounce lemon juice
½ ounce passion fruit syrup
½ (or ¼) ounce grenadine
cherry and lemon wedge

Shake bourbon, lemon juice, passion fruit syrup and grenadine with 1 cup of crushed ice for five seconds and pour into a Collins glass or small tiki mug. Garnish with a cherry and a lemon wedge.

For a slushier texture, pulse in a blender (but be wary of "blender explosions," as bartender Ty Wenzel calls them). Passion fruit syrup is available from at least one vendor, B.G. Reynolds, or can be easily made. Raspberry syrup can be substituted for the grenadine.

Polynesian Spell

Another original drink attributed to Sandro Conti, this is a non-rum-based beverage, as well. It is essentially a gin cocktail.

1 ounce grape juice
¾ ounce fresh lemon juice
¼ ounce triple sec
¼ ounce peach brandy
½ teaspoon sugar syrup
1½ ounce dry gin

Shake well with ice cubes. Strain into a champagne glass.

Kahiki Bahía

From an unsourced, undated newspaper clipping.

2½ ounces (¼ cup plus 1 tablespoon) unsweetened pineapple juice
1 ounce (2 tablespoons) fresh lemon juice
1 ounce (2 tablespoons) canned coconut cream
2 ounces (¼ cup) light rum
1 scoop shaved or crushed ice
pineapple-cherry fruit stick

Place all but fruit stick in shaker glass; shake well. Or mix in blender. Decorate with fruit stick. Makes 1 serving.

Kahiki's Jungle Fever

From an unsourced, undated newspaper clipping.

½ banana
1 ounce (2 tablespoons) light rum
1 ounce (2 tablespoons) fresh lime juice
1 dash maraschino cherry liqueur
1 dash sugar syrup
1 scoop shaved or crushed ice
banana slice and cherry

Combine all but banana slice and cherry in blender; mix until smooth. Serve as is or freeze until slushy. Garnish with banana slice and cherry. Makes 1 serving.

Kahiki Smoking Eruption

This drink dates from about 1980.

In a blender, mix:

1 ounce guava juice
1 ounce pineapple juice
1 ounce passion fruit juice
1 ounce light rum
1 ounce vodka
1 ounce Appleton Punch Rum
½ ounce rock candy syrup
½ ounce lemon juice
dash red food coloring

Add crushed ice and blend slightly. In a smaller glass (to fit inside the one you will serve in), place a small amount of dry ice. Put this smaller glass into the larger one, and just when prepared to serve, put hot water into the glass containing dry ice. This will create bubbling water and "smoke" (fog).

The Kahiki Outrigger

½ ounce grapefruit juice
½ ounce falernum
¾ ounce cinnamon syrup
2 ounces golden rum

Shake all ingredients with a ½ cup of ice and pour into an old-fashion glass.

Polynesian Martini

This isn't a recipe per se but rather the story of a drink. Bartender Tommy Joseph had one particularly difficult customer who would come in every day, pound the bar and say, "Give me a Polynesian martini." After he had downed it, he would complain about how bad it was and then walk away without leaving a tip. One day, a condiment salesman came in with jars of pepperoncino peppers that were especially hot, and Tommy talked him into giving him two of them. The next time his problem customer came in, Tommy skewered the peppers on a spear, dropped them in the martini and told him they were Polynesian olives. The man replied, "Well, you've finally got it" and popped the pepper in his mouth. "You could see his face turn red," Bill Harrison said. "I'm not sure, but there must have been wax coming out of his ears, and I know his nose was running. And he took the entire four ounces of gin and, in one fell swoop, sucked it down." Tommy remarked, "You really go for those Polynesian martinis." The customer never came back.

APPENDIX C
CUBAN ADVENTURE

Given Bill Sapp's fondness for Old Havana (La Habana Vieja), the Kahiki Supper Club might just as easily have had a Cuban theme. When they were initially staffing the restaurant,

> *Sandro* [Conti] *and I flew down to Miami and stayed at the Columbus Hotel for about three weeks and hired mostly Cuban refugees. I would say that 75 percent of the people that opened the Kahiki were Cuban refugees. There were doctors, lawyers, musicians and everything. They came up here and worked very diligently. They were great workers…The Cubans are great people. They are very industrious people and full of rhythm. They love to dance.*

According to Bill Harrison, one very distinguished-looking gentleman who worked at the Kahiki had been the president of the Bank of Cuba before Castro took over. He remained at the restaurant until he had learned English and saved enough money, and then he went down to Miami and opened a bank there.

However, Bill Sapp nearly became a refugee himself. While it doesn't exactly fit in the story of the Kahiki, it does show that Don The Beachcomber wasn't the only adventurer in the tiki bar business.

> *Well, we just went on one of our regular junkets to Cuba, which we did often because we had so much fun down there. So we moved into the "old"*

section of Havana because that's where we liked it the most. Sandro and I were going out. My wife was tired, so she said, "I'm going to stay in the room." So Sandro and I go out, and in the meantime—this is when the revolution was going on—so the revolutionaries start storming "old" Havana, shooting and everything. Sandro and I were in some bar, and we wanted to go to another bar—and we didn't care about any damn revolutionaries. So we went out and hailed a cab, and this cab stopped. But [the cabby] *said, "I ain't taking you anyplace; I'm afraid that they'll kill me." So Sandro says, "If you don't take us where we want to go, we're gonna kill you right now!" So he took us to this other bar, where we stayed for a while, and anyways it starts to get daylight so I'm thinking the wife's gonna be furious. So we get back to the hotel, and there's an iron gate there and we can't get in. So we rattled this gate for an hour. Finally, the caretaker comes because he thinks the revolutionaries are trying to break in. We assured him that we were tourists and guests of the hotel, so finally he lets us in. Well, we get into the hotel, and the elevator doesn't work. We were up on the eleventh floor, so we go up the stairs. And by the time we got to the room, we were both just beat. So anyway, I go in and go to bed. The next morning my wife screams, "Bill, Bill get up." I said, "What's the matter?" She says, "Look at this!" I looked out the window. And they had* [hanged] *somebody down there, and he was swinging in the breeze. My wife said, "Let's get out of here." We decided it best to get out of there, so we changed our reservations and got on the last plane out of there. Just as we were taking off, we get up and immediately dropped back down from Havana to Varadaro Beach, the airport there. Some guys had gone down the canal and were shooting machine guns, or something, and the pilots were afraid they were going to shoot the plane out of the air. There* [were] *some people, I guess, on the plane that shouldn't have been there, so they lined us all up and they poked us with guns and searched everything. Everybody was scared. Finally, we were able to get back on the plane, and we took off for Miami.*

NOTES

1. Howard Johnson started the ball rolling five years earlier with the first restaurant franchise.
2. The first theme restaurants made their appearances in the Montmartre section of Paris during the 1880s.
3. This long-popular tourist attraction closed at the end of 2013.
4. Since a recipe is little more than a list of ingredients, it cannot be copyrighted unless it incorporates some measure of literary expression.
5. It was revived in 1993.
6. After dying out completely, the Don The Beachcomber name has been resurrected within the past decade.
7. The Thorntons clearly believed in the adage "Go big or go home." The Mai-Kai was the most expensive restaurant built in 1956.
8. Although interracial marriages were prohibited, forty "racially ineligible" women did manage to marry their American boyfriends in defiance of U.S. military policy.
9. Hawaii was as far from the U.S. mainland as Colonel Tom Parker, Presley's manager, would allow him to venture. There were never any overseas tours because Parker, an illegal immigrant from Holland, did not have a passport and would not have been able to accompany him.
10. In 1999, Sapp sold the Top to attorney Steve Yoder Kenny Yee, owner of Wings Restaurant, a Bexley institution that had originally opened in the 1920s as the Far East Restaurant.

11. They later sold the house on the lot to Grover Schmidt for $100, and he moved it.
12. "What type of decadent, perverted minds, what sort of people, can find pleasure in mocking the bones of those who have died before them?…Bad taste and sordid vulgarity have reached their nadir in Columbus, Ohio," wrote S.R.B. Cole from St. Louis, Missouri.
13. Founded by Ed Schmid in 1963, Funni-Frite Industries of Columbus, Ohio, was a manufacturer of carnival fun houses. In 1970, the company introduced Voo Doo Trail, a walk-through fun house that might have been at least partially inspired by the Kahiki. There were twin moai, and thrill-seekers would enter through the mouth of one and exit through the mouth of the other.
14. The monkey pod tables were made by Benson Company of Long Beach, California.
15. It was invented circa 1885–89 by Joseph Kekuku'upenakanai'aupunioka mehameha Apuakehau, or Joseph Kekuku for short.
16. The Columbus Senior Musicians Hall of Fame was co-founded by Robert D. Thomas and David Meyers.
17. Some of the men who married former Mystery Girls think they have the "ultimate collectable."
18. For some reason, Michael Tsao replaced the large gong with a smaller one and, later, a drum.
19. This does not include the eruption of Coach Woody Hayes when the Ohio State Faculty Council voted not to send the Buckeye football team to the 1962 Rose Bowl game.
20. Salinger was the White House press secretary during the Kennedy and Johnson administrations.
21. Many of them stayed at the Olentangy Inn and received flowers from the Livingston Flower Shop, according to contemporaneous advertisements.
22. As William Shatner, Rob Lowe and others have pointed out, Kenley's personal life was more theatrical than his shows. He lived in the Midwest during the summers as John Kenley and in Florida during the winters as Joan Kenley.
23. Wednesday nights they dined across the street at the Desert Inn. They also participated in "meet and greets" at the Lazarus Department Store Assembly Center. John Kenley kept his stars busy.
24. Originally a tap dancer, Styles was a Borscht Belt comedian born in Columbus, Ohio. His wife was the actress and singer Mary Hatcher.
25. The Water Works on North Front Street, another themed restaurant where customers sat in claw-footed bathtubs, also had a backgammon club.

26. A critical success, "Son of Heaven" ended up costing local taxpayers $1.67 million, which was less than the $2 million loss it sustained in Seattle.
27. *Trouble in Tahiti*, a one-act opera by Leonard Bernstein, concerns the breakdown of a marriage.
28. In March 1977, Duncan would find the Columbus Board of Education guilty of operating a segregated school system, paving the way for forced busing to balance the racial composition of the schools.
29. A turnkey is the person in charge of the keys.
30. Mark Pi is a Columbus restaurateur who has operated several successful chains of Asian restaurants.

BIBLIOGRAPHY

Anaconda (Montana) Standard. "The Hawaiian Speech." September 25, 1898.

Bartell, David. "I Owe Ohio." http://www.kevdo.com/maitai/reviews/kahiki.html (accessed on October 20, 2013).

Berry, Jeff. *Beachbum Berry's Grog Log.* San Jose, CA: SLG Publishing, 1998.

Blundo, Joe. "Adventures in Paradise—Readers Revel in the Kahiki's Ersatz Polynesian Pleasures." *Columbus Dispatch,* May 6, 2000.

Burlingame, Burl. "He's 'Uke Kook.'" *Honolulu Star-Bulletin,* 1997.

Business First. "House of Frozen Food." January 12, 1998.

———. "Kahiki Restaurant Is Nominated as One of the Top 50 'Best of the Best' Restaurants and Receives a Five-Star Diamond Award from the American Academy of Restaurant Sciences." March 16, 1992.

Cadwallader, Bruce. "Prank Leaves Two Men Wounded by Shotgun." *Columbus Dispatch,* January 31, 2003.

Chenault, Jeff. "Tiki Pioneer Bill Sapp—Original Owner of the Kahiki Supper Club." *Tiki Magazine* 4, no. 1 (Spring 2008).

Chenoweth, Doral. "Kahiki Has Advocate in Downtown Diner Owner." *Columbus Dispatch,* May 2, 2000.

———. "The Kahiki, 3583 E Broad St., Is Accepted for Listing onto the National Register of Historical Places." *Columbus Dispatch,* December 29, 1997.

———. "Owner on Top of Business Year-Round." *Columbus Dispatch,* February 19, 1996.

———. "Trio Takes Columbus Cuisine to the Top." *Columbus Dispatch,* February 18, 1998.

Chilcoat, Beth, and Cindy Kusmer. *A Taste of Columbus*. Columbus, OH: Corban Productions, 1978.

City of Columbus, Plaintiff-Appellee, v. Samuel E. Bryant, Defendant-Appellant; City of Columbus, Plaintiff-Appellee, v. Joan Johnson, Defendant-Appellant. Court of Appeals, Tenth Appellate District, Franklin County, June 30, 1977.

Cohen, I. David. *Sorry, Downtown Columbus Is Closed*. Columbus, OH: self-published, 2009.

Columbus Dispatch. "Allen Taylor Jr., 25, of 1079 Bryden Rd, Is Arrested in Connection with a Shooting Involving His Estranged Wife Alice, 22, in the Parking Lot of Kahiki, 3583 E Broad St." September 14, 1961.

———. "Armed Robber Gets an Estimated $10,000 from Offices of the Kahiki Restaurant, 3583 E Broad St." November 10, 1969.

———. "Burglars Use a Cutting Torch to Open a Large Safe at the Kahiki Supper Club, 3583 East Broad St and Escape with an Undetermined Amount of Cash." February 17, 1969.

———. "The Municipal Airport Commission Rejects a Request of the Kahiki Restaurant to Set Up a Polynesian Hut with a Hostess in the Terminal and Asks for More Information on a Toy Shop." November 22, 1961.

———. "Police Arrest Todd A. Pahel, 19, a Former Employee of the Kahiki, Inside the Restaurant at 3583 E Broad St. and Charge Him with Breaking and Entering." November 7, 1978.

———. "75 Union Members Picket at the Kahiki Supper Club, 3583 E Broad St.; They Are Miffed at the Non-Union Construction of the Wine Cellar, on E Dublin-Granville Rd., by Owners of Kahiki." August 14, 1971.

———. "Thieves Enter the Kahiki Supper Club, 3583 E Broad St., by Breaking a Side Window, Ransack the Second-Floor Office and Leave a Large Amount of Cash on the Accounting Room Floor." April 2, 1963.

———. "Waiter Found Shot to Death." May 29, 1990.

Curtis, Wayne. "The Tiki Wars: How Do We Distinguish the Historic from the Sentimental?" *Atlantic Monthly* (February 2001).

Decker, Theodore. "Police Seek Tips in Kahiki Waiter's Death." *Columbus Dispatch*, August 4, 2008.

Diez, Deborah J. *Kahiki Catalog: Volume Two*. Columbus, OH: self-published, 2001.

Eaton, Dan. "Volcanos, Waterfalls, Tiki Torches. Lessner's Latest Downtown Eatery Boasts Polynesian Flair." *Business First*, October 31, 2011.

Frank, Peggy. "Small Businesses, Like Kahiki Supper Club, Raise Start-Up Capital Through a 'Regulation A' Stock Offering Designed for Small Co. and Called Scor (Small Corp Offer Registration)." *Business First*, August 7, 1995.

Gibson, Elizabeth. "10 Years After Torches Go Out, Kahiki Memories Live." *Columbus Dispatch*, August 25, 2010.

Hayes, Christine. "Bringing the Tropics to Central Ohio: The Kahiki and the Tiki Lit." *Short North Gazette* (March/April 2014).

Hoekstra, David. "Chef-O-Nette, Columbus, Ohio." November 18, 2007.

———. *The Supper Club Book: A Celebration of a Midwest Tradition*. Chicago: Chicago Review Press, 2013.

Jacksonville Florida Times Union. "Historic Theme Restaurant Closing Doors. New Drugstore to Occupy Space." August 25, 2000.

Leonard, Martha. "Kahiki Lives: Frozen-Food Business Thriving." *Business First*, September 20, 2004.

Lietzke, Ron. "Wine Cellar Operator Mum on Reopening." *Columbus Dispatch*, March 22, 1989.

Looney, Douglas S. "A Big Loss for a Gambling Quarterback." *Sports Illustrated*, May 30, 1983.

Meck, Stuart. "Dates Declined with Infinite Excuses." *Ohio State Lantern*, May 17, 1967.

Meyers, David, and Elise Meyers Walker. *Historic Columbus Crimes: Mama's in the Furnace, The Thing & More*. Charleston, SC: The History Press, 2010.

Meyers, David, Beverly Meyers and Elise Meyers Walker. *Look to Lazarus: The Big Store*. Charleston, SC: The History Press, 2011.

Meyers, David, Candice Watkins, Arnett Howard and James Loeffler. *Ohio Jazz: A History of Jazz in the Buckeye State*. Charleston, SC: The History Press, 2012.

Meyers, David, Elise Meyers Walker and James Dailey. *Inside the Ohio Penitentiary*. Charleston, SC: The History Press, 2013.

Mollard, Beth. "Kahiki Supper Club Inc. Wins Contract to Provide State Food." *Business First*, March 11, 1991.

Montaigne, Renee. "Interview: Michael Tsao Discusses the Closing of Kahiki Supper Club, His Tiki Bar in Columbus, Ohio." *NPR Morning Edition*, August 23, 2000.

Motz, Doug. "History Lesson: The History of Columbus' Most Famed 'Lost' Restaurant. The Kahiki." http://www.columbusunderground.com/history-lesson-the-history-of-columbus-most-famed-lost-restaurant-the-kahiki. September 11, 2012.

National Register of Historic Places Registration Form for the Kahiki, 1997.

Oliver, Douglas. *Polynesia in Early Historic Times*. Honolulu: Bess Press Inc., 2002.

Parsa, H.G., Amy Gregory and Michael "Doc" Terry. "Why Do Restaurants Fail? Part III: An Analysis of Macro and Micro Factors." Orlando, FL:

Dick Pope Sr. Institute for Tourism Studies, University of Central Florida Rosen College of Hospitality Management, 2011.

Rakauskas, Christine. "From Hometown to Nationwide, Duff's Keeps Original Flavor." *(Kissimmee) Sentinel*, July 14, 1990.

Rampell, Ed. "'Hawaii Calls' Again on Two Audiences." *Chicago Tribune*, February 28, 1993.

Schmidt, Kristen. "Do or Die: Whitehall." *Columbus Monthly* (May 2013).

Senn, Nicholas. *Tahiti: The Island Paradise*. Chicago: W.B. Conkey Company, 1906.

Shook, Carrie. "Kahiki Supper Club Inc. Signs on Two Food Distribution Services to Ship Its Cuisine to Stores; New $1 Mil Food Processing Plant Behind Restaurant Increases Food Production." *Business First*, February 27, 1995.

Slatzer, Bob. *The Life and Curious Death of Marilyn Monroe.* New York: Pinnacle Books, 1974.

———. *The Marilyn Files.* New York: S.P.I. Books, 1992.

Stern, Michael. *The Encyclopedia of Bad Taste*. New York: Harper Collins, 1990.

Tebben, Gerald. "Mansion Once Stood as Promise of Ohio's Ability to Meet Debts." *Columbus Dispatch*, March 24, 2012.

Teitelbaum, James. *Tiki Road Trip: A Guide to Tiki Culture in North America.* 2nd edition. Santa Monica, CA: Santa Monica Press, 2007.

Tennenbaum, Robert. "The Hustler Goes to Bexley." *Columbus Monthly* (April 1976).

Thomas, Bob. "Columbus Recollections: City's Earliest Airport. Arabian Gardens and Nick Albanese's Showboat Bar Were Nearby." *Columbus Dispatch*, March 31, 1996.

Thomas, Robert D. *More Columbus Unforgettables*. Columbus, OH: self-published, 1986.

Troost, J. Maarten. *Getting Stoned with Savages: A Trip Through the Islands of Fiji and Vanuatu.* New York: Broadway Books, 1906.

Trowbridge, Denise. "Kahiki Revisited—Hills Market Brings Back Polynesian Landmark for a Day, with Samples, Demonstrations, Dinner." *Columbus Dispatch*, April 27, 2010.

Von Stroheim, Otto. "Bon Voyage, Kahiki: Tiki News Bids Farewell to an Icon." *Tiki News*, n.d.

———. *Tiki Art Now! A Volcanic Eruption of Art.* San Francisco, CA: Last Gasp, 2004.

———. *Tiki Art Now Volume III: Modern Art Inspired by a Primitive Past.* San Jose, CA: SLG Publishing, 2006.

———. *Tiki Art Two: The Second Coming of a New God*. San Francisco, CA: 9mm, 2005.

Wenzel, Ty. *Behind Bars: The Straight-Up Tales of a Big City Bartender*. New York: St. Martin's Press, 2003.

Whitaker, Jan. "Ohio + Tahiti = Kahiki." Restaurant-ing Through History, May 28, 2013. http://restaurant-ingthroughhistory.com/2013/05/28/ohio-tahiti-kahiki.

Williams, Brian. "The Kahiki Supper Club Inc.'s Latest Venture Is Producing Its Own Frozen Foods, Under the General Tsao Label, in a New Plant." *Columbus Dispatch*, November 27, 1995.

Wolf, Barnet D. "Kahiki Lite: Tropical Bistro Tries to Recapture Feel of Polynesian Favorite." *Knight Rider Tribune Business News*, March 28, 2006.

———. "Kahiki Plans Stock Offering to Construct a Separate, 8,000-Square-Foot Processing Operation Behind Its Restaurant at 3583 E Broad St." *Columbus Dispatch*, April 9, 1992.

INDEX

C

D

E

F

G

H

I

J

K

L

M

N

ABOUT THE AUTHORS

A graduate of Miami and Ohio State Universities, David Meyers has written a number of local histories and various works for the stage. Among the former are *Columbus, the Musical Crossroads* and *Ohio Jazz: A History of Jazz in the Buckeye State* while the latter include *The Last Oz Story* and *The Legend of Sleepy Hollow Condominium Association, Inc*. He has also collaborated with his daughter, Elise, on *Central Ohio's Historic Prisons*; *Historic Columbus Crimes: Mama's in the Furnace, The Thing & More*; *Look to Lazarus: The Big Store*; *Columbus State Community College: An Informal History*; and *Inside the Ohio Penitentiary*.

Elise Meyers Walker is a graduate of Hofstra University. While in college, she was a freelance writer for several national magazines and also performed in a professional theater troupe based on Long Island.

Having attended the Recording Institute of Detroit, Jeff Chenault is a music producer, recording engineer, writer and musicologist. He is known throughout the country for his expertise in exotica music and has written articles for *Tiki News*, *Cool and Strange Music Magazine* and *Tiki Magazine*. Jeff is also a prominent member of the Fraternal Order of Moai, Kahiki Chapter.

Doug Motz is the president of the Columbus Historical Society. Much in demand as a leader of local history tours, Doug also attended Ohio State University and writes a regular "History Lesson" column for columbusunderground.com.

Visit us at
www.historypress.net

This title is also available as an e-book